For Chris,

as ever,

Seamus

Space and the Irish Cultural Imagination

Also by Gerry Smyth

DECOLONISATION AND CRITICISM: The Construction of Irish Literature

THE NOVEL AND THE NATION: Studies in the New Irish Fiction

Space and the Irish Cultural Imagination

Gerry Smyth
Senior Lecturer in Cultural History
Liverpool John Moores University

First published 2001 by
PALGRAVE
Houndmills, Basingstoke, Hampshire RG21 6XS and
175 Fifth Avenue, New York, N. Y. 10010
Companies and representatives throughout the world

PALGRAVE is the new global academic imprint of
St. Martin's Press LLC Scholarly and Reference Division and
Palgrave Publishers Ltd (formerly Macmillan Press Ltd).

ISBN 0–333–79407–9

This book is printed on paper suitable for recycling and
made from fully managed and sustained forest sources.

A catalogue record for this book is available
from the British Library.

Library of Congress Cataloging-in-Publication Data
Smyth, Gerry, 1961–
    Space and the Irish cultural imagination / Gerry Smyth.
        p. cm.
    Includes bibliographical references (p.) and index.
    ISBN 0–333–79407–9
    1. Ireland—Historical geography. 2. Space perception—Social
aspects—Ireland. 3. Deane, Seamus, 1940– Reading in the dark.
4. Northern Ireland—Historical geography. 5. Popular culture–
–Northern Ireland. 6. Northern Ireland—In literature. 7. Space
and time in literature. 8. Personal space in literature. 9. Popular
culture—Ireland. 10. U2 (Musical group) Joshua tree. I. Title.
DA969 .S69 2001
941.50824—dc21
                                                        2001021721

10 9 8 7 6 5 4 3 2 1
10 09 08 07 06 05 04 03 02 01

Printed and bound in Great Britain by
Antony Rowe Ltd, Chippenham, Wiltshire

For Lizzie and Esther,
with all my love

Contents

List of Maps

List of Abbreviations

AFM   John O'Donovan (ed.), *Annala Rioghachta Eireann: Annals of the Four Masters of the Kingdom of Ireland from the Earliest Period to the Year 1616*, 7 vols (Dublin: Hodges & Smith, 1848–51)

CDIL   Various Arrangers, *Contributions to a Dictionary of the Irish Language* (Dublin: Royal Irish Academy)

INP   P.W. Joyce, *The Origin and History of Irish Names of Places* (Dublin: McGlashan & Gill, 1869)

MD   Edward Gwynn (ed. and trans.), *The Metrical Dindsenchas: Parts I–V* (Dublin: Hodges, Figgis & Co., 1903, 1906, 1913, 1924, 1935)

MM   Eugene O'Curry, *Lectures on the Manuscript Materials of Ancient Irish History* (1861; Dublin: Four Courts Press, 1995)

OED   *The Oxford English Dictionary* 2nd edn., prepared by J.A. Simpson & E.S.C. Weiner, 20 vols (Oxford: Clarendon Press, 1989)

Ireland

Some Aphorisms and Definitions

[There] is ground for taking the house as a *tool for analysis* of the human soul ... [for] by remembering 'houses' and 'rooms', we learn to 'abide' within ourselves.

Gaston Bachelard (1994: xxxiii, original emphasis)

The city is a map of the city, / Its forbidden areas changing daily.

Ciaran Carson, from 'The Bomb Disposal' (1988: 32)

ballyboe (ballybetach) (Ir. *baile biataigh*, 'residence of a food provider'), a medieval territorial unit, a subdivision of the cantred, of varying extent, depending on the quality of the soil and the nature of the terrain.

from S.J. Connolly (1998: 34)

Representation becomes the auratic process by which a place that had been misrepresented or not represented at all finally achieves presence.

Seamus Deane (1994: 132)

Every story is a travel story – a spatial practice.

Michel de Certeau (1988: 115)

The present epoch will perhaps be above all the epoch of space.

Michel Foucault (1986: 22)

History is the chronicle of man's concern for 'place'.

Martin Heidegger (1971: 24)

There is always a figure in the landscape.

J. Hillis Miller (1995: 4)

History, Stephen said, is a nightmare from which I am trying to awake.

James Joyce (1922: 42)

Deliverance, oh Lord; Deliverance or Death – Deliverance, or this island a desert!

James Fintan Lalor (1921: 57–8)

To finally escape from the English shadow, we must fashion a new sense of political, cultural and economic space for ourselves.

J.J. Lee (1985a: 94)

Space is becoming the principal stake of goal-directed actions and struggles.

Henri Lefebvre (1991: 409)

Ireland is something that often happens elsewhere.

Fintan O'Toole (1994: 27)

All that we can do is re-collect and creatively juxtapose, experimenting with assertions and insertions of the spatial against the prevailing grain of time.

Edward Soja (1989: 2)

Preface and Acknowledgements

In an essay written at the beginning of the 1990s the historian Kevin Whelan suggested that '[the] last decade has seen a surge of interest in Irish local places' (1992: 13). In this book I would like to suggest that such an interest has continued into the new millennium. I submit further that a concern with 'local places' has in fact been extended to the wide range of spaces which bear upon experiences and practices across the island. This study is premised on the impression – anecdotal and observational in the first instance, scholarly and critical at a later stage – that modern Ireland is in fact obsessed with issues of space, and that this obsession may be understood to function at a number of interrelated levels.

In geopolitical terms it registers in issues such as the Republic's role within the European Union, the relations between the northern and southern parts of the island, the status of its huge emigrant population, the increasing interpenetration of island and global economics, and the crisis of the nation-state as a unit of international territorial organisation. Emigration, for example, has created a situation in which, as Fintan O'Toole puts it, 'the people and the land are no longer co-terminous. In this sense, the map of Ireland is a lie' (1994: 18–19). Or again, the population of the Republic awoke one morning in January 1999 to find that as citizens of a state which had signed up to the single European currency, they had suddenly become inhabitants of a new geographical entity called 'Euroland'. This entity was related in many complex ways to other spatial units which already impacted upon Irish life. As a result of ideologically motivated decisions, and without any corresponding shift in the earth's tectonic plates, the relations between (and hence meanings of) places such as Dublin, London and Brussels had altered significantly overnight.

At an interim level, there is much concern about urban and rural development, and also about the impact of infrastructural changes on established practices. One thinks of the controversies surrounding the construction of bungalows in (environmentally and economically defined) 'sensitive' landscapes, or the erosion of small-farm culture and its subsequent impact on the landscapes which sustained it and were in turn sustained by it. In an urban context, it would be an understatement to say that the civic institutions have not as a rule kept pace with the rapid conversion of Dublin from city to city-region since the 1960s. Then there is the issue of regionalism as a post-national administrative paradigm. In 1999, two new super-regional authorities were established in Ballaghaderreen, Co. Roscommon and Waterford City. Many consider regionalism to be a positive development. On the one hand, it is seen as an acknowledgement of the ideological limitations of the nation-state, and thus a contribution to the restoration of permanent peace on the island. More pragmatically, regional bodies offer both a more efficient and a more sensitive means of organising the expansion of the Celtic Tiger beyond the metropolitan areas. However, some critics see regionalism less as an attempt at administrative decentralisation along continental lines, and more as a fairly blatant redeployment of the existing geography designed to maximise financial benefits from the European Union.

At the more interpersonal level first identified by Whelan, Irish people seem to have become fixated with issues of individual, local and private space. The local history movement continues to grow, and it is no longer only the descendants of emigrants who are concerned with family history. Geography – the need to know *where* and in relation to *what* – has always been a significant aspect of these historical and genealogical concerns. This spatial dimension was accentuated in the latter decades of the twentieth century when rapid social, economic and political change encouraged an appreciation of the fact that *where* you come from, and the places in which you live, work and socialise, define in great measure *who* you are. Twenty-first century Ireland has developed (temporarily perhaps) into a society in which there is big money and little room, and the organisation of the latter in relation to the former has as a consequence become one of the most pressing issues for modern Irish people.

All these factors, moreover, are related, so that the modern Irish person's experience of and relation to individual space is subject to a number of influences which radiate outwards in a series of decreasingly discernible though no less impactful contexts. One of the goals of this book is to track those influences and contexts. As Doreen Massey writes, 'we need to conceptualize space as constructed out of interrelations, as the simultaneous coexistence of social interrelations and interactions at all spatial scales, from the most local level to the most global' (1993: 155). Everyone needs a home, whether it be an apartment in Temple Bar or a caravan on the side of the road. Everyone needs to travel, whether to pick up a benefit cheque or to close a deal. Everyone knows an emigrant – perhaps a returned one – either in their own family or amongst their acquaintances. Despite spectacular economic growth, an inordinate percentage of the population still consider emigration to be a viable option. At the same time, only the most insular and/or the most myopic remain unaware that German monetary policy is related in some arcane fashion to their lifestyle options. Whether it be the Tallaght housewife or the Belfast businesswoman, the Clare farmer or the Donegal musician, the Kerry politician or the Cork hurler, issues of space bear visibly upon Irish people's lives to a greater extent than at any point in the past.

These areas will be elaborated throughout the course of *Space and the Irish Cultural Imagination*. But it is also my impression that a *cultural* concern for space has been mirrored by important changes within the *critical* institutions which attend the study of Irish culture. In Chapter 1 I outline a number of intellectual and institutional initiatives which bear upon the re-emergence of space as a crucial category for the study of Irish cultural history. In the meantime, it might be claimed with some justification that the study of space, Irish or otherwise, is not really within the ambit of a cultural historian whose principal research interests to date have been literary criticism and postcolonial theory. I am not a geographer, not even a cultural geographer. I simply do not possess the methodological resources to pronounce with authority on many of the things which have interested me over the course of researching and writing this book. The category of 'space', I hear, should be the legitimate concern of researchers with more appropriate training in fields such as geography, built environment, sociology, politics and anthropology.

So what, then, are my credentials for this kind of study? In many ways, my previous research has always been infused with spatial concerns, though not in any self-conscious or systematic way. Literary critics and cultural historians may not acknowledge it, but the texts which form the basis for most critical analyses are obviously produced and consumed in places; they describe real and imagined places; they are 'placed' in certain institutional locations with reference to specific research projects; critics and historians 'travel' between theories as they look to expedite certain analyses. This latter issue is particularly relevant as it raises the question, as J. Hillis Miller points out, 'of the degree to which a given theory is rooted in one particular culture, able to function only in a specific place' (1995: 5). At the same time, space and its related *topos* have always been irreducibly discursive. For example, Seamus Deane noted the way in which nineteenth-century attitudes towards Ireland were reflected in different terminologies, with the words 'territory', 'land' and 'soil' emerging from coexistent, often competing, discourses of statehood, economics, and cultural nationalism respectively (1997a: 70). A scholar trained in close textual reading may be better equipped to make this kind of analysis, *and* to work through the implications of this kind of imaginative division, than scholars from supposedly more 'appropriate' disciplines.

I think I can best answer the above question, however, by quoting the American geographer Jay Appleton who, in his book *The Experience of Landscape* published in 1975, described an approach to the study of space which strikes me as broadly resonant of the position adopted in the present study:

> [What] we need is someone to trace the threads which run across the boundaries of the various disciplines, connecting geology with aesthetics and animal behaviour with the history of art. Such a person must be prepared to invade territory with which he is not altogether familiar and to make at least tentative statements which he may not be able adequately to support. This sort of undertaking is not any more likely to commend itself to an established scientist anxious to preserve an academic reputation than to an up-and-coming arts man still seeking to establish one. . . . The Jack-of-all-trades who attempts this task should therefore be a person with modest professional aspirations which, preferably, he has already achieved. For the limitations of his knowledge of subjects other than his own, compensation must be provided by an interest in, even a love of, landscape in the widest possible sense. . . . He must be an optimist and he must accept the stark implication of rushing in where angels fear to tread . . . and if he is immodest enough to go into print, his arrogance must at least stop short of deceiving him into the belief that he is doing anything more ambitious than thinking aloud. (1975: 5)

Appleton's call for a form of analysis ambitious enough to range over once discrete disciplinary boundaries in pursuit of different kinds of knowledge was answered by the emergence during the last decades of the old century of just such a Jack-of-all-trades 'discipline': cultural studies. With regard to 'immodesty' and 'arrogance', I couldn't possibly comment. More seriously, neither am I sure if what I am doing here could be described as 'cultural studies'. But I do know that the research process was interdisciplinary and organic in so far as I engaged with materials from a wide range of contexts which seemed best to suit my requirements and which at the same time seemed to be demanded by the texts, practices and events I chose to study. I shall expand upon the point in Chapter 1, but it should be clear from the outset that an acknowledgement of the significance of space does not entail a rejection of the category of history. It is true that spatial analysis is a kind of formalism, concerned with synchronic rather than diachronic phenomena. But this does not mean that it is divorced from or antithetical to temporal concerns. To adapt Roland Barthes: a little space takes one away from history, a lot takes one back towards it again.

Space and the Irish Cultural Imagination is organised in such a way that the largely descriptive-theoretical material of early sections provides the context for the analyses of later chapters, which are intended in turn to reflect back upon and mitigate earlier pronouncements. The book thus has a narrative (which is to say, temporal) dimension which is in some ways opposed to its spatial subject matter, but which in other ways supports that theme in so far as successful engagement depends upon the synchronic apprehension of disparate issues. Like all language use, in other words, this book both tells a story and creates an image, and it is up to the reader to decide which aspect of the critical discourse to stress at any given point. I would like to thank Faber and Faber Ltd. for permission to quote from Seamus Heaney's poem 'Toome', included in his collection *Wintering Out* (1972).

Given the eclectic nature of the materials engaged in this study, inspiration has come from a number of sources. A hint here, a reference there, a sceptical glance from more than one bemused colleague, all have helped to feed to some degree the critical vision underpinning this book. I would like to thank the following people for the support, inspiration and love offered during the researching and writing of *Space and the Irish Cultural Imagination*: Jeff Adams, T.G. Ashplant, Sam Ball, Jim Barnard, David Beck, Marion Beck, Georgina Byrne, Dymphna Callery, Sean Campbell, Peter Childs, Mary Corcoran, Jo Croft, Michael Cronin, Eve-Anne Cullinan, Graham Dawson, Fatima Fernandez, Carmel Flahavan, Amanda Greenwood, Fe Hinton, Wendy Hyde, Matt Jordan, Richard Kirkland, David Llewellyn, Trevor Long, Frank McDonald, Willy Maley, Joe Moran, Pam Morris, Ron Moy, Glenda Norquay, Pádraig Ó Riain, Shaun Richards, Helen Rogers, Joe Saunders, Berthold Schoene-Harwood, Mick Simpson, Christine Smyth, George Smyth, Kevin Smyth, Mike Storry, Lisa Tierry, Billy Webster, Paul Webster, Roger Webster.

1
Irish Cultural Studies and the Re-emergence of Spatial Analysis

The coalescing of a number of critical discourses in the closing decades of the twentieth century made the study of Irish cultural history amenable to spatial analysis. This included the rediscovery of the spatial imagination within the work of a number of established philosophical systems, a reinvigorated Marxist geography, the growth of environmentalism and the emergence of postmodern (often called 'new') geography. Together, these provided the methodological and theoretical bases for the high profile that 'space' came to enjoy as an analytical category in such fashionable modern fields as cultural studies and postcolonial theory. This cluster of critical discourses has fed into this book at a number of levels, providing a rich array of techniques and languages with which to undertake an overview of Irish culture's spatial imagination.

In this chapter I wish to explore these developments at greater length, outlining their chief concerns and assumptions, before going on to speculate on their relevance for the nascent discipline of Irish cultural studies. It should be understood immediately that the issues and examples introduced here are not intended to be exhaustive of the so-called 'spatial turn' which has overtaken many fields within the humanities in recent years. They are profiled, rather, because they inform the analyses undertaken in later chapters.

Philosophy

Nomadism, imperialism, feudalism, capitalism, colonialism, nationalism, fascism, globalism: each of these socio-political systems connotes a specific way of viewing history, but also a specific way of organising and negotiating space. Moreover, although the connection is not always made, these systems are frequently underpinned by systematic philosophical speculation. Philosophers, like literary critics and historians, have always made use of overtly topographical metaphors, such uses invariably eroding or modifying earlier references and connotations. But as one of the two existential coordinates (the other being time) regulating human experience of and in the natural world, space has also attracted the attention of philosophers since ancient Greece in terms of its physical and abstract properties. As with many other fields of human enquiry, however, philosophical engagement with space has suffered during the modern period in relation to the widespread assumption that time and its related tropes (regularity, frequency, repetition, duration, and so on) constitute the most significant aspect of human experience.[1]

The traditional philosophical conception of space promulgated by thinkers as diverse as Descartes, Newton and Kant amounts to a coercive realism in which places can supposedly 'speak' for themselves, and in which each place has *a* meaning amenable to analysis. It is, in the frank words of Neil Smith and Cindi Katz, 'quite literally the space of capitalist patriarchy and racist imperialism' (1993: 79). Human activity is understood to take place within a politically void 'absolute space' (ibid.: 75), which merely provides the backdrop for real politics, whether this be the politics of class, gender or race. Philosophy underpins politics, which in turn maintains the social and cultural networks which delimit human activity. This conception has formed the basis for both traditional philosophical engagements with space in the West, and for a range of social and political initiatives which, over the years, have taken their cue from such engagements. Even when the meaning of a particular place is contested, as for example in Northern Ireland, the idea informing it invariably adheres to this conception of 'absolute space' – simultaneously real, empty and unproblematic.

Of the many challenges to the dominance of 'absolute space', four are of particular relevance for present purposes. The first emerges from the thought of Martin Heidegger, a German philosopher whose roots lie in phenomenology but who is also regularly hailed as one of the founders of existentialism. For a thinker whose major work is entitled *Being and Time*, Heidegger also had much to say (admittedly later in his career) about 'being' and space, although this latter relationship is implicit throughout his *oeuvre*. In a series of dense essays, Heidegger proposed that an intimate relationship between abstract space and specific place is one of the most fundamental elements of human life. In 'An Ontological Consideration of Place', he differentiated between 'horizontal' place, determined by the state and socio-political discourse, and 'vertical' place, connoting the subject's existential reality. Heidegger insisted that '[each] dimension in itself is an abstract generality which can be conceived but not realized without the other' (1956: 21). He saw the category of 'place' as exemplary of 'the relationship between the onto-logical dimension of being and the political structure of human existence' (ibid.: 18). Empirical place and ontological place, that is to say, repre-sent linked yet conflicting dimensions of being. The resolution of these 'horizontal' and 'vertical' dimensions will result in 'a house in which being can unfold and manifest its Being' (ibid.: 26). 'House' is employed here in literal and metaphorical senses, representing the physical struc-ture wherein 'the political, social, or economic aspects of existence' are engaged, but also the existential location wherein may be revealed 'the freedom of man' (ibid.).

Another name for 'house' is 'dwelling', which Heidegger comprehends as a complex dialectic of human spirit and material object. 'Dwelling' is the primal human faculty, the ability to be *in* and *of* a place; it can be achieved, however, only through (a) building, which is itself always geared towards 'dwelling'. Dwelling is also a synonym for 'home', and for Heidegger, as Edward Relph explains:

> Such places are indeed foundations of man's existence, providing not only the context for all human activity, but also security and identity for individuals and groups. We can change places, move, but this is still to look for a place, for this we need as a base to set down Being and to realise our possibilities – a *here* from which the world discloses itself, a *there* to which we can go. Without such relationships, human existence, while possible, is bereft of much of its significance. (1976: 39, original emphases)

All that is 'authentic' in the way of human art and culture emerges from the reality of dwelling. It is this authenticity that modern life threatens, admitting a widespread condition of 'homelessness' or 'placelessness', which undermines our ability to live with, and care for, the earth. Loss of the capacity to dwell entails a loss of roots, which in turn leaves us bereft of the spiritual nourishment necessary for an authentic (in this sense, happy and fulfilled) life. Heidegger's proto-existentialist 'dwell-ing' informs much of postmodernism's interest in place, and especially the attempt to (re)discover alternatives to late capitalism's reification of time and space. 'Place', in any event, remains fundamental, providing both the actual physical terrain as well as the abstract conceptual basis upon which the empirical and ontological dimensions of human experience meet, compete and compromise.

Heidegger's spatial concerns make him an attractive figure for contemporary philosophers, geographers and environmentalists looking for weapons in the struggle against what many see as the destructive nexus of historicism and humanism. This is especially true in the light of his insistence that '[to] dwell, to be set at peace, means to remain at peace within the free, the preserve, the free sphere that safeguards each thing in its nature. *The fundamental character of dwelling is this sparing and preserving*' (1971: 149, original emphasis).

A major problem with any attempt to deploy Heidegger's thought in these terms, however, is his well-publicised support for Nazism. Away from the lofty reaches of philosophical enquiry, Heidegger's concern with authenticity led him to espouse beliefs and undertake actions which leave his otherwise potentially enabling thought tainted by what John Kerrigan calls a 'dark Romanticism' (1998: 152). 'Dwelling' – defined as a caring relationship with an authentic place – can in fact foster feelings of resentfulness and possessiveness which, when articulated to a political programme, can in turn degenerate into enmity and eventually aggression. Neither Irish cultural history nor contemporary Green politics is a stranger to such feelings or programmes. One recurring question, then, must be the extent to which Heidegger's extra-scholarly record compromises any engagement with his thought, including quite centrally, as Kerrigan notes, his 'ideal of a life lived in accommodation with the earth' (ibid.: 146).

Gaston Bachelard was another twentieth-century thinker interested in space as a philosophical concept. His book *The Poetics of Space* (1958; 1994) is a study of intimate human space emerging from the same phenomenological tradition to which Heidegger himself was significantly indebted. Bachelard began by asking: how does the human mind encounter the properties of size, distance, shape, and so on, that bear on that most fundamental of spatial locations, the house? His main proposition was that what he called 'the topography of our intimate being' could in fact be accessed through 'topo-analysis' (1994: xxxii), that is, close study of the human encounter with space, and more especially, domestic space. Topo-analysis focuses upon 'the space we love' (ibid.: xxxi), or what he also called 'images of felicitous space' (ibid.: xxxii), to discover the ways in which humans use the house, and to consider what emotions, practices and memories are associated with its various aspects and features: secret rooms, cellars, garrets, wardrobes, and so on: '[There] is ground for taking the house as a *tool for analysis* of the human soul,' Bachelard wrote, for 'by remembering "houses" and "rooms" we learn to "abide" within ourselves' (ibid.: xxxvii, original emphasis).

But how is the phenomenologist to set about using this 'tool for analysis'? Positivist research is incapable of engaging with the imaginative manipulation of space that occurs in domestic situations. Having rejected science as 'an insufficient basis upon which to found a metaphysics of the imagination' (ibid.: xiv), Bachelard turned to the poetic imagination which, he claimed, offers 'a phenomenology of the soul' (ibid.: xvii) – hence the title of the study: *The Poetics of Space*. His unique take on the phenomenological method enabled a deeper, more empathetic understanding of the kinds of emotions invested in, and the kinds of meanings produced by, the house. The suggestion is that the house in fact embodies the most primal resonances of the human experience – sanctuary, love, reason – while also providing spatial form for that which resists empirical analysis. 'We must,' he claimed,

> experience the primitiveness of refuge and, beyond situations that have been experienced, discover situations that have been dreamed; beyond positive recollections that are the material for a positive psychology, return to the field of the primitive images that had perhaps been centers of fixation for recollections left in our memories. (ibid.: 29–30)

Bachelard argued that the figures best equipped to engage with this 'field of ... primitive images' are not historians, planners or political scientists, not even philosophers like himself, but poets. 'Evidence' and 'reason' are flawed categories in this regard for they are incapable of engaging with the uncertainty, what he referred to as the 'hesitation of being' (ibid.: 214), which constitutes the fundamental human imagination of space. Bachelard's self-appointed task in *The Poetics of Space* was to '[demolish] the lazy certainties of the geometrical intuitions by means of which psychologists sought to govern the space of intimacy' (ibid.: 220).

Michel de Certeau was another figure more concerned with the practicalities of intimate space than with abstract positivist models. De Certeau was interested in 'the practice of everyday life', that is, 'the ways in which users – commonly assumed to be passive and guided by established rules – operate' (1988: xi). He speculated that people routinely subvert such established rules, 'not by rejection or alteration, but by using what is given with respect to ends and references foreign to the system they had no choice but to accept' (ibid.: xii). The everyday is political, that is to say, although not in any programmatic way. Politics emerges rather as a poetics, a system which may be intended but which is often semi-conscious or unconscious. And much like Bachelard, who found the 'poetry' of intimate domestic space impervious to traditional disciplinary analysis, so de Certeau speculated that everyday life, both within and beyond the house, constitutes a form of poetry in which people become 'silent discoverers of their own paths in the jungle of functionalist rationality' (ibid.: xviii).

One of the principal means by which subversion occurs is in the everyday use – or rather, misuse – of the rules established with regard to space. Simply walking in the city, for example, constitutes a creative use of public space in which subjects 'make innumerable and infinitesimal transformations of and within the dominant cultural economy in order to adapt it to their own interests and their own rules' (ibid.: xiii–xiv). People necessarily use established spaces, that is, but in so doing they modify those spaces in line with their own fears and desires. Cities are planned, virtual spaces, apprehensible in terms of 'the "geometrical" or "geographical" space of visual, panoptic, or theoretical constructions' (ibid.: 93). But every step taken by city walkers as they weave their own personal urban poem represents a potential subversion of those constructions. A 'metaphorical' (ibid.: 110) city thus comes to occupy the same space as the planned city, answerable not to an abstract disciplinary vision but to concrete practices. This process of modification can never be part of a programme, however, but is instead opportunistic and partial, dependent upon what de Certeau called 'tactical' action, which is itself a response to the context of an event. Space may thus be 'tactically' reappropriated in ways that exceed and resist technocratic 'discipline'. This includes the 'discipline' of traditional cultural critique, a discourse that simply does not possess the techniques or languages to engage with such a seemingly quotidian level of action.

One final figure worth mentioning here is Michel Foucault who, although primarily focused on a series of historical problematics, remarked on a number of occasions on the importance of space as an analytical category and its relative neglect within the dominant intellectual and philosophical systems of the modern world (1980; 1984b; 1986). In autocritical mode, Foucault called for a systematic critique of the 'devaluation of space that has prevailed for generations. . . . Space was treated as the dead, the fixed, the undialectical, the immobile. Time, on the contrary, was richness, fecundity, life, dialectic' (1980: 70). His observation that '[the] present epoch will perhaps be above all the epoch of space' (1986: 22) provided the imprimatur which would animate and inspire other scholars with more appropriate skills working in more appropriate disciplines.

Although this interest was never systematically developed, Foucault made a number of suggestive methodological speculations with regard to the analysis of space in relation to the power/knowledge problematic that informed his properly scholarly work elsewhere. One of the most interesting of these throwaway speculations was the 'heterotopia', which he defined as either 'a space of illusion that exposes every real space' or 'a space that is other, another real space, as perfect, as meticulous, as well arranged as ours is messy, ill-constructed, and jumbled' (1986: 27). He observed that certain salient social places, such as boarding schools, prisons, cemeteries, gardens, museums, fairgrounds and ships, are essentially heterotopic spaces and might be observed to function in terms of this elemental dialectic of illusion and/or otherness. Most interestingly for present purposes, he wondered 'if certain colonies have not functioned somewhat in this manner' (ibid.). Although my observations remain likewise speculative for the most part, the possibility of viewing Ireland as an 'illusionary' and/or 'other' space of the British heterotopic imagination during their long historical association is something with which I wish to engage throughout the course of this study.

Ecocriticism

Since at least the 1960s, concern about the environment (or, more accurately, human abuse of the environment) has been growing throughout the West. It seems clear in retrospect that an environmental, or 'green', conscience constituted the major and most enduring element of the hippie movement and its various offshoots. Subsequent decades witnessed the development of this green conscience in a wide range of social and political arenas, with many disillusioned Marxists in particular making the move from red to green (Bate 1991: 8; Feher and Heller 1984).[2] Environmentalism itself is concerned in large part with explicitly spatial issues, for example, the relationship between local and global economies, the disparity between morphological and bureaucratic geography, and the impact of technology – say, 'advances' in road construction – upon the human experience of space.

The emergence of an international green politics has been shadowed within the academy by the development of critical techniques specifically focused upon issues of culture and environment. The relatively modern discourse of ecocriticism represents 'enviromentalism's overdue move beyond science, geography and social science into "the humanities"'; its principal task is 'to evaluate texts and ideas in terms of their coherence and usefulness as responses to environmental crisis' (Kerridge and Sammells 1998: 5). The premise underpinning ecocriticism is that all human activity is fundamentally rooted in the physical environment, but that this dimension has been systematically marginalised in what has emerged as the most powerful and influential arena of human culture since ancient times: the West. Having 'reached the age of environmental limits' (Glotfelty and Fromm 1996: xix), however, it is no longer possible (or indeed rational) to ignore the symbiotic relationship between humanity and nature, between the human capacity for communicating thought and the physical contexts out of which such thought arises. Thus, the role of environmentally aware literary critics extends beyond asking 'What role does the physical setting play in the plot of a novel?' (ibid.) – although this certainly remains a valid question; rather, their most important contribution is the reconnection of categories that have been expediently sundered, including that most insidious of connections: critic and context.[3]

The advent of a literary-critical discourse self-consciously focused on issues of the environment is ironic in the light of the fact that, as Tony Pinkney points out, '[from] one end of twentieth-century critical or cultural theory to the other, unacknowledged spatial presuppositions or metaphors continue to generate and structure the official theoretical argument' (1990: 14). But a green sensibility has become influential in fields other than literary criticism, albeit with the same emphasis upon the specific, situated subject over and against a general, universal consciousness. Max Oelschlaeger (1997) argues that a reinvigorated 'radical' geography, informed by a properly ecological consciousness, could salvage philosophy from the ancient temporal and humanistic biases inherited from the Greeks. As many green commentators have pointed out, these biases were installed as the paradoxically 'natural' bases for mankind's cultural evolution during the Renaissance and the Enlightenment (Dobson 1990: 8). Summing up a position that is widespread at the outset of the twenty-first century, however, Oelschlaeger suggests that post-Hellenic philosophy's vain infatuation with the timeless and the universal must be replaced by a concern for 'the concrete and particular, the local and seasonal', which is to say, for 'the grounded immediacy of human perception in particular places' (1997: 377). Traditional philosophy (as noted in the previous section) focused on 'Man Apart' and his drive to master an existentially blank, morally indifferent nature. Geography must reawaken the notion of a situated humanity and its attempt to dwell on and with the earth. This is because humans, contrary to a 2,000-year metaphysical tradition, are 'inextricably caught up with the larger context of bio-material relations that make and sustain life' (ibid.: 384).

Oelschlaeger's insistence that '[the] human and the cultural (including the ethical, theological, and philosophical) are linked with the material and organic' (1997: 384) is echoed in Simon Schama's study of the reciprocal impact of landscape and the human imagination throughout western history. 'Landscape,' Schama states bluntly, 'is the work of the mind' (1995: 6); the natural world is 'irreversibly modified' (ibid.: 7). Nature is never pristine; landscape is never encountered, only re-encountered. 'It remains a common error,' as Raymond Williams pointed out, 'that substantial interference with the natural environment began only with the industrial revolution' (1989: 211). The guilt which underpins our awareness of the extent of human encroachment on nature – a guilt which may be said to inform many ecocritical analyses, if not the entire modern environmentalist project (Smyth 1999) – is obviated by the fact that 'nature' has always been to a greater or lesser extent a human product. Culture has not eclipsed nature, moreover, merely sublimated and disguised it. The myths and cults which informed earlier western societies – encompassing landscape aspects such as the forest, the river and the mountain – are, Schama insists, 'in fact alive and well and all about us if only we know where to look for them' (1995: 14). *Landscape and Memory* is predicated on the belief that the core myths which inform the human imagination of nature may be discovered throughout the modern world.

So, philosophy and history have begun to register the impact of ecological considerations. At the same time, a powerful 'ecofeminist' critical discourse has emerged which, in its simplest terms, looks 'to interrogate the Eurocentric convention that positions Man over and above Woman and Nature' (Salleh 1997: ix). If nature is in a crisis characterised by overconsumption and lack of respect for difference, this is in large part because history continues to be dominated by the thinking of dead, white, heterosexual men. Paternalistic societies invariably configured the earth, nature and landscape in feminine terms, and this in turn allowed for the emergence of seemingly 'natural' gender relations organised around the notions of the passive, nurturing female and the active, aggressive male. Ecofeminism contends that such an ideology may be seen to be active within discourses as diverse as political colonialism and cultural romanticism, and that it continues to underpin a blatantly exploitative relationship with the natural world.[4]

Again, such a critique finds particular purchase in a country like Ireland where gender has been such a powerful agent in the formation of certain images and identities, and where, in line with developments elsewhere, '[nature], landscape, femininity and the unknown are figured as objects of masculine desire and fear, and thus linked to senses of loss and lack across which male subjectivities are produced and managed according to psychoanalysis' (Nash 1996: 155). In terms broadly resonant of ecofeminism, Catherine Nash has traced what she understands to be 'the diverse origins of the feminisation of Ireland': '[these] representations of Ireland as female,' she claims, 'have been predominantly produced by men in order to stabilise versions of masculinity and naturalise their power over women' (1997: 111, 116). To combat this, and without falling into the idealist trap of claiming nature and/or landscape as 'a universal source of identification for all women' (1996: 157), Nash calls for a renegotiation of the Irish landscape in ways that disrupt the paternalistic gaze which has dominated it for so long.

One of the arguments of this book is that the study of the relationship between culture and environment overlaps significantly with the study of Irish cultural history, and more specifically with analysis that addresses the issue of Irish space. There are tactical as well as practical reasons for this. The impact of a global environmental crisis on modern Irish life offers an alternative focus to Irish cultural critics who wish to challenge the exceptionalism which has fed discourses of division and domination throughout the island. It also encourages concern with issues that emphasise the island's wider fortunes rather than its internal constitution. The issues which currently occupy Irish Studies, and which appear to have evolved from discretely national or regional concerns, in fact engage significantly with many of the issues that inform the modern international discourse of ecocriticism.

As an aggressive First World economy, for example, the 'Celtic Tiger' is implicated in the pressure placed upon non-renewable resources by a highly mobile, post-Fordist capitalism. At the same time, all sides in the peace process have been obliged to consider the role of history in the formation of identity and difference in Northern Ireland. The resulting focus on established narratives of identity interfaces significantly with the growth of scepticism towards the historical imagination in the West, something which in turn facilitated the emergence of the spatial awareness informing ecocriticism. Furthermore, modern studies of the production and impact of gender discourses in Ireland resonate with international ecofeminism's concern to trace the systematic privileging of a masculine perspective which continues to inform human attitudes and practices, and which has contributed in large part to the current environmental crisis. Finally, and perhaps most tellingly, the 'special relationship' between people and place, signalled (as we shall see) in so many accounts as *the* defining feature of Irish cultural history, echoes ecocriticism's concern to re-establish that same relationship in a modern international context in which, because of prevailing economic and political conditions, people and place are routinely sundered.

All told, it seems likely that Irish Studies and ecocriticism will have much to say to each other, in so far as many of the issues that occupy the latter have traditionally been part of the former's remit, albeit in other forms and guises. Geographical peculiarity and historical discontinuity produced a situation in Ireland in which questions concerning space, landscape, locality, gender, urban and rural experience, nature, and so on, became central to both the cultural and the critical imagination (Carpenter 1977; Harmon 1984; Duffy 1997). When the Irish writer describes a landscape in terms of gender, therefore, or when a critic addresses the ambivalent overlapping of public and private spaces in an Irish text, they are in fact 'doing' ecocriticism. They are doing it, moreover, in concrete situations which realise the abstractions of a discourse which, by the nature of its subject matter, is obliged to focus on the bigger picture and thus risk much of its affective potential.

Postmodern geography

In 1989 the American geographer Edward Soja published *Postmodern Geography*. This influential text functioned primarily as a polemic against the historicist bias within twentieth-century Marxism and social science. Soja took up where Foucault left off, indicting the 'carceral historicism of conventional critical theory' (ibid.: 1), and calling for '[a] critical discourse in which space "mattered", in which human geography was not entirely subsumed within the historical imagination' (ibid.: 6). For too long, he suggested, time had been the privileged master-narrative dictating the shape of 'reality' for both critical and cultural practices. The task of deconstruction was made all the more difficult, moreover, by the fact that '[the] quiet triumph of historicism has ... deeply shaped Western intellectual history over the past hundred years' (ibid.: 31). During the nineteenth century, he argued, the discourses which attempted to critique capitalism became subsumed within its own temporalist logic. Marxism and social science learned to view capitalistic production as an essentially historicist problematic, thus gradually losing a sense of it as a set of social and political practices which depended as much upon the manipulation of space as upon the unfolding of history. It is this spatial sense which, Soja claimed, must be rediscovered.

Besides tracking the emergence of history's institutional and intellectual hegemony, *Postmodern Geography* offered an account of the potential benefits ensuing from a reinvigorated geographical imagination. Historicist analysis alone, Soja maintained, could not adequately engage with the complexity of people's experience of capitalism, or indeed any regime of power/knowledge. There remains a synchronic dimension to power – a dimension which impacts on day-to-day experience in the form of protocols surrounding mobility, access, usage, and so on – with which geographical analysis is better equipped to deal. At the same time, one of the strengths of the book was that it neither professed nor pursued a wholesale rejection of history – the stick with which Marxists and humanists alike beat postmodernists throughout the closing decades of the century. Soja was keen to avoid berating historicist analysis for what many were coming to see as its collusive vision (Attridge, Bennington and Young 1987: 1–11). Rather, *Postmodern Geography* represented an attempt to reconfigure the prevailing categories into a more enabling critical matrix. As he wrote in the Introduction: 'I attempt to spatialize the conventional narrative by recomposing the intellectual history of critical social theory around the evolving dialectics of space, time, and social being: geography, history, and society' (ibid.: 3).

One influential proposition that emerged in the wake of Soja's study was that modernism was time-oriented – as manifested in the theoretical premises of great 'father figures' such as Darwin, Marx, Einstein and Freud – while postmodernism was space-oriented. The latter's task was to disrupt the (temporal) maps which had been so painstakingly drawn during earlier periods according to established physical and social principles. At the same time, the theoretical underpinning of the 'new geography' also differed significantly from earlier models. Whereas the supposedly 'radical' spatial initiatives of the previous generation tended to be structuralist in outlook, focused upon the relations between identifiable synchronous phenomena, the 'new geography' was informed for the most part by a poststructuralist sensibility in which space was a 'text' subject to myriad cross-referenced, but ultimately unauthorised, meaning systems. The task became, in the words of Derek Gregory, '[to] uncover the underlying multivocal codes which make landscapes cultural creations, to show the politics of design and interpretation, and to situate landscape at the heart of the study of social process' (1994: 45).

Soja's call for a truly radical geographical discipline was heard by scholars from a wide range of disciplines who had begun moving more or less independently towards a recognition of space as a crucial category for contemporary critical practice. Understood more as a 'discourse' than a 'discipline', geography became one of the success stories of the 1990s with the publication of a great number of edited collections and monographs on various aspects of what rapidly came to be known as 'new' or 'postmodern' geography.[5] In this expanded sense, to quote Gregory again, '[geography] ... is not confined to any one discipline, or even to the specialized vocabularies of the academy; it travels instead through social practices at large and is implicated in myriad topographies of power and knowledge' (1994: 11). Because its subject matter was itself dispersed and polymorphous, cultural geography had to become transdisciplinary. Cultural geography, in other words, began to 'colonise' other disciplines and other areas of scholarly interest possessed of apparently no 'natural' propensity towards the spatial.

The principal focus for postmodern geography quickly became the question of identity in relation to place. 'Identity' (and the closely related notion of 'the subject') had been established by earlier generations of theorists as a crucial political and cultural category. But this category, even when supposedly grounded in terms of a specific location, was invariably invoked in historicist terms. In Irish Studies, for example (and as we shall shortly see at greater length), it is fair to say that 'identity' has been, and by and large remains, an historical issue. Which is to say: 'Irish identity' has traditionally been addressed in terms of the factors bearing upon the evolution of that category over time. Much less frequently engaged are the actual spatial factors (such as topography, landscape, movement, proximity, location) which have delimited the composition and evolution of Irish identity. When such factors were invoked, it tended to be within the theoretically impoverished models of traditional cultural geography, a discipline hitherto mortgaged to essentialist notions of identity and thus incapable of doing justice to the multiply determined, radically ambivalent subject posited by modern poststructuralist theory. Identity in these latter terms, as Michael Keith and Steve Pile put it, 'is always incomplete, always subsumes a lack, perhaps is more readily understood as a process rather than an outcome' (1993: 28). Identity, that is to say, is never contained in essences; rather, it is maintained through practices; and it is this model of contingent, radically contextualised identity to which postmodern geography addresses itself.

In these two respects – poststructuralist theory and transdisciplinarity – geography became an integral part of the late twentieth century's most successful institutional initiative: cultural studies. No self-respecting commentator, it seemed, could afford to ignore the spatial dimension to any social or cultural practice. Identity became 'emplaced identity', definitionally contextual, necessarily spatial. And perhaps the most significant area in which this attempt to challenge established epistemological maps manifested itself was the field of postcolonial theory. On both macro and micro levels (it was argued), the world had been ordered in terms of the unequal power/knowledge capacities of coloniser and colonised. Cultural studies, informed and enabled by cultural geography, could provide the best conceptual and methodological tools with which to begin to deconstruct that order. It was possible to show that the geographical division between 'West' and 'East', for example, had been produced as a 'meaningful' concept in the same way that 'meaning' is an effect produced by the matrix of text, reader and reading context. Both the characteristics and qualities with which (macro) 'eastern' subjectivity has traditionally been identified, and the (micro) spaces occupied by that subjectivity, were thus amenable to a species of textual analysis, capable of being 'read' by the postcolonial theorist in the same way that a literary critic 'reads' a novel, an anthropologist 'reads' a custom, or a sociologist 'reads' a community.

But herein lie the seeds of some familiar problems. 'Postal' theorists begin to 'read' socio-political phenomena as texts, only to be attacked by more established critics (both progressive and conservative) for initially making, and subsequently disseminating, a fundamental category error. Space is not a 'text' but the site of fears and desires which are historically traceable, politically organised and socially effective. Poststructuralist theory disdains coherence, whether it be in the subject or in society at large, but in so doing it risks undermining the coherent, stable discourses around which resistance to domination frequently mobilises. As Catherine Nash puts it, '[poststructuralism] does not disallow the *critical* use of the concept of identity' (1993: 50, original emphasis). We are all decentred, it might be said, but some of us are more decentred than others, and poststructuralist analysis routinely elides the practical political differences which still support discourses of domination and subordination, and which still order the ability to speak and act in space. At the same time, poststructuralism tacitly supports those forms of postmodern power which, rather than being challenged by incoherence, actually thrive upon it. It has been further argued that while poststructuralist theory deploys spatial metaphors to expose historicism's bad faith and the impossible metaphysical coherence of the modern world, it reproduces the fundamental hierarchy which sees an active, masculine temporality set over and against a passive, feminine spatiality.

The impression of space that emerges most strongly from postmodern geography is one of incompleteness, contingency and partiality. The sequentiality of time is always mitigated by the simultaneity of space. 'Negotiation' and 'production' become key concepts. The subject negotiates her/his identity in relation to a range of competing social and political discourses, and this process of negotiation emerges in term of her/his use of space. This process of negotiation enables acts of spatial usage ranging from complete identification – the 'right' person doing the 'right' thing in the 'right' place – to complete de-identification – acts that consciously (or are retrospectively seen to) challenge spatial orthodoxy. And because space itself is dialectically produced, with neither the subject nor the context categorically privileged, so geographical research should also be dialectical and strategic. The cultural, the economic and the political cannot be separated for practical critical purposes. Rather, research should address itself both to the institutional and ideological discourses which attempt to delimit the uses of social space – private and public, built and natural, leisure and professional – and to the ways in which those spaces are used by subjects located in social units ranging from the individual through a series of numerically greater 'imagined' communities – family, neighbourhood, village, townland, county, province, region, state, country, class, race, gender.

Marxism

Soja argued that '[for] at least the past century, time and history have occupied a privileged position in the practical and theoretical consciousness of Western Marxism and critical social science' (1989: 1). Marxism, after all, was first and foremost an historicism, an attempt to understand the process of change through time. Space was existentially vacant until infused with properly meaningful (that is, temporal) considerations. Despite this historicist bias, over the course of the twentieth century a scholarly discourse did evolve within the western academy which looked to bring the basic assumptions of Marxism to bear upon spatial phenomena. 'Marxist geography' retains a faintly oxymoronic ring, however, in so far as the temporal imperative of the first term is more often than not at odds with the spatial connotations of the second. This was the context in which Soja suggested that Marxist intellectuals should 'break out from the temporal prisonhouse of language and the similarly carceral historicism of conventional critical theory to make room for the insights of an interpretive human geography, a spatial hermeneutic' (ibid.: 1–2).

Postmodern Geography remains the most developed attempt to rethink the basic Marxist categories in terms of space. Despite Soja's disappointment with earlier work, however, the immediately prior generation had in fact produced two remarkable interventions which were influenced to a large degree by the Marxist project. Simultaneously polemic, plea and prolegomena, Henri Lefebvre's *The Production of Space* (1974) attempted to lay the ground for a properly dialectical analysis of the ways in which western space functioned in terms of power understood with reference to the core Marxist categories. Against a metaphysical tradition 'running from Descartes to the present day via Hegel, a tradition that has been successfully incorporated into a society based on *raison d'état*, and at the same time into a particular conception of space and a particular spatial reality', Lefebvre proposed a theory which,

> carrying reflection on the subject and the object beyond the old concepts, [would re-embrace] the body along with space, in space, and as the generator (or producer) of space. To say that such theoretical thinking goes 'beyond discourse' means that it takes account, for the purpose of a pedagogy of the body, of the vast store of non-formal knowledge embedded in poetry, music, dance and theatre. (ibid.: 406–7)

Like Bachelard and de Certeau, that is, Lefebvre was concerned less with spatial knowledge than with spatial practices. In *The Production of Space* he explored the possibilities of redeploying traditionally non-formal practices against a reality conceived in terms of a coercive, power-oriented discourse for which space was always scientific and instrumental. Although working within basic Marxist terms, however, this latter discourse does not equate to capitalism for Lefebvre. As he was at pains to point out, no single force or agency was capable of shaping space worldwide. Rather, 'space' itself was the space – simultaneously micro and macro, immediate and abstract – wherein different forces and agencies vied for power. And because space was radically ambivalent, unfinished and incoherent, it could become the site of resistance as well as domination.

Lefebvre's enduring contribution was to install the category of space as a crucial element for any truly radical social analysis. If space was socially produced, he insisted, then society was also and equally spatially produced. This, as we have seen, was the premise from which postmodern geography emerged. In the anglophone world meanwhile, Raymond Williams pursued a similar line with his *The Country and the City* (1973), which explored the emergence of cultural representations of urban and rural space within modern British history. The central premise of this study, as Williams was later to describe it, 'was that these two apparently opposite and separate projections were in fact indissolubly linked, within the general and crisis-ridden development of a capitalist economy, which had itself produced this division in its modern forms' (1989: 227). At the same time as he was developing the critical system that would become known as 'cultural materialism', Williams was also laying the basis for a kind of 'green socialism', based in part on his analysis of the urban/rural divide but more fundamentally on his recognition that Marxism would have to develop a cogent green dimension if it were to be able to critique the uses and abuses of spatial power inevitably generated by late capitalism (Wainwright 1999). As he stated in a late interview:

> A new theory of socialism must now centrally involve *place . . . place* has been shown to be a crucial element in the bonding process – more so perhaps for the working class than the capital-owning classes – by the explosion of the international economy and the destructive effects of deindustrialization upon old communities. When capital has moved on, the importance of place is more clearly revealed. (1989: 242, original emphases)

The work of Lefebvre and Williams demonstrated that there were Marxist scholars (albeit of an independent cast of mind) who were willing to embrace space as an active, dialectical category rather than time's politically vacant 'other'. But perhaps the most telling intervention with regard to the category of space and the organisation of modern (or more specifically postmodern) capitalist culture was produced by the American cultural critic Fredric Jameson. In a key essay for the emergence of anglophone postmodernist critique, 'Postmodernism, or the Cultural Logic of Late Capitalism', Jameson raised the issue of 'cognitive mapping', which he described as 'a pedagogical political culture which seeks to endow the individual subject with some new heightened sense of its place in the global system' (1984: 92). The premise here (and in the later essay entitled 'Cognitive Mapping' [1988]) was that, to function successfully, most living organisms need to develop a sense of their own location in relation to both the immediately visible environment and also to the world beyond the range of their senses. Jameson then produced a Marxist rationale for the kinds of spatial practices that have dominated the lives of the majority of western humans in the modern era. The geometrical Cartesian space of classical market capitalism gave way to the dispersal of economic reality across a number of sites which was characteristic of modernist capitalism. This model was in turn super-seded by a postmodern, post-Fordist capitalism, one 'that involves our insertion as individual subjects into a multidimensional set of radically discontinuous realities, whose frames range from the still surviving spaces of bourgeois private life all the way to the unimaginable decentering of global capital itself' (1988: 351).

Which is to say, different economico-political systems produce different socio-cultural spaces within which subjects are obliged to function. Jameson's earlier essay remains one of the most forceful analyses of the aesthetic discourses which have developed within the context of late capitalism and its peculiar spatial dynamic. The task of the cultural critic or social commentator, he suggests, is to communicate a sense of social totality and thus to enable subjects to map themselves in relation to the social and political spaces within which they live. In the context of the postmodern city-dweller, for example, cognitive mapping constitutes 'a dialectic between the here and now of immediate perception and the imaginative or imaginary sense of the city as an absent totality' (1988: 353). The subject's sense of self, in other words, is produced from a combination of his immediate sensual perceptions and his imaginative reconstruction of a range of spaces and places – a reality – located at a greater or lesser remove from their corporeal experience.

As with even the most advanced Marxist science, however, this dialectic is determined in the last instance by considerations of power and economics understood with reference to the classic categories of capital and labour. Now, although most postmodern geographers would probably accept the attractiveness of 'cognitive mapping' as a strategy of self-empowerment for both individuals and groups, many would also wish to resist the model of power upon which Jameson's theory is prem-ised. This is because of their insistence upon the radical contingency of the subject and the multiplicity of forces which bear upon, and compete for, meaning in the postmodern world. Jameson is a seriously reconstructed materialist, responsible in large part (along with Williams) for dragging anglophone Marxism into the late twentieth century. Yet he seems unwilling (unlike Soja, say) to countenance postmodernism as an enabling paradigm which, despite its many obvious social and political limitations, might also be possessed of an emancipatory potential, if only the critic knows where to find it and how to deploy it.

In any event, even while retaining Jameson's emphasis on the changing nature of space in relation to economic organisation throughout the modern period, and his insistence on the considerations of power which inform every spatial negotiation, it is not necessary to adhere to his originary Marxist narrative to engage meaningfully with the concept of cognitive mapping. It retains certain methodological advantages when invoked in alternative critical contexts. It is my sense that the 'here and now of immediate perception' in early twenty-first century Ireland interacts with 'the imaginative or imaginary sense' of a range of spaces that continue to be widely invoked throughout Irish culture. Part of the process of any radical Irish cultural studies would be the production of cognitive maps which enable Irish people to locate themselves in relation to both their own local environments and to the series of increasingly larger networks of power which bear upon those environments.

Ireland and the 'special relationship'

In Chapter 2 we shall be examining in depth a number of Irish cultural practices in terms of their engagement with the philosophical, political and institutional issues raised above. Before moving on to that, how-ever, and by way of conclusion to this chapter, I want to signal the existence of a paradox concerning the relationship between time and space at the heart of Irish Studies. This paradox resides in the fact that although the formal study of Irish culture has been dominated through-out the modern period by a methodology organised around issues of chronology, duration, order, frequency, disruption, inheritance – in other words, issues of history – the subject matter of that study has been invariably geographical, concerned (even when it seemed not to be the case) with the existence and influence of a 'special relationship' between community and environment permeating Irish life.

It seems clear that the vision of Irish cultural practice invoked in the latter part of the eighteenth century under the auspices of an Anglo-Irish-inspired cultural revival was one in which history was the primary conceptual consideration. This vision remained dominant throughout the nineteenth century, and was indeed augmented by the influential artistic and political visions of the leading figures from the first half of the twentieth century, including W.B. Yeats, James Joyce, Padraig Pearse and Eamon de Valera. History's institutional hegemony was then consolidated after independence by the emergence of a cadre of pro-fessional male scholars who succeeded in installing temporality as the dominant factor in any consideration of island life, past or present, urban or rural (Brady 1994).

The dominance of time for the understanding of Irish culture remained more or less intact down to the end of the twentieth century. Despite (or perhaps because of) the ultimately sterile – because categorically irresolvable – debate on revisionism which animated the work of so many commentators since the 1970s, history, as Gerald Dawe wrote, remained 'the central focus of Irish Studies programmes: the study of Ireland is mostly a study of the historical story of the country's founda- tion – failed Rising in Dublin in 1916, followed by a War of Independ- ence and a Civil War – before the modern state was established (albeit partitioned) in 1922' (1998: 222). Another commentator, S.J. Connolly, pointed out that '[works] of academic history have found their way onto the Irish bestseller list. Historical debates have been covered by press, radio and television. There is a thriving market for heritage centres and summer schools. Local history societies proliferate' (1997: 44). Both Irish culture and its attendant critical discourses, that is to say, are still driven principally by the talismanic properties of dates, names and events from the past.

As indicated above, however, such a methodological emphasis is curious in so far as the primary theme of Irish (cultural, political and social) history would appear to be not historical but geographical – specifically, the presence and function of a 'special relationship' between people and place. As Soja and others have argued, this theme was implicit from the outset in the romantic nationalism which set the agenda for the understanding of Irish history during the modern period. With its roots in the writing of Johann Herder, the idea grew throughout the nineteenth century that landscape and humans are locked in a sym- biotic relationship that was established in pre-history. History was thus the record of emplaced humanity, that is, of agency and character apprehensible with reference to environment and landscape (Williams 1980: 86–102).

The Irish experience merely represents one highly developed form of this truism. The form of cultural nationalism which came to dominance in Ireland during the nineteenth century fostered, in Catherine Nash's words, 'the idea that there is only one true Irishness and that this depends on a stable and secure relationship to place' (1997: 109). From the first postglacial migrants, through the first division of the island by the legendary Scythian invader Parthalón, and on into the historical era, matters of space are widely understood to have been of the utmost importance in the formation of Irish character and culture. Irish history could thus be engaged with reference to what Smadar Lavie and Ted Swedenburg describe as 'the old certainty that there is an immutable link between cultures, peoples, or identities and specific places ... [a] homology between a culture, a people, or a nation and its particular terrain' (1996: 1). Many perceive this homology, moreover, as continuing to inform Irish cultural, political and social practices down to the present day, albeit in hidden or mysterious ways.

Benedict Kiely, for example, has argued that although not confined to Ireland, it is possible that '[the] attachment to place, to the home places, even the mythologizing of place-names ... may be more emphasized in the case of island people, and made more poignant when their destiny takes them far from the island of their earliest associations and affections, Ithaca or Ireland' (1982: 96). He goes on to state that the earliest Irish literature clearly shows the presence of an irrevocable and mystical relationship between dwellers and island. In Kiely's reading, moreover, this mystical relationship embraced the whole island. He thus introduces an overtly nationalistic agenda: 'it is idle,' he insists, 'to say that the idea of one island, united, bound in by the triumphant sea was merely a modern political notion. Whatever the trampling of later generations and invasions may have done the idea was there in the beginning as clear as blossom on a spring morning' (ibid.: 97).

Although avoiding such florid language, James Charles Roy concurs with regard to the existence of 'a Celtic fascination with landscape and topography' (1997: 228). Indeed, so fundamental was this 'fascination' that it remains beyond the purview of rational scholarly inquiry. The Celtic peoples who colonised the island were themselves responding to '[the] more ancient shards of a lost pre-Celtic tradition', a tradition in which landscape was *the* primary force in community life: 'dramatically situated, instantly recognizable, [a passport] to a different though accepted sphere of everyday life, the magical' (ibid.: 235). Roy does not share Kiely's understanding of the special relationship between landscape and people as a vindication of the one-island state, however. He asserts that '[the] notion of a united Ireland ruled by a single high king – or later by a single bishop such as St. Patrick – is revisionist history of absolutely no relation to fact' (ibid.: 238). In any case, the relationship itself is fading in effect. In a variation on the 'placelessness' theme advanced by Relph (via Heidegger), Roy argues that the ancient fascination with landscape has been severely eroded in post-Independence Ireland. Changes in the island's wider political and cultural experience have effected 'radical breakdown in this traditional affection – and even familiarity – with the land'; affection and familiarity, as a consequence, are 'only available now as parody' (ibid.: 228).

It would be easy to fall in with a critical line which argues 'the weakening of distinct and diverse experiences and identities of places' (Relph 1976: 6). Loss and nostalgia, as we shall encounter time and again throughout this study, would appear to be the *sine qua non* of both ecocritical and heritage-based analyses. No doubt many traditional spatial affinities and identities have been lost, in Ireland as elsewhere; no doubt irreversible damage has been, and continues to be, done to traditional landscapes and the ways of life they support. I would have no hesitation in saying that from an ecological perspective much of this change should be resisted. But this is not the same as saying that 'loss' is in itself bad, nor that it is indicative of some deep failing on the part of the island communities, however they are imagined. As old spatial practices die out, new ones arise, based not, perhaps, on Roy's implicitly enriched feelings of 'affection and familiarity', but on more contestable (and thus potentially more interesting) feelings of attraction, repugnance, and all points in between (Graham 1997: 1–15). The fear of, and desire for, space has not disappeared, only mutated under pressure from changing circumstances in the developing social, political and cultural spheres. Indeed, contrary to the nostalgia of Roy and like-minded observers, interest in Irish space and place surged rather than diminished in the latter decades of the twentieth century (Whelan 1992). Some of this interest was obviously based on received narratives of belonging and identity; but much more of it, I suggest, emerged from the confused matrix of spatial affiliation, alienation and negotiation which came to form the basis of modern Irish cultural experience, and which in different yet related ways also provided the basis for the emergence of a 'postmodern geography'.

As stressed in the preface, this book does not represent an attempt to reverse the methodological polarities which have structured analyses of Irish life during the modern period. Geography without history would be just as flawed as history without geography. Rather, and to quote Soja for a final time, this book constitutes '[an] intention to tamper with the familiar modalities of time' (1989: 1) which have dominated the study of Irish culture throughout the modern period. My argument is that it is not so much the case that concern for history has been lost, but rather that under pressure from a combination of factors, issues of space have more or less organically re-emerged alongside the temporal considerations which so successfully dominated the Irish critical and cultural imagination for so long.

Conclusion

'There is always a figure in the landscape', as J. Hillis Miller writes (1995: 4). That figure, moreover, is always modifying the landscape in some way, always *doing* something with, to or on it: crossing it, admiring it, fighting for it. Even the attempt to 'conserve' a landscape or a cityscape in some supposedly better or more authentic form represents human agency undertaken in the name of some narrative of how space *is* or *should be*. Such practices then become the subject of a range of critical discourses and philosophical systems – competing and conflicting – some of which we have encountered above. Having constructed a broad theoretical and methodological context for the study, it is now time to look at some specific practices which have impacted throughout history upon the Irish imagination of space.

2
Space and the Irish Cultural Imagination

Chapter 1 provided a context within which a study focusing on issues of space, culture and identity in modern Ireland might be undertaken. In this chapter I want to take an overview of some of the ways in which discourses of place and space have been addressed in Irish critical, cultural and political practices over the years. Of the many potential areas of interest, I have chosen to focus on four: travel and tourism, mapping/naming, poetry, and the imagination of urban and rural space. Each of these fields and practices is vast in itself and I can do no more than briefly indicate, with a few illustrations, their significance. One recurring theme, however, concerns the relationship between the historical practices which continue to bear upon the ways in which space is imagined and organised in modern Ireland and the changes that are overtaking traditional spatial practices at the outset of a new millennium.

Travel and tourism

Travel and tourism are related spatial practices which have impacted heavily on the Irish cultural imagination throughout history. More recently, these practices have moved to the centre of the postcolonial critical agenda, with a number of incisive studies tracing both their emergence and their discursive properties. One of the most influential, Mary Louise Pratt's *Imperial Eyes: Travel Writing and Transculturation*, introduces '[the] possibilities and perils of writing in what I like to call "contact zones", social spaces where disparate cultures meet, clash, and grapple with each other, often in highly asymmetrical relations of domination and subordination.' Pratt goes on to focus upon 'European travel and exploration writing, analysed in connection with European economic and political expansion since around 1750' (1992: 4). It is instructive that, beginning even earlier yet covering substantially the same period (from around the middle of the eighteenth century to the present), a body of British travel writing about Ireland emerged, which performed many of the same tasks identified by Pratt as operating throughout the wider colonial world.

The roots of inter-island travel, however, lie further back in time. There is evidence of widespread trading and raiding between Ireland and Britain from before the coming of the Celts during the Iron Age (Duffy 1997: 10). In some ways, indeed, the writings attributed to St Patrick can be looked on an as early form of travel literature; he was, after all, bringing Christianity to 'the ends of the earth' (Hood 1978: 49). Patrick's description of Ireland has resonated down the centuries, initiating what might be called a problem-centred tradition of English travel-writing about Ireland. As John McVeagh points out, '[most] English contact with Ireland before [the eighteenth] century had been undertaken for military reasons, and was directed towards a colonial objective' (1995: 16). The fundamental hostility of the vast majority of early modern British accounts of Ireland (including most notably those of Sir John Davies and Edmund Spenser) should therefore come as no surprise. Thereafter, encouraged by 'the likelihood of personal safety, which in turn depended on political stability' (Foster 1997a: 62), the eighteenth century witnessed an explosion of English travel discourse on Ireland, including paintings and prints, road-books and road-maps, and of course prose accounts. Into the nineteenth century and beyond, however, the focus remained very much on 'the problem' of Ireland, and on what kinds of attitude were available to the British subject when confronted with this problem (Harrington 1991: 9ff).

Another early contributor to the tradition of problem-centred travel accounts was Giraldus Cambrensis (Gerald of Wales), the twelfth-century cleric who witnessed the early Norman incursions in Ireland. This formidable medieval figure set the tone for much of what followed when, casting doubt on classical and first millennium accounts of Ireland, he wrote: 'For it is only when he who reports a thing is also one who witnessed it that anything is established on the sound basis of truth' (O'Meara 1982: 35). In other words, 'go and see' is the message for those who require knowledge of Ireland; and certainly, 'rely more on those who have been and seen for themselves'. Gerald's *The History and Topography of Ireland* thus sets in motion what Pratt calls 'a rhetorics of presence' (1992: 205). The British traveller's desire to 'know' Ireland is structured in terms of this grammar and this rhetoric, so that such 'knowledge' is generated within the metropole's specific (instrumental) terms. For what does it mean to 'know' a country? What will happen to such knowledge? What is it for? What relationships of power does it enable? How does it structure itself as a body of knowledge, and how does it position itself in relation to the object which comes to be known?

These are obviously Foucauldian questions to some extent. As Foucault would no doubt have been the first to point out, the emergence of the post-Renaissance European subject can itself be largely understood with reference to the encounter between the privileged traveller, increasingly equipped with a range of practical tools and professional languages, and an 'unknown' other who constitutes a threat by virtue of their very 'unknownness'.[1] Colonial travel, as Nicholas Thomas puts it, 'is much more than movement across space'; it is rather a series of 'self-fashioning exercises' through which the coloniser attempts to formulate the identities and dictate the terms upon which exchanges across the colonial divide will take place (1994: 5ff). That 'contact zone' described by Pratt represents a space in which identities of domination and resistance are initiated and subsequently consolidated. It is the space wherein the discursive technologies designed to facilitate these identities are formulated. Travel to, and knowledge of, the non-European world is thus an essential factor of second millennium world history. And this holds good for the British encounter with an Ireland, as in Cambrensis, 'inevitably' destined to be less powerful than its neighbour.

Imperialism, as Derek Gregory writes, is 'a discourse which privileges vision' (1994: 171), and many accounts from the 'contact zone' contain instances of what Pratt terms 'the-monarch-of-all-I -survey' scene (1992: 201ff). This is the moment in which the European traveller encounters a particular landscape or edifice, usually from a height, which somehow encapsulates the identity of the non-European other whose territory is being traversed.[2] It is always a telling scene in the travel account for it offers a frozen, concrete image of the relationship between those who gaze and those who are gazed upon, the discoverer and the discovered. The local landscape is recruited for a discursive economy which limits it to those attributes and emotions set in place at the point of (supposedly) 'first' contact: exoticism, quaintness, danger, colour, primitiveness. This is a profound moment for both colonial and colonising subjects, as it confirms (and with each new account reconfirms) the identity of those categories and the relationship between them.

We find this 'monarch-of-all-I-survey' scene played out time and again in eighteenth- and nineteenth-century travel accounts of Ireland, with Killarney and environs providing a particularly popular locus. The anonymous author of *Ireland in 1804* 'set out immediately after break-fast, to walk to some eminence where I might survey the beauties of the lake at a single glance; and without expense sail in fancy over the lake, soar with the eagle among the rocks, or pursue the echoes to their most distant caves' (Grimes 1980: 50). That 'single glance' from 'some emin-ence' encapsulates the imperialist attitude towards the native culture, consisting, as Pratt says, 'of a gesture of converting local knowledges (discourses) into European national and continental knowledges asso-ciated with European forms and relations of power' (1992: 202). Anon.'s fantasy of sailing, soaring and pursuing masks the significant passivity of the experience: the complete English subject encounters the finished Irish landscape and interprets it from a position of privilege and power, symbolised by his promontory location. At the same time, the land-scape *exists* only by virtue of the traveller's presence, his ability to look upon and order it into a meaningful experience (what is included, what it omitted), and of course by virtue of the written account in which the landscape itself is realised (made real) for a (metropolitan) readership removed in time and space. The British gaze upon the exotic landscape of Killarney thus involves what Michael Cronin calls an intellectual and emotional act of translation, 'converting the experiences of the other place and people into the traveller's own native currency' (1993: 57). Making a similar point, Pratt calls this act of translation a 'relation of mastery' (1992: 204), a moment in which the landscape is simultaneously evaluated and constructed, judged for its beauty (in terms of contem-porary British tastes) and reproduced for the implied British reader.

The British traveller's home country is in fact never far away in this or indeed most of the eighteenth- and nineteenth-century accounts of Ire-land. Because of their relative geographical proximity, colonial relations between the main islands has been structured by a sensitive discourse of familiarity and exoticism in which, to speak figuratively, Ireland was white but not quite, black but not so black that it suffered the vili-fication reserved for more distant colonies (Lebow 1976; Murphy 1996). Thus, another feature of the rhetoric of travel discourse is the manner in which these exotic locations are described and oriented in terms of more familiar landscapes. Earlier in his tour Anon. had referred to Grafton Street as 'the Cheapside of Dublin' (Grimes 1980: 17), and opined that the poverty in Thomas Street makes St Giles (in London) seem like 'a palace of comfort' (ibid.: 20). Likewise, surveying the landscape from the summit of Turk his first thought (after the characteristic self-deprecating gesture of doubting his own literary ability) is to liken the panorama to the English lakes, and later he again draws comparisons with 'Cromack and Buttermere'. Finally, as he is about to descend, he thinks:

> I was now at the furthest extent of my tour, and if at each remove I had dragged a lengthening, although a pleasing chain, no wonder that I leaped down the sides of the mountains with a speed that outstripped and surprised the guide. Every step was now shortening my chain, and bringing me nearer home. (ibid.: 54)

The limitations of the guide's 'vernacular peasant knowledge' (Pratt 1992: 5) – which Anon. needed in practical terms to attain his monarch-of-all-I-survey moment – are here exposed in the face of a narrative drive towards closure (home), which functions as a textual analogue of colonial power. Anon. enjoys his tour in Ireland (despite the echoes of recent military conflict and political upheaval), but it is clear that the island he depicts exists only in terms of its relation to the larger island to the east, and only as an effect of his consciousness of the differences in power and knowledge enabled by that relation. Having made it to the heart of difference ('the furthest extent'), mastered (by describing and understanding) what he saw there, he will now return home to write up an account in which the colonial effects he experienced in 'reality' are reinscribed at the textual level.

What of the actual form of this and other travel texts? By 1804 it had become possible to give the political relations between Ireland and Britain an aesthetic gloss. Anon. writes of Killarney's 'beauties', the islands 'richly covered' with woods, 'delightfully situated' houses, the oars of a 'majestically' moving boat, the sound of which 'ravish the senses' (Grimes 1980: 52–3). He is engaging, in other words, with a long-established tradition of travellers from the colonising community who responded to Killarney using this kind of language. In 1758, for example, even Richard Pococke had suspended his attempt at an otherwise highly objective discourse to extol the beauties of the area, various aspects of which he found 'most Romantick', 'most delightful', 'wonderful', 'extraordinary' and 'charming' (McVeagh 1995: 182, 184).[3] In fact, 'beautiful' is the word occurring most frequently in Pococke's account of the Killarney landscape. But 'beautiful' was an imperial word; which is to say, it was a word routinely employed throughout the eighteenth century to describe improved British landscapes. Those places on the Celtics margins, however, whether in the Cairngorms, Snowdonia or west of the Shannon, needed another language to describe their vast, unimproved, dangerous status.

Thus we find interwoven with Anon.'s language of plenitude and sensuality a different level of engagement. One lake perpetually wears 'a gloomy and solemn appearance, from the dark, sullen shadow of Turk, which frowns upon it'; the mountains surrounding Killarney conceal 'horrid recesses', and the upper lake has a character 'rough, horrid and sublime' (Grimes 1980: 52–3). The notion of the sublime had received its official British debut in the year before Pococke's tour, with Edmund Burke's *Philosophical Enquiry*, a book which, as John Wilson Foster points out, 'stimulated a new generation of landscapers, who sought the picturesque qualities of roughness, irregularity and surprise' (1997a: 61). Within a few years, Burke's distinction between the sublime and the beautiful – and the different orders of pleasure afforded by each – had taken hold on the British (and indeed the European) imagination. The distinction was, moreover, frequently articulated to wider ideological concerns, including most significantly religion and politics. Landscapes described in terms of the sublime (with associations of divinity, vastness and solitude) and the beautiful (with associations of civilisation, order and balance) became physical symbols of supposedly different human (but soon national and regional) characteristics. (That other great late eighteenth-century aesthetic category, the picturesque, would impinge on representations of Killarney in due course.) Each had their attractions and their functions; each represented a particular way of engaging with the world which, when grounded in something so 'natural' as landscape, became powerful discursive symbols.

Killarney did not have to wait long for the sublime.[4] Like many before and since, Arthur Young was struck by the beauty of the area on his tour of 1776, and he employed the familiar battery of adjectives to describe it. Alongside and interspersed with the 'beautiful', however, he found a scenery that was not beautiful but that nevertheless commanded his respect as a viewing subject. He wrote: 'There is something magnificently wild in this stupendous scenery, formed to impress the mind with a certain species of terror. All this tract has a rude and savage air, but parts of it are strikingly interesting' (1892: 348). The beautiful – that which is pleasing and has been improved from Nature – exists alongside the sublime – that which through sheer magnitude surpasses human comprehension. Young wins these insights during a classic monarch-of-all-I-survey scene, ascending to 'one of [the] heights' surrounding the lakes from which he can survey the surrounding landscape and pass judgement upon it. He finds the prospect 'savage and dreadful . . . a scene of wild magnificence' (ibid.: 349). As Pratt points out (1992: 204), the monarch-of-all-I-survey metaphorically paints a scene for the safely tucked away imperial subject, and Young does actually invoke a painterly metaphor on a number of occasions (1892: 349, 354). The representational issues are thus similar to those of artistic discourse. Confronted with this sublime landscape, Young is 'both the viewer there to judge and appreciate it, and the verbal painter who produces it for others' (Pratt 1992: 205). What he decides to include is all there is; what he excludes does not exist, cannot be seen, heard or imagined. Killarney is in fact being relocated within what Iain Chambers calls 'the physical, psychic and imaginary landscapes of the "West"' (1997: 78). Indeed, it is as if Killarney *exists* so that it may be viewed by Young from the particular vantage point that he, as active agent, has chosen.

Despite his engagement with the sublime, Young could not rid his discourse of the rhetoric of 'improvement' which grew in fashion throughout the eighteenth century (Andrews 1961: 13). Even when gazing upon Killarney, 'the wildest and most romantic country I had anywhere seen', he noted certain less rugged areas which 'proved that these mountains were not incapable from climate of being applied to useful purposes' (1892: 348). The only thing missing, it appeared, was native skill and/or inclination. Young thus engages with a recurring motif in British representations of Ireland, summed up by John McVeagh in his introduction to Pococke's travelogues: 'admirable country, unadmirable people' (1995: 18). Again, we might look back to Cambrensis for the roots of this motif. While he found much of interest and merit in Ireland, the inhabitants were 'a wild and inhospitable people ... [who] live like beasts' (O'Meara 1982: 101). With regard to agriculture, Cambrensis explained: 'The wealth of the soil is lost, not through the fault of the soil, but because there are no farmers to cultivate even the best land.... The nature of the soil is not to be blamed, but rather the want of industry on the part of the cultivator' (ibid.: 102). The improper exploitation of such 'wealth' formed the basis of the Norman (and many another) colonial enterprise, for here, surely, was a landscape 'mutely pleading,' as Mary Hamer puts it, 'for the imperial helping hand of civilized England' (1989: 187). At a stroke, we are also introduced to what will become the familiar figures of the lazy native and the industrious coloniser.

By the middle of the nineteenth century this motif had evolved in some curious ways. The intention of John Hervey Ashworth's *The Saxon in Ireland* was 'to direct the attention of persons looking out either for investments or for new settlements, to the vast capabilities of the Sister Island, and to induce such to visit it, and to judge for themselves' (1852: unpaginated preface). Ashworth adopts the role of a bankrupt intending to emigrate to the New World, but induced instead to follow the advice of a curate friend to visit Ireland; for, as the latter explains, '[the] want of capital and enterprise are the main causes of all the evils existing in that unhappy country.... It is an admixture of Saxon habits and feelings, and the importation of English capital, that Ireland requires' (1852: 6). Later, the curate predicts that 'the English ere long will discover how much better it is to settle in Donegal or Mayo, than to seek their fortunes beneath burning suns, or in the land of the wild Indian' (ibid.: 105). Ireland is of a kind with India and America, it seems, an unimproved wilderness occupied by primitives of greater or lesser ignorance, awaiting only the guiding hand of an informed English administration.

At the same time, of course, Ireland is also unique in that it possesses tiers of colonial culture *in situ* – old English, Planters, Cromwellians and Glorious Revolutionaries. But for Ashworth, earlier colonialism is indicted by absenteeism and the inability of the contemporary colonial community to prevent the Famine, the full impact and extent of which was only beginning to emerge as he was writing. The landscapes Ashworth describes in his travel account are still admirable, in need of both 'understanding' (with all the connotations of surveillance and mastery) and 'development'. If the people remain unadmirable, however, this is the fault of inefficient colonial management. His book tacitly scorns the coerced 'Union' of 1800, but anticipates Ireland's willing entry into 'the strictest union with her sister island – when the same laws, the same usages, the same language, the same feelings will prevail in both' (1852: 106–7). In other words, the greater familiarity encouraged by travel and colonial migration is the natural analogue of greater political and cultural amalgamation.

Mention of the Famine leads on to the issue of late twentieth-century tourism. The packaging of that particular historical event in the Famine Museum at Strokestown, Co. Roscommon, as well as the recruitment of the 'Great Hunger' for various high-profile media 'events' during the 1990s, is indicative of the fact that no aspect of Irish historical experience is beyond the ken of the island's burgeoning tourist industry. Many people remain suspicious of the success of that industry, however, arguing that it trades upon 'a very selective and exclusively aesthetic representation of Ireland', a representation 'in which there is a constant attempt to discover what is visually appealing and exotic' but which '[ignores] poverty and conflict' (Sheerin 1998: 43). Having internalised traditional representations of Ireland as a series of picturesque landscapes and quaint natives, modern tourist discourse replays a relationship between native landscape and the privileged tourist gaze which may in fact be ultimately consequent upon relations between the coloniser and the colonised. Alongside the rhetoric of remembrance and healing that accompanied the 150th anniversary of the Famine in 1995, for example, another discourse – to do with figures, image, representation and management – was clearly at work. In short, as Barbara O'Connor puts it, 'Ireland has been, and continues to be, constructed as "other" to cater for the leisure needs of the metropolitan centres of Europe and North America. The construction has...a number of negative implications for the local population in terms of their sense of identity and self-worth' (1993: 69).

John Urry, author of *The Tourist Gaze*, writes that in modern western societies,

> much of the population in most years will travel somewhere else to gaze upon it and stay there for reasons basically unconnected with work. Travel is thought to occupy 40 per cent of 'free time'. ... It is a crucial element of modern life to feel that travel and holidays are necessary...Worldwide tourism is growing at 5–6 per cent per annum and will probably be the largest source of employment by the year 2000. (1990: 5)

The importance of tourism, then, in both material and theoretical terms, should not be underestimated. Urry traces the emergence of a range of modern tourist practices in relation to 'normal society' (1990: 3), showing how each informs and in part depends on the other. He argues that the notion of travel motivated by leisure has important implications for the organisation of modern society and for the awareness of those people who comprise society. A wide range of factors characteristic of late capitalist society currently impinges on tourist discourse, one of which is increasing urbanisation and the concomitant valorisation of rural life as a somehow more 'authentic' form of experience. Another significant influence is the sociological phenomenon known as the 'greying' of the population – that is, the changes wrought on established demographic patterns in the West by earlier retirement and longer life (1990: 128). At the beginning of the twenty-first century there are more people than ever before with more money to spend, many of whom are looking for 'quality' experiences to bring meaning and perspective to their later lives.

Even in Arthur Young's time, there was a sizeable tourist trade in Ireland, as the proliferation of travelogues, companions and maps throughout the latter part of the eighteenth century attests.[5] This industry grew during the nineteenth century, since which time 'Ireland has been popularly regarded as a place of great natural beauty worthy of the traveller's gaze' (O'Connor 1993: 69). Especially since the 1960s, tourism has been targeted by successive administrations, north and south, as a key area for economic growth. Despite the institution of a Department of Tourism, Sport and Recreation in the Republic of Ireland, however, responsibility for the development of the industry appears to be distributed across a number of government bodies. Amongst other things, the Department has responsibility for Bord Fáilte Éireann (the Irish Tourist Board), and CERT (the State Tourism Training Agency). The Heritage Council, however, comes under the auspices of the Department of Arts, Heritage, Gaeltacht and the Islands, while An Bord Pleanála (the Planning Board) and the Environmental Protection Agency are run from the Department of Environment and Local Government. The Office of Public Works, responsible for conserving and protecting built and natural environments on the one hand, and commissioning and building many heritage and interpretive centres on the other, operates out of the Department of Finance. Other relevant areas, including agriculture, transport and natural resources, are likewise dispersed. The story is similar in Northern Ireland (McArt 1998: 71–2). This organisation of affairs makes for conflict and confusion when tourist-related issues are raised.

However, even a perfunctory glance reveals that tourism was certainly a growth industry throughout the island during the 1990s. Various factors may have contributed to this, such as the prospect of peace in Northern Ireland and a more aggressive marketing policy by the concerned bodies. There is also the fact that, although the land mass has not altered, 'Ireland' has grown in terms of what there is to see and the kinds of things now considered worthy of the tourist gaze. Although the so-called Celtic Tiger has developed in large part on the strength of manufacturing industry (O'Hearn 1998), in many areas the production of tourist-worthy objects and landscapes appears to have superseded the production of goods. In the mid-1990s, Ruth McManus reckoned that 'tourism in the Republic accounts for one in twelve of all jobs' (1997: 91). Whereas in 1960 there were fewer than 1.5 million tourists to the Republic of Ireland (Gillmor 1994: 18), over 5.2 million visited during 1997, bringing over 1.5 billion punts to the national economy (McArt 1998: 251). The number of registered heritage-based attractions in both the Republic and Northern Ireland showed a sharp increase during the 1990s; tourists now have a wide range of historic houses and castles, interpretive centres, museums and folk parks, nature and wildlife parks, and heritage gardens from which to choose (Sheerin 1998: 40). Under the Republic's *Operational Programme for Tourism* (1994–99), there were plans to invest 125 million punts in what was called 'Natural/Cultural Tourism', seemingly part of an 'all-weather' strategy designed to extend the tourist season (Government of Ireland 1994). Given the growth of the economy in the south and the increasing number of people wishing to visit the island, these trends can only be expected to continue into the foreseeable future.

Tourism has also contributed to major changes in Irish transport policy, as laid out for example in an earlier *Programme* (Department of Transport and Tourism 1988). While the link between tourism and transport has a long history in Ireland, the introduction of roll-on, roll-off ferries between Ireland, Britain and the European mainland during the 1960s had a profound impact on travel to and from the island in the late twentieth century. There has also been a sustained attempt to upgrade the internal transport infrastructure, financed in part by the European Union and in part by the private and public sectors (Kneafsey 1998: 111). One significant development has been the construction of a motorway network around Dublin to facilitate traffic flow into and out of the city region. A significant divide has thus emerged between those more 'romantic' (that is, less well off) tourists who prefer to travel light, and those car tourists who are no longer reliant on the vagaries of the national public transport system. Many of the former evolve in time into the latter, and this also has implications for the kind of tourists attracted to the island and the nature of the gaze they bring to bear upon it. Meanwhile, from being one of the most expensive air spaces in the world, air travel to Ireland (especially from Britain and Europe) was liberalised towards the end of the 1980s, encouraging a level of fares and a range of independent airlines accessible to many more, and different kinds of, potential tourists. Besides large international airports in Belfast, Cork, Dublin and Shannon, there are smaller regional ones in Derry, Donegal, Galway, Kerry, Knock, Sligo and Waterford. These provide access portals for better-off tourists who wish to bypass the bigger cities and reach the 'real' Ireland as fast as possible.

There have also been a number of factors impacting on the tourist practices of Irish people themselves. The same global economic factors that have precipitated new patterns in visits *to* the island have also affected the indigenous population and their sense of spatial orientation, with regard to their own country and to the rest of the world. Resorts such as Courtown and Tramore on the 'Irish Riviera', Salthill near Galway City, Bundoran in Co. Donegal and Ballybunion in Co. Kerry continue to attract many Irish tourists. However, with the upturn in the economy during the 1990s and the development of cheap, fully inclusive package holidays, many people are now just as likely to head for Tenerife, Rimini or Corfu (Corcoran, Gillmor and Killen 1996). And while the numbers holidaying abroad continue to rise, the same is by and large true of those travelling from Ireland for other reasons, such as business and visiting (McArt 1999: 254). North America, the destination of so many emigrants during the 1980s, is now also a hugely popular destination for their friends and relatives. These developments, like the upsurge in tourism to continental Europe, have been precipitated by cuts in the cost of air travel; indeed, 'improvements' to road and rail transport and falling air costs have made weekend inter-state commuting a viable possibility for many at the beginning of the twenty-first century.

Although numbers still warrant the designation 'mass tourism' (especially on an island with such a relatively small population), it seems clear that Ireland attracts (in the Althusserian sense, 'hails, calls into being') different kinds of tourists in search of different kinds of experience. There are, as the brochures remind us, any number of reasons for visiting the island, and the industry has encouraged the development of a number of specialist areas, including leisure (especially fishing and golf), heritage, culture, roots and environment. Tourism represents only one potential use of the modern Irish landscape, but it is itself fragmented into numerous sub-areas, each competing to convert amorphous 'spaces' into particular 'places'. The same limited landscape has to be imaged and produced in numerous different ways to maximise the number of potential visitors, even those 'post-tourists' who profess to adopt the tourist gaze from an ironic perspective. And as with the administration of the tourist industry, fragmentation of the image of Ireland produces a situation in which there are many points of overlap and contradiction.

At its most basic, tourism may be understood 'as a use of landscape as a resource' (Kneafsey 1995: 136). But a resource for what? If Foucault set the theoretical agenda for debates on travel, then Freud can perform the same task for tourism, prompting us to ask: What does the tourist want? Put another way: what induces large amounts of peoples to uproot periodically and travel to another place to gaze upon something which they have previously only read or heard about, or seen on television? One answer to that question must be: the pursuit of the 'authentic', a category with a long and troubled career in Irish cultural history (Graham 1999). Urry's argument, that '[it] seems incorrect to suggest that a search for authenticity is the basis for the organisation of tourism' (1990: 11), applies principally to Britain and other late capitalist formations; tourism in Ireland, on the other hand, does not yet appear to have evolved to that particular stage of post-tourism, and it still operates by and large upon a fetishisation of the 'authentic' and the 'typical'.

But what is 'authentic' and what is 'typical' in Ireland, and how could one tell? One traditional answer sees the rural elevated above the urban as a sign of Irishness, as if national identity were a quantifiable phenomenon. Which is to say, modern Irish tourist discourse encourages a practice in which 'people in urban capitalist society can feel a superiority over the traditional, at the same time as they seek "authentic experience" in it – an "authenticity" which is no longer possible in their everyday life' (O'Connor 1993: 77). Rural Ireland offers an ideal retreat for the metropolitan mind exhausted by the rigours of the 'real' world. You may observe the comely maidens and athletic youths, the fine old women and the pensive old men, in their natural environment – you can even temporarily immerse yourself in that environment if you are feeling particularly in need of refreshment and have the financial wherewithal to indulge yourself – and thereby come to a fuller sense of who you are and where you fit in the world as it is currently organised. That, after all, is in large part what tourism is for: an exercise is self- and other-formation.[6] However, the bad faith of such a practice creates what one commentator calls 'a primary breeding ground for deceit, exploitation, mistrust, dishonesty and stereotype formations' (cited in O'Connor 1993: 77). This breeding ground is shared by tourist and native, for if the former implicitly supports a discursive agenda founded on the asymmetrical power of centre and periphery, the latter is increasingly caught between established cultural patterns and the financial attraction of playing up to the stereotype. With tourism becoming of increasing importance to the Irish economy, it seems inevitable that the imagery produced by the industry will have a greater impact upon the identity of the places and the people it is trying to sell (Kneafsey 1998).

O'Connor points out that the key element of modern Irish tourist discourse is the representation of life on the island 'as a pre-modern society' (1993: 70). One of the discursive mechanisms through which this effect is realised is the 'chronotope', described by Joep Leerssen (after Bakhtin) as 'a place with an uneven distribution of time-passage, where time is apt to slow down and come to a standstill at the periphery: that emerges as one of the formative notions in the literary and historical imagination of Ireland' (1996: 226). What Leerssen is referring to here is the impression that not only is the island physically removed from 'real' life, but also that time functions differently there. Modern Irish tourist discourse, that is to say, employs a kind of 'spatial grammar' – inherited from earlier travel accounts and from certain developments in nineteenth-century cultural nationalist discourse – in which the movement westwards in space figures simultaneously as a movement backwards in time.[7] The chronotope is thus the basis of the peculiar mythology surrounding 'the West' in modern Irish culture, a belief that somehow a particular spatial location affords a qualitative difference in knowledge and experience.[8] As we shall see throughout this study, this difference can be inflected in a number of ways – from 'bad' primitive-ness to 'good' simplicity and all points in between.

But of course, the 'peripheral' and the 'central' are not stable locations; they are merely effects of their relation to other places, depending upon who is looking, from where, and that subject's particular sense of how space and place are organised. Thus Galway is 'peripheral' to Dublin, which itself is 'peripheral' to London. But London is not 'naturally' the centre of the Atlantic archipelago, it only seems that way through the projection of a way of seeing which has its roots in imperial history. As Leerssen goes on to argue, all space is in fact subject to many different yet coexistent temporalities, so that what appears quaint and primitive for one – say, nineteenth-century Dublin for the English traveller newly arrived from London – will seem the acme of modern speed and bustle for the Galwegian. 'In the case of Dublin,' he continues, 'the work of James Joyce offers an interesting example how one and the same place can be seen as peripheral at one moment, central at the next, and how the attendant registers of description match that contradictory construction' (1996: 227).

The tourists' demand for authenticity, and the tourist industry's willingness to supply (or manufacture) it at all costs, has resulted in the development of the concept of 'heritage' (now serviced by organisations such as Dúchas) as a key concept for modern Irish tourist discourse. Because of its wide usage, however, the term comes loaded with ambiva-lence and controversy (Fladmark 1993). Among other things, one remarkable aspect of modern Irish tourist discourse is the flourishing of the concept of 'heritage' in a context which is economically and cultur-ally buoyant; in some cases, in fact, economic success is sought quite specifically by means of a heritage-led approach to local redevelopment (Kneafsey 1994, 1998; McManus 1997). This contrasts with the estab-lished academic view, which understands heritage emerging and thriving 'in a climate of decline', while simultaneously stifling 'the culture of the present' (Urry 1990: 109). However, it seems clear that in modern Ireland at least, the 'culture of the present' has made significant gains by trading – literally and metaphorically – on particular constructions of the culture of the past.

There is a danger, however, that such a programme will function piecemeal and unevenly, whilst eroding (sometimes literally) the 'heritage' that is ostensibly the basis of attraction for privileged outsiders. Ireland is not the only place where a desired balance between conservation and development has proved easier to theorise than to implement (McManus 1997: 93). Heritage represents a highly selective version of tradition, marginalising some aspects, but focusing on those which contribute to the most attractive, most cost-effective 'experience' in the present. 'Authentic' representations have to be packaged in entertaining ways, and this latter imperative impacts in numerous ways on the 'meanings' such representations communicate. In a related point, many argue that the industry is founded upon a fundamental contradiction in so far as the (increasingly successful) attempt to attract tourists from relatively well-developed western countries to experience 'authentic' ways of life in 'authentic' Irish locations in itself constitutes a threat to local communities and environments (MacManus 1997; Kneafsey 1998). This is all the more ironic in so far as one of the recurring images employed to sell Ireland as a desirable location is precisely the absence of mass tourism. Short-term gains may have grave implications for local rural communities attracted to tourism as a panacea for the decline in traditional ways of life.

So, having once asked 'What does the tourist want?', and come up with the answers 'heritage' and 'authentic culture', another question presents itself: 'Who decides how to interpret?' (Kneafsey 1995: 149). In other words, how is the past to be brought before the tourist gaze? How will it be organised and packaged? What kinds of people will be involved? And how will the interpretation of landscapes and artefacts produced by the discourse of heritage relate to other competing interpretations produced by those with different concerns? These questions have both theoretical and practical implications. 'Interpretation' carries the entire critical baggage of modern European critical theory, loaded with issues of representation, point of view, point of departure, translation, and so on. 'Interpretation' is also a key term in heritage discourse, impacting upon local job opportunities, the location of amenities and services, and so on. Given the importance of tourism to the Irish economy, the tendency has been, as Moya Kneafsey argues, that '[ultimately], the final decision will rest with professionals who may have different agendas depending on the perceived use of the heritage' (1995: 149). Emer Sheerin agrees: 'heritage creates a deep division between professionals involved in heritage representations and both the visitors and the local populations surrounding the heritage sites.' Lacking access to the language of the professionals, she concludes, local residents are in danger of becoming in effect 'mere spectators of their own past.'[9]

To combat these dangers, Bord Fáilte has emphasised the concept of 'sustainable tourism'. The Department of Tourism, Sport and Recreation aims, among other things, 'to contribute to Ireland's economic and social progress by developing a sustainable tourism sector that promotes high standards in marketing, service quality and product development' (reproduced in McArt 1998: 71). The goal is a commercially viable industry based on a balance between professional conservation and 'bottom-up' development. Heritage tourism will continue to focus in large part upon 'tradition', but should be organised in such a way as to pose no threat, material or otherwise, to traditional ways of life (Bord Fáilte 1992). On the contrary, the positive view of tourism's impact on local communities holds that it 'can play a major role in reinforcing pride in rural areas, which in turn leads to a greater desire to develop traditional skills and abilities, and to share them with others' (Kneafsey 1994: 115). Heritage may have become indissolubly linked with tourism, but it also performs an important civic role in educating local communities as to the significance of the built and natural environments in which they live. Moreover, it is possible that focusing tourist attraction in purpose-built heritage centres may help to alleviate pressure on 'real' heritage sites (McManus 1997: 92). It would be an ironic but not unwelcome development if the influence of global tourism contributed to the rehabilitation of local communities in relation to the mid-range political and cultural institutions – such as the nation-state – through which they have for so long been misrepresented and marginalised.

For critics, however, such arguments are a rationalisation by an industry that is increasingly profit-led. Cultural systems, no less than natural ones, are immensely sensitive and susceptible to any kind of incursion, be it linguistic, material, environmental or whatever. The danger is that the particular 'thought worlds' sustained by such cultural systems may collapse under 'the weight of the tourist "gaze"',[10] thus killing the goose that lays the golden egg. Despite the rhetoric of 'sustainable tourism' and the commitment to local engagement, modern Irish tourism remains a use of landscape as a resource by those with no sentimental interest in, and only an instrumental – albeit specialised – knowledge of, those landscapes. Indeed, the danger is that the phrase 'sustainable tourism' may turn out to be oxymoronic.

Colonialism, as O'Connor points out, remains a key trope for the analysis of tourist discourse as it impacts upon a small, fragile economico-cultural formation such as Ireland:

> Apologists for colonial expansion regarded the land marked out for plantation as empty and therefore available for stamping their own mark on 'virgin territory'. So, too, in a contemporary tourist context, areas and countries are represented as exclusively available as a pleasure paradise for tourists – a place in which they can engage in carefree play for the duration of their holidays. (1993: 71)

This certainly represents one dimension of modern tourism in Ireland, and has been engaged as such by critics and cultural commentators. But while it remains possible to regard tourism as colonialism by other means, it is also necessary to maintain a sense of 'the complexity by which different visitors can gaze upon the same set of objects and read them in a quite different way' (Urry 1990: 111). No one, and least of all the professional critic, should rush to cast the first stone. It may be, as Kneafsey argues, that '[rather] than simply (re)constructing or destroying previously fixed and stable place identities, tourism contributes to on-going processes of change, whilst at the same time being mediated through the elements of continuity which exist within place identities' (1998: 114). One thing is certain, however: in a world where some form of travel, leisure and tourist-gazing are within the compass of more people than ever before in the West – including Ireland – we are all tourists now, none more so than those with secure notions of just exactly where 'home' and 'away' are.

Mapping/naming

We have already encountered the concept of 'cognitive mapping', the process whereby the subject comes to an impressionistic sense of her/his location in relation to a range of unevenly empowered environments. In this section, however, I am principally concerned with the production and use of real maps: texts which enable the map-reading subject to negotiate space by offering seemingly practical knowledge of the world – its shape, size, physical properties, and so on. Closely related to this is the process of naming, which invariably accompanies the production of maps. As a language-using species, humankind registers space, distance and topographical features only when these have been granted the fundamentally human property of the name. As Tim Robinson, a cartographer of whom I shall have more to say later, puts it: 'Placenames are the interlock of landscape and language' (1996: 155). J. Hillis Miller makes the same point rather more formally: 'topographical consider-ations, the contours of places, cannot be separated from toponymical considerations, the naming of places' (1995: 1). In what follows, therefore, I shall employ the rather awkward locution 'mapping/naming' to maintain a sense of the functional cognation of these practices.

If travel and tourism represent important elements for a contemporary Irish cultural studies alert to the possibilities of space, the same is no less true of mapping and naming, discourses with a long and eventful history within the Irish cultural imagination. Each has emerged from recent relative academic obscurity in sub-disciplines such as cartography and folkloristics to become crucial elements for many engaged contem-porary critical practices. In much the way that 'narrative' and 'discourse' were buzzwords from earlier periods in the theoretical revolution, so one finds 'mapping' widely evoked, both as actual cartographical practice and metaphorical figure (Gregory 1994; Smith and Katz, 1993: 69–70; Soja 1989). Indeed, one commentator goes so far as to suggest that '[the] "cartographic connection" can ... be considered to provide that provisional link which joins the contestatory theories of post-structuralism and post-colonialism in the pursuit of social and cultural change' (Huggan 1995: 411).

The argument in this section will be that the mastery of space implied in official maps/names is one of the principal means through which hegemony is both asserted and contested. In deconstructive terms, '[topography]', as Hillis Miller puts it, 'is a logocentric practice through and through' (1995: 303). The rhetorical force of the map/name is to the effect that '*these* places mean *these* things, don't they?'; but such a formulation is always open to the possibility of a negative response. The map may be read, as Catherine Nash suggests, 'as a manifestation of a desire for control which operates effectively in the implementation of colonial policy' (1993: 49); but it is also a site of confrontation and struggle between various 'official constructions of identity and power' (Graham 1997a: 183) and unofficial usages which attempt to question the authority of the map/name in terms of popular cultural requirements and practices.

The conversion of abstract empty space into meaningful historic places by the twin processes of mapping and naming would in fact appear to be one of the most fundamental aspects of human life. Place-naming represents the humanising of the landscape; '[space]', as Edward Relph put is, 'is claimed for man by naming it' (1976: 14). We may presume, for example, that the communities of hunters and fishers who settled in the Bann Valley in Northern Ireland during the Mesolithic had intimate links with a limited physical terrain, a terrain they must have known – that is, mapped either mentally or by means of some crude technology – if they were to survive. It was only when these terrains were named, however, that landscapes began to take on specific personalities, atmospheres, connotations – in short, meanings. Space that is unmapped and unnamed is chaotic and dangerous, lacking the coordinates necessary for a meaningful engagement. Relph argues that 'space' only becomes 'place' when it is named, and it is only named when it is considered 'in terms of some human task or lived experience' (ibid.: 15).

Commentators point to the implicit instrumentality of the map/name, its function as an image of certain selected aspects of the world (Harley 1988; King 1996; Wood 1992). Like any text, that is, the map/name is not a neutral reflection but an engaged representation of the world, countenancing by inclusion certain materials, interests and experiences. The map/name offers us something useful we could not otherwise have – an impression of space and distance beyond the range of our senses – but what it actually delivers is an impression of power made supposedly 'natural' by its own materiality. This is because both the concept of the map/name and the signs it employs to naturalise that concept are highly contingent (King 1996: 37ff). Every aspect of the map/name, from its ostensible subject matter (every map is *of* something; every name *names* something) to the material from which it is made, represents what Denis Wood calls a '[moment] in the process of decision-making' (1992: 185), a moment in which *this* feature (for example, coal, taxable property, religious persuasion) is deemed worthy of surveillance while others are ignored, in which *this* technology (the eye, triangulation or satellite photography) is deemed 'better' – more accurate, more useful, more lucrative – than others, and in which *this* system of representational signs (symbols, relief or colour-coding) is established at the expense of others. In short, the knowledge embodied in the map 'is socially constructed' (Wood 1992: 18).

As might be expected, mapping was a crucial aspect of the modern imperial enterprise. Intrepid early explorers traversed supposedly 'empty' space in the 'new' world, claiming and naming wilderness for the empire as they proceeded. Mapping/naming was an integral part of the process by which the empire was legitimised, for not only did it possess crucial tactical value (in the struggle with other imperial powers

and with the aborigines who paradoxically occupied the 'virgin' territory); it also lent substance to the imperial imagination, fleshing out the
culture of colonialism with a set of symbolic representations that was
simultaneously familiar and exotic (Carter 1987). Maps were used, as
Bruce Avery notes in the context of early modern British imperialism in
Ireland, 'both as tools for the expansion of empire and the fostering of a
nationalistic attachment to territory' (1990: 263). It was only later, in the
wake of Enlightenment and the growth of the historical imagination in
the West, that colonising projects began to

> split between assimilationist and segregationist ways of dealing with
> indigenous peoples; between impulses to define new lands as vacant
> spaces for European achievement, and a will to define, collect and
> map the cultures which already possessed them; and in the defin-
> ition of colonizers' identities, which had to reconcile the civility and
> values of home with the raw novelty of sites of settlement. (Thomas
> 1994: 2–3)

Imperialist Europe became fascinated with 'native' cultures, and many a
scientific and artistic career was built upon the raw material of empire.
Of course, engagement with these exotic cultures was a two-way exercise,
for the more the imperialist represented the native – either in the 'hard'
language of science or the 'soft' language of art – the more his identity
as empowered subject was consolidated, and the more the asymmetrical
relationship between the categories was cemented.[11] Which is to say, at
precisely the same time as the native landscape was mapped/named as
'native', the mapping/naming subject mapped/named himself as 'mapper/
namer' – that is, as an empowered subject possessing both the ability
and the right to appropriate unfamiliar landscapes through a process of
mapping/naming. Like travel and anthropology, then, mapping/naming
has 'frequently affirmed the values and precedence of the centre, under
the guise of taking a "genuine"' critical interest in the different spaces
of the exotic' (Thomas 1994: 6).

Imperialist mapping/naming attempted to construct 'a homology
between a culture, a people, a nation and its particular terrain' (Lavie
and Swedenburg 1996: 1). This homology functioned in turn as the
'reality' upon which a whole series of hierarchical oppositions was formulated and deployed: nature/culture, male/female, civilised/barbarian,
developed/primitive, and so on. The map/name of the native landscape
was thus represented in terms of a functional realism in which the
'truth' produced by the text was supposedly the 'truth' embodied in the

actual landscapes in question. The native terrain 'spoke' its own subjection, and the imperialist power had the maps and the names to prove it. With the emergence of postcolonialism as a critical paradigm during the 1970s and 1980s, however, attention has shifted from processes of domination to strategies of resistance, from the ways in which imperialism constructed the fiction of stability and security to the ways in which the colonised culture challenged and undermined received 'reality' by exposing the contradictions of colonial discourse.

As part of this shift, much work has been done since the 1970s on resisting, or 'deconstructing', the map (Harley 1992; Huggan 1995; King 1996: 167–85). Official maps/names cannot be summarily discarded, because we do not yet possess an alternative cartographical imagination capable of enabling us to survive in the world as it is currently established. However, they may be read in such a way as to expose their gaps and inconsistencies, with the effect that the map-reader/name-user becomes aware of the constructed nature of the 'reality' that is being represented in the text. As Catherine Nash writes in a specifically Irish context: 'However tainted the concept of landscape is by colonial and masculinist discourse, a poststructuralist understanding of identity allows its re-appropriation. Postcolonial and feminist remapping and renaming do not replace one authoritative representation with another but with multiple names and multiple maps' (1993: 54). The idea, then, is not to substitute a 'good' map/name for a 'bad' one, but to displace the terms in which different versions of 'reality' are asserted. Only in this way can 'reimpositions of domination or fundamental inequality ... be avoided', and at the same time 'new and more equitable mappings, cartographies that in time could gain a similar hold' (King 1996: 185) be established.

Besides the essentially negative process of 'deconstructing the map/ name' – the act of *de*territorialisation in which imperial maps/names are challenged and undermined – postcolonialism also pursues a process of positive *re*territorialisation, reconstituting (remapping and renaming) both individual and social perceptions in the spaces vacated by the colonial power. Despite its heritage as one of the principal engines of imperialism, that is, mapping/naming may be celebrated 'as an agent of cultural transformation and as a medium for the imaginative revisioning of cultural history' (Huggan 1995: 407). Reterritorialisation should not be cast in that naively realist mode characteristic of early forms of anti-imperialism, however, in which 'proper' maps and names are produced in an attempt to rectify imperialism's ideological imposition (and in implicit imitation of imperialist maps/names). Rather, the map/name should function 'as a locus of productive dissimilarity where the provisional connections of cartography suggest an ongoing perceptual transformation which in turn stresses the transitional nature of post-colonial discourse' (ibid.: 408). We cannot do without maps/names; but instead of producing entirely new ones which are in danger of replicating the old systems of thought, the goal should be '[a] new, deconstructive reading of the existing map...in which the arbitrary status of the existing boundaries is apparent' (King 1996: 172). The postcolonial map/name, in other words, must forgo the traditional claims on 'truth' and attempt instead to express both the historical contingency and the ontological hybridity of space; for if hybridity and contingency were exacerbated by the historical encounter between coloniser and colonised, they appear to constitute the natural condition of landscape and of the language used to describe landscape.

As many commentators point out, moreover, imperial (or indeed any) maps/names do not require deconstruction from some privileged point in the present. Arguing from Derrida, it is possible to show that the map/name, like any text, is self-deconstructive if examined closely enough. 'The landscape "as such" is never given,' as Hillis Miller puts it, 'only one or another of the ways to map it [is]' (1995: 6). But history shows that the map/name has always been addressed on the ground (so to speak) with a mixture of 'faith and doubt' (Wood 1992: 27), that is, with a set of functional expectations produced by the authority of the map/name, but at the same time with a scepticism which gives rise to a determination to question and potentially subvert the power encoded in the map/name. Official maps/names offer what Michel de Certeau calls 'a "state" of geographical knowledge [which] pushes away into its prehistory or into its posterity, as if into the wings, the operations of which it is the result or the necessary condition' (1988: 121). Or as Mary Hamer puts it: '[an] abstracted and standardized representation of terrain challenges direct local experience and removes, as it were, the terrain from the cognitive ownership of those who inhabit it' (1989: 184). The map/name, to repeat, is an ideological construct, masking its disparate, contingent histories under the guise of a seemingly inevitable 'state'. But de Certeau discerns a gap between the usage of maps/names in 'everyday culture' (1988: 121) and the abstract topographical and toponymical discourses of official culture. People occupy by necessity 'all forms of an imposed order' (ibid.: 122); but in 'the practice of everyday life' they use these forms in ways that exceed and subvert official *diktats*.

Such rejoinders to the traditional authority of the map/name have in their turn elicited critical responses from those who consider the postmodernist and postcolonialist celebration of supposedly free radical acts of mapping/naming as a dangerous fantasy. Postmodern geography attempts to collapse the boundaries between 'good' and 'bad' maps/ names by showing that all such endeavours are ultimately expressions of certain privileged representations of the world. Yet such a division is still apparent in the implicit differentiation (as evidenced by the words 'should' and 'must' in the previous paragraphs) between (good) maps/ names which short-circuit their own assumptions and (bad) ones which do not. The postmodern celebration of reterritorialisation is, moreover, liable to ignore the 'power relations, the continued hegemony of the center over the margins' (Lavie and Swedenburg 1996: 3) that still structures most people's perception of contemporary space.

For some, 'postal' theory has colluded in the production of a situation in which the map/name is more important than the territory of which it is ostensibly a representation. Geoff King talks of 'the map that precedes the territory', and continues: 'Rather than the map being a product *of* the territory, as it is usually understood, coming only after it – both temporally and conceptually – and remaining answerable to it, there has been a curious reversal' (1996: 1–2, original emphasis). Such is the technology of representation and reproduction, actual physical landscapes may come as a bit of a disappointment to those expecting a soundtrack and regulated temperature to accompany their spatial adventures.[12] In other words, typically of western cultural production in the postmodern age, the simulation has come to replace the referent in discursive priority (Baudrillard 1983; Eco 1983). If things, places, names are not on the map, in some important senses they do not exist. The older paradigm of spatial politics, to which the 'deconstruction of the map/name' was addressed, is by and large defunct at the beginning of the twenty-first century. In the meantime, loss of faith in the notion of secure mappable/nameable coordinates has undermined any attempt to resist the new systems which are overtaking the spatial and temporal organisation of the postmodern world.[13] Hence, the absolute necessity to restore 'a clear distinction between map and territory' (King 1996: 14).

What has been Ireland's experience of mapping/naming? The earliest known map of the island was produced by Claudius Ptolemy in Alexandria in the middle of the second century (1991: 48–9, 172). Since then the island has been continuously mapped/named, the materials in question covering every instance of human concern from the rough, pre-battle outline of a medieval fortification to the sophisticated modern tourist map/name of a relatively small urban area such as Temple Bar in the heart of Dublin. Before going on to consider the role of mapping/

naming in modern Irish history, however, it is worth mentioning once again the 'special relationship' which many have discerned between community, place and name in early Gaelic society, and in subsequent Irish cultural history. John Wilson Foster has argued that:

> Named places, sometimes defined and identified by a natural feature (a mountain, a bog, a strand, a river, a natural well, etc.), did not generate simply local lore, but also a topography intimately bound up with families, ownership, genealogy. ... Places, place lore, place-names: the landscape of Ireland was *seen* and *read* by the Irish through powerful cultural lenses. (1997a: 43, original emphases)

Such practices, he continues, bespeak 'the ancient assumption of an intimate traffic between human beings and nature' (ibid.: 45), certain aspects of which survived the demise of the culture supporting that assumption and the onset of a new scientific paradigm. It was these remnants that eighteenth- and nineteenth-century folklorists 'discovered', and which fuelled in part both the first and second Celtic Revivals. From the beginning, however, many such analyses were cast in a declensionist mood, to the effect that the Celtic 'fascination with landscape and topography' (Roy 1996: 228) is lost and gone forever, only available in the modern world in the form of parody or nostalgia. In later times, '[the] colonial mapping of Ireland in the nineteenth century, the concurrent Anglicization of Irish place names, and the decline of the Irish language provide the historical background for the expression of themes of cultural loss and recovery in contemporary Irish culture' (Nash 1993: 40). Space and place, in this reading, have been crucial both to the experience of individuals and to the organisation of society on the island from the beginning of recorded history, although their significance and impact continues to shrink with every generation.

One of the conventions through which the Gaelic relationship with landscape was expressed was '*dinnshenchas*'. This term describes both a general tendency in early Gaelic literature and (when prefixed with 'the') a body of Middle-Irish toponymic literature known as *Dinnshenchas Erenn* assembled during the twelfth century. Roughly translating as 'the traditional, legendary lore of notable places' (Mac Giolla Léith 1991: 158), *dinnshenchas* developed from onomastic (placename traditions) and aetiological (origin legends) discourses derived from early Celtic culture. Edward Gwynn pointed out that 'knowledge of the place-names of a particular neighbourhood was from very early times an essential part of the education of the higher orders of society' (1935: 91), while Seán O Tuama claims that '[no] poet was accounted educated if he was not fully acquainted with the *dinnsheanchas'* (1985: 24). Such knowledge would have been valuable currency within a society so significantly shaped by issues of blood and land. Given their important role as conveyors of ritualised memory, poets would have been especially concerned with landscape. The canon of early Irish literature is in fact infused with topographical and toponymical matter.[14]

The formalisation of onomastic and aetiological tendencies in *Dinnshenchas Erenn* combines history (derivation and tradition) with geography (topographical feature), and learned disquisition with native folklore.[15] The discourse itself, however, proceeds by means of some rather 'fanciful' (Gwynn 1935: 92), if not 'entirely spurious' (Mac Giolla Léith 1991: 160) etymology. A place-name could have any number of legends regarding its origins, while Middle-Irish scholars were notorious for the 'ingenuity' of their interpretations, even (or especially) if they required an element of invention. Nevertheless, it is the manifestation of topographical and toponymical knowledge in Irish writing of the early and middle periods that usually forms the basis for claims regarding the special relationship between place and identity in Celtic/Gaelic/ Irish life. Much modern critical and theoretical debate focuses on the extent to which Irish literature from the nineteenth century to the present testifies to some innate need within the Irish psyche to express this special relationship. The question of accuracy is incidental; indeed, 'accuracy' as an analytical category belongs to a mentality which has come to threaten older paradigms of knowledge, in Ireland and elsewhere. Yet sympathetic commentators remain adamant that (the) *dinnshenchas* reflects an understanding in which place and identity are inseparable, and that this understanding has survived in part the demise of the culture which fostered it.

Kevin Whelan has written that 'Gaelic society never evolved a cartographic tradition – it knew the country by heart in its enduring *dinnshenchas'* (1992: 403). Around about the same time as *Dinnshenchas Erenn* was being compiled, however, Ireland was experiencing the first incursions from Norman Britain.[16] And as in similar imperial contexts, the technology of map-making developed alongside the technology of conquest. But mapping/naming in Ireland from the twelfth century on was in fact a process of hegemonic accretion as well as 'an instrument of active appropriation' (Hamer 1989: 188). With every advance in the conquest and with each individual act of confiscation, Gaelic Ireland was mapped/named – that is, *known* – within the terms of the colonising power. The (disputed) meanings of the spaces and places of Gaelic Ireland, much of the time encapsulated within their (disputed) names, were slowly displaced by a different set of concerns which shifted the Irish cultural and political imagination from one spatial paradigm (tribal and caste-based) to another (feudal and colonial). This was not the result of a process of outright domination and displacement, of course. Much of the time, the systematic programme of confiscation and resettlement – as for example during the wars and plantations of the sixteenth and seventeenth centuries (Avery 1990) – was 'superimposed on and somehow reconciled with' indigenous spatial knowledge, thus securing 'the double benefit of co-opting the native past and diminishing the likelihood of resistance to the new order' (Hamer 1989: 189). Established Gaelic space was colonised by new British space, creating a subtle series of overlappings and redoublings, which yet never lost sight of the power of the latter over the former.

The watershed in the history of modern Irish mapping/naming was the 'Down Survey' produced by Sir William Petty in the years after the Confederate Wars of the mid-seventeenth century (Andrews 1961: 9–11). The maps/names produced by Petty's team were accurate and functional, designed to expedite a programme of systematic confiscation. At a deeper level, they represent the first attempt to formalise a scientific dimension to the colonial relationship, '[fixing] the "other",' as Nash puts it, 'and [neutralizing] the threat of difference by the apparent stability of the map's coherence' (1993: 50). Impelled by the widespread practice of land (especially estate) surveying in a country where land was both materially and ideologically central, the Anglo-Irish contribution to the discourse of scientific cartography grew in significance (Andrews 1985; Foster 1997a: 45ff). During the eighteenth century especially, science and colonisation advanced alongside each other; if 'unknown' lands provided the impetus for the development of a new scientific imagination, the latter (along with religion) provided the former with a rationale for its drive towards discovery and conquest. The mapping/ naming of the island by Anglo-Irish cartographers in the relatively peaceful century after the Treaty of Limerick was one area in which the two discourses significantly overlapped.

The key development in terms of the history of Irish mapping/ naming was the commissioning and execution during the first half of the nineteenth century of a series of Ordnance Survey maps of the country 'on the unprecedentedly large scale of six inches to one mile' (Andrews 1961: 16). All existing mapping/naming projects, whether civilian or military, were deemed obsolete in the face of this huge scientific undertaking. Fieldwork began in 1825 under the directorship of Colonel Thomas Colby in London and (after 1828) of Lieutenant (Captain after 1840) Thomas Larcom in Dublin; 2,139 people were employed at the peak of the project in 1839. By the time the final sheet (of 1,906 in all) was produced in 1846, the entire island and its coastal waters had been systematically surveyed at the expense of the British Exchequer. Besides its main cartographical mission, the survey was also instrumental in the development of a number of disciplines – including archaeology, orthography, geology and philology – that were to be significant in the emergence of a particular version of 'Irish' identity later in the nineteenth century. Alfred Smyth claims that the first Ordnance Survey initiated the discipline of modern Irish historical geography and provided the impetus for subsequent scholarly analysis of Irish history (1982: 1).

Smyth refers to the 'Anglo-Irish Ordnance Survey' (ibid.), however, and this is indicative of the fact that the project may also be viewed as one of the most symbolic points of confrontation between modernity and tradition in Irish colonial history. For one thing, the appeal to 'science' masked, as usual, a much more active agenda. The fact that Ireland was singled out for such a 'prestigious' undertaking signalled the need to contain this radically othered space on the Empire's own doorstep, so that it might be known, named and mapped within the Empire's own limiting terms. The island's very amorphousness demanded a steady, controlling British hand, a metaphor concretised time and again by the manipulation of the theodolite during the process of triangulation.

Hamer has suggested quite bluntly that the ideology underpinning the enterprise was Protestant, Unionist and landowning (1989: 186). She goes on to argue, however, that the interests of the Gaelic-speaking, non-landowning Roman Catholic population were not so much erased as coopted. The Ordnance Survey was responsible, for example, for the consolidation of the townland as the principal administrative unit of territory in Ireland. Yet the claims of this traditional land division (62,205 of which were recorded in all) were in many instances subordinated to the cartographical demands of the survey; new townlands were created, old ones subdivided, boundaries straightened, extended and erased (McErlean 1983). Irish place-names, likewise, 'were a major feature of the map but they bore no witness to Irish ownership of the soil. They endorsed, rather . . . the state of the Union between Britain and Ireland and the power of the English Protestant landowners, the ascendancy class, in Ireland' (Hamer 1989: 186). Irish scholars were recruited to bring their philological and toponymical expertise to the exercise, but denied real executive power. The Ireland they helped produce was one 'subtly regulated by the discourse of ethnology' (ibid.: 188). The landscape and its Gaelic inhabitants became passive objects of the privileged imperial gaze, denied agency, depth, subtlety and contradiction.

For whom were these maps intended, after all, and for what purposes? The answer cited in the Spring Rice Report of 1824 (the document produced by the House of Commons Select Committee on Irish Finance) was 'the relief which can be afforded to the proprietors and occupiers of land from unequal taxation' (cited in Andrews 1975: 308). It is possible, however, to view the entire undertaking as an exercise in colonial-military power, the representation of a landscape which by virtue of its subaltern status was incapable of speaking for itself. All in all, the maps/names produced by the Ordnance Survey were textual evidence of the survival of native knowledge within a new political dispensation – the Union – and thus a fitting symbol of the way old and new, Irish and British, could be meaningfully reconciled. 'The effect,' Hamer concludes, was 'both to privilege and alienate the past' (1989: 193).

One of the by-products of the Ordnance Survey was a renewed interest in place-names. The Irish scholars such as John O'Donovan who were recruited to the project were charged with assessing the evidence of the native literature as well as earlier mapping/naming endeavours to produce definitive names for the places and spaces mapped by the field workers. These names were then anglicised – 'the great betrayal' according to Tim Robinson (1996: 160), although such a process seems to have been occurring for centuries in any case. Building on the work of the Survey (including two of its stalwarts, George Petrie and Eugene O'Curry), P.W. Joyce produced his pioneering *The Origin and History of Irish Names of Places* in 1869, since which time the field has continued to attract the interest of both amateur and professional scholars. The intrepid researcher could awaken the 'original' names (and alternative meanings) lying dormant within the English versions – what Richard Kearney called 'the stored heritage of local history which each Gaelic name recollects and *secretes*' (1983: 38, original emphasis) – and thus contribute to the revitalisation of Irish culture. However, whereas Joyce was certain that the 'great name system . . . such as it sprang forth from the minds of our ancestors . . . exists almost unchanged to this day' (1869: vi–vii), subsequent place-name research in Ireland has been haunted by what Catherine Nash perceives to be '[a] sense of loss and recovery' (1993: 51). Nash is not alone in thinking that the desire to retrieve the 'original' meaning which is an implicit aspect of place-name research, to call forth the ghost hidden in the word, has contributed to the maintenance of many discursive forms and figures which have been disabling for postcolonial life across the island.

Two English men and one Northern Irish text possess particular significance when questions of mapping/naming are raised in contemporary Irish Studies: the scholar John Andrews, the cartographer Tim Robinson and the play *Translations* by Brian Friel. Andrews is a 'colossus' (Whelan 1992: 379) within the field of Irish map history. After studying historical geography in Cambridge and London, he moved to Ireland in 1954 to take up a post as assistant lecturer in the Department of Geography at Trinity College Dublin. There he found 'the great wealth of the Irish cartographic tradition' (ibid.: 385) almost untouched, and dedicated his subsequent career to its research and exposition. His 1975 book *A Paper Landscape* introduced the early nineteenth-century Ordnance Survey of Ireland to a wide audience with no specialised knowledge of (and probably little interest in) issues of mapping/naming. It would not be overstating the case to say that this text significantly shifted the focus of subsequent Irish critical and creative endeavour. By and large pre-dating (at least in Irish Studies) the impact of postcolonial theory, the scrupulous scholarship and engaging readability of his *magnum opus* provides a benchmark for those who might wish to engage with the significance of mapping/naming in Irish political and cultural history but at the same time remain aware of the pitfalls awaiting any unselfconscious 'deconstruction' of the map. In the same way that the Ordnance Survey sheets themselves provide an empirical representation of the landscape upon which alternative spatial practices, past and present, may be superimposed, so Andrews' historical researches offer an established critical language with which to begin to address the issues of Irish mapping/naming.

One contemporary map-maker who continues to use official cartography (albeit the later survey of the 1890s) as the basis for his otherwise highly original work is Tim Robinson, cited by Andrews as a figure possessing 'a poetic appreciation of landscape all too rare among geographical communicators in any country' (1997: 203). Describing himself as a 'discriminating earth-worshipper' (1996: 70), Robinson left London with his partner in 1972 to move to the west coast of Ireland. He has spent the time since mapping and writing widely about various parts of that area. His map of 'Árainn', the largest of the Aran Islands, was published in 1976 (a second version appeared in 1980), followed by *Stones of Aran* (1990, 1995) an incredibly – almost desperately – in-depth, two-volume description of both the shoreline and interior of the same island. Robinson explains that the more accepted name for this island,

'Inishmore', 'was apparently concocted by the Ordnance Survey for its map of 1839, as a rendering in English phonetic values of the Irish "Inis Mór", big island, a name which did not exist previously but is now replacing "Árainn" even in the island's own speech' (1990: 3). Árainn, Inis Mór, Aran, Inishmore: same landscape, different names. Part of Robinson's work involves uncovering the ways in which name, place and meaning function for both the community and the individuals who together comprise the community.

According to Fintan O'Toole, Robinson has produced '[the] most potent maps of recent years . . . records, not merely of topography, but of the people he met, the stories he was told, while making them' (1994: 25). With regard to his own map-making abilities, however, Robinson admits that 'cartography, in the sense of a general desire and competence to make maps, remains alien to me' (1996: 75). Part-scientist, part-ethnographer, part-hippie,[17] he is none the less admired and respected for his ability to ground the necessary abstractions of map-ping/naming in what he refers to as 'the texture of immediate experi-ence' (1996: 77). The maps tend to be of places that he can see from his own home, 'elaborated and externalized versions of the mental sketchmaps one makes to situate oneself, cognitively and emotionally, in a new locality' (1996: 75). Although an 'outsider' by birth, Robinson's maps are an attempt to capture what William J. Smyth in a related context referred to as 'the rounded sense of place as experienced by the insider', an experience involving 'all the senses – of seeing, feeling, of sound, of touch and taste' (1985: 4).

Likewise, when researching place-names Robinson insists that analysis of textual sources must be accompanied by fieldwork so that name, place and meaning may be locked into 'the physical and histor-ical context of the place' (1996: 156). Sounding a bit like Heidegger, he claims that '[seeking] out place-names, mapping, has become for me not a way of making a living or making a career, but of making a life; a mode of dwelling in a place' (1996: 164). As the name of the publishing imprint he founded with his partner suggests, maps are a kind of 'folding landscape', terrains that have been captured in textual form and represented for an observer removed in time and space from the terrain itself. And if he can do it, the implicit message is, so can the map reader: everyone their own cartographer. We have both the right and the responsibility to map/name the places we inhabit in terms of the events and concerns that have shaped us, and in contention with official representations of the same spaces. Added to this is the central recognition that the map is never finished; it is in the cartographer's own words nothing more than an 'interim report on the progress of its own making'.[18]

In all this kind of work, however, there is the old difficulty of privileging one particular name or one particular representation of the landscape above others as the oldest, the most authentic, the most descriptive, or whatever. Robinson insists on the survival of 'matted and tenacious roots . . . deeper than any economic or legal realities' (1996: 70–1), buried deep in the landscapes he maps/names. As with so much commentary on the west of Ireland, these roots are perceived to be under threat from modernisation, on the one hand, but also and more insistently from their own attractiveness to a modern sensibility in danger of withering from lack of authenticity. But Robinson's own maps and essays, conceived perhaps as exercises in reclamation and preservation, paradoxically contribute to this modern sensibility, construing Aran, Connemara and the Burren as landscapes retaining a special significance which may still be accessed by those from less existentially enriched environments. The danger is that the 'primitive' landscapes of the west are romanticised *vis-à-vis* other, somehow more mundane, less human (or sometimes all *too* human) landscapes, thus contributing to the notion of that region as a haven of authenticity in a world swamped with simulacra. There should be no doubting Robinson's commitment to the landscapes he remaps/renames; what happens to those texts when they escape the deeply personalised, face-to-face context in which they were conceived and executed is another matter. 'Everyone should be the mapper/namer of their own environment' may be the intended message; 'Come to the West of Ireland and save your soul' may be how the work is actually being interpreted.

Brian Friel's *Translations* is an immensely evocative text in terms of the mapping/naming-related issues broached in this section, and indeed in terms of any number of the recurring themes of contemporary Irish Studies. Set in 1833 in the fictional Donegal village of Baile Beag (or Ballybeg), the play explores the relationship between the members of an Ordnance Survey team and the master and pupils of a local hedge-school. A number of characters in the play appear to be drawn from historical figures involved in the survey. Although based on an arche-typal, even melodramatic, structure (Murray 1997: 211), Friel manages to wed technical brilliance with critical insight in an artistic vision which engages with the discourses of language, place and identity so powerfully invoked by the work of the Ordnance Survey. The play's concern with these issues, and especially with the central metaphor of translation, places it in intertextual dialogue with the entire tradition of

Irish art and criticism (Kearney 1983). Just as Friel speaks backwards to (say) Yeats's vision of an island culture balanced between pastoral and aristocratic spatial practices, so he speaks forward to the postmodern Irish subject and the dangers attending either the loss or the retention of the ability to name where you live.

Translations has been criticised, by Andrews among others, as a crude artistic rendering of a complex socio-political initiative (Friel, Andrews and Barry 1983; Connolly 1987). He accepts that 'the Ordnance Survey is only a dramatic convenience' for Friel, and also that the play genuinely helps to reveal how that operation, like so many earlier map-making undertakings in Ireland, 'has perverted the science of cartography by making it an instrument of imperialism' (1983: 121). He goes on to suggest, however, that Friel distilled fiction and history in his play to produce a simplistic colonial (if not frankly Republican) context for the work of the survey. The playwright's vision of imperial imposition meeting subaltern resistance on the ground is anachronistic, possessing no sense of the actual historical manoeuvring and compromising involved on all sides. Such a reading is resisted, however, by those who argue that although Friel acknowledges the significance of the Gaelic traditions lost during the survey (and indeed during the whole process of colonisation), there is no wish to convert those traditions into a measure of the 'real' Ireland which must be recovered and celebrated at the expense of what came after. For Declan Kiberd, *Translations* is not about – or not *only* about – loss and displacement, but about the practicalities of surviving in a colonial situation. He quotes approvingly the schoolmaster Hugh's verdict as he shows the book of new placenames to his class: 'We must learn where we live. We must learn to make them our own. We must make them our new home' (Friel 1981: 66). The power and privilege encoded into the Ordnance Survey maps/names are implicitly deconstructed in *Translations*, but the reconstruction which must follow is revealed as an emotionally and politically fraught process, full of personal and political pitfalls.

For Shaun Richards, likewise, Friel's theatre exposes the shallowness of poststructuralist and postcolonial critiques of national identity as passive, strategic or reactionary. In *Translations* the past is accessed not for any nostalgic or redemptive ends but as a resource which may be deployed in the active remaking of present and future. Tradition (or rather the fetishisation of one highly selective tradition) may have become a problem for the postcolonial community, but 'too rapid a rush to rejection of the past results in a cynicism towards tradition which effects a withering act of cultural deracination' (n.d.: 7). 'Critical traditionalism'

(Richards 1997: 64) is the only means through which the postcolonial subject can come to an initial sense of its own temporal and spatial identity; what happens after that is another story. Postcolonial theory rightly warns against any kind of naive quest to discover the original, authentic map/name of the landscape. Friel acquiesces, but insists on staging the politics of translation in all its violence and bad faith, and in the name of what Richards calls 'a meaningful, but not naive, authenticity' (1997: 56).

It seems that humans could not exist in the world without maps/ names. Some of the species' most basic requirements depend upon a spatial awareness structured in terms of the accessibility and relative location of particular places, as well as the associations and significance of the names attached to those places. The beliefs and practices that develop around these basic requirements inhere in our cultural and political discourses, from the overtly instrumental military map to the subtlest toponymical resonance in a place-name. The evidence of both prehistorical and early Celtic civilisation on the island of Ireland, as well as the later experience of (anti-)colonialism, provide particularly interesting examples of the ways in which the different beliefs and practices of various mapping/naming cultures clash and overlap, persist and disappear. It is therefore important that the student of Irish cultural history should develop an awareness of the hegemonic processes that activate different mapping/naming practices, remaining alert to the ways in which seemingly incidental usages of mapping metaphors or place-name citations may in fact signify highly charged cultural aspirations and/or political affiliations.

Poetry

If there is one cultural practice which over the years has laboured – in all its primary and secondary forms: composition, translation, criticism, and so on – under the weight of a supposed 'special relationship' between place and Irish identity, it is poetry. From Dallán Forgaill to Eiléan Ní Chuilleanáin, from Mary Monck to Ciaran Carson, Irish poetry is widely construed as a discourse overdetermined by spatial concerns. John Montague's famous verse from *The Rough Field* encapsulates an attitude which remains by and large dominant at the beginning of a new millennium:

> The whole landscape a manuscript
> We had lost the skill to read,

A part of our past disinherited;
But fumbled, like a blind man,
Along the fingertips of instinct.
(1990: 35)

As with Andrews, the landscape is imagined here as a text, in this case a 'manuscript' telling the story of a certain kind of Irishness which, owing to a history of neglect and oppression, can now be only barely read and faintly understood. The underlying message is that not only has an authentic Irish identity been 'disinherited' and 'lost'; the cultural forms (such as poetry) through which that identity could be articulated are themselves increasingly alienated. In this respect, *The Rough Field* (like all contemporary Irish poetry) is a monument to its own failure.

This attitude squares with an historical and philosophical tradition which argues that the success of any work of art depends upon the degree to which it is rooted in a familiar landscape. For Heidegger, as John Kerrigan puts it, '[what] a bridge is to riverbanks, poetry is to dwelling.... A poet brings language into a state of at-homeness with dwelling' (1998: 145). But this, as we noted in Chapter 1, threatens a 'dark Romanticism' susceptible to dangerous ideological inflection. Yet it was this tradition that Yeats invoked when he argued that '[there] is no great literature without nationality' (1934: 103–4). 'Nationality' here is merely one hypertrophic version of the 'organic community', an age-old spatial concept in which the individual, the community and the landscape are figured in some kind of empathetic relationship, mutually supportive and mutually expressive. As Raymond Williams once remarked, however, the thing about the organic community is that it is always gone (1979: 252). It thus tends to be invoked (with greater or lesser levels of sophistication) either in terms of tragic loss or potentially triumphant recovery. This is essentially the same binary of 'loss and recovery' that Catherine Nash perceives operating in respect of Irish place-name research (1993: 51). Likewise, the history of Irish poetry from its earliest manifestation can produce no shortage of examples cast in each of these modes.

The discourses of literary criticism and literary theory are only slowly coming to terms with the fructifying interaction of historical and geographical discourses in Irish (or indeed any) poetry. This is due in part to the marginalisation of space as a relevant analytical category throughout the twentieth century when these discourses were evolving into their current forms. 'One of the major tasks of a newly spatialized cultural studies', writes Tony Pinkney, 'would be a wholesale rewriting of twentieth-century literary theory, operating upon it the kind of "spatial deconstruction" that Soja practises upon historical materialism' (1990: 13). At the same time, an historically sensitive geocriticism must avoid, as Chris Fitter puts it, 'a reckless atavism, reducing man's topographic imagination to that of a beast, and...studies of poetic landscape that package the forms and features of the literary surface in disconnection from the mental climate that generated them' (1995: 2). Which is to say: even as its own spatial consciousness is developing, criticism has to begin the task of engaging with literary texts in terms of the few, often obscure clues emerging from spatially engaged disciplines such as geography, philosophy and etymology. It is towards just such a critical engagement on the one hand, and a 'spatial deconstruction' of cultural theory on the other, that this section (and indeed this entire book) is working.

To begin, then, let us consider the following text:

Suibne the Lunatic
My little oratory in Tuaim Inbir, it is not a full house that is...
with its stars last night, with its sun, with its moon.
Gobban hath built that – that its story may be told to you –
my heartlet, God from Heaven, He is the thatcher who hath thatched it.
A house wherein wet rain pours not, a place wherein thou fearest not spearpoints,
bright as though in a garden, and it without a fence around it
                    (reproduced in Stokes and Strachan 1903: 294)

This is a translation of a fragment found in a ninth-century codex preserved in the Benedictine monastery of St Paul-in-Lavanttal on the shores of Lake Constance, in the province of Carinthia (Kärnten), Austria. The manuscript consists of four leaves of old Irish writing, and the text in question has the words *Suibne Geilt* – 'Sweeney the Lunatic' or 'Sweeney the Wild Man' – written in the left margin. The poem is thus one of the earliest references to the Middle-Irish tale *Buile Suibne* (*The Frenzy of Suibhne*). Suibne (Sweeney in English) the 'King' of Dál nAraide, deranged by the noise of the Battle of Moira (*Cath Maige Rath*, AD 637) and cursed by a cleric (subsequently saint) named Rónán whom he had attacked, turns into a bird and takes to the wilderness. The man-bird wanders across the island lamenting his fate and praising nature by turns. Eventually he is received into the Christian faith by a cleric (subsequently saint) named Moling in the place named after him (St Mullins) in Co. Carlow. The tale of Suibne's madness is believed to date from the seventh century. The text relating the tale originates in the twelfth century, although materials other than this fragment had been accumulating since at least the ninth century. The MS in which the full legend is preserved, however, was written in Co. Sligo in the late seventeenth century (O'Keefe 1913: xiii–xvii).

This much anthologised fragment resonates with all the mystique, romanticism and controversy of latter-day Celticism.[19] It is possible, for example, to interpret Suibne's fate as an allegory of the confrontation between pagan Ireland and the new Christian dispensation introduced by Patrick and promulgated by his heirs, Colum Cille and Brigit. In the introduction to his translation of the tale, J.G. O'Keefe suggested that 'the original story attributed the madness to the horrors which [Suibne] witnessed in the battle of Magh Rath, and that the introduction of St Ronan and St Moling may be a later interpolation' (1913: xxxiv). Introducing his own translation, Seamus Heaney refers to 'a tension between the newly dominant Christian ethos and the older, recalcitrant Celtic temperament' (1984: unpaginated). Elsewhere he suggests that early Irish poetry 'is sustained by a deep unconscious affiliation to the old mysteries of the grove, even while ardently proclaiming its fidelity to the new religion' (1980: 186).

At the same time, the simplicity and sheer *jouissance* of this poem, as well as the apparent endorsement of nature above culture, render it profoundly emblematic of the 'special relationship' between place and identity which many see as the as the critical key to Irish cultural history.[20] Heaney goes on to read Suibne's fate as a symbol of the artistic struggle between personal imagination and social obligation, an insight he revisited in the poems collected as 'Sweeney Redivivus', part three of *Station Island* (1984a).[21] In ecocritical discourse, however, it is also possible to read the legend as symbolic of the confrontation between an older, more integrated view of nature and one (developed during the classical era) in which nature becomes increasingly subservient to a man-shaped God.[22]

As throughout *Buile Suibne*, of which it ostensibly forms a part, an actual geographical location is invoked: Tuaim Inbir. Joyce has no reference to such a place, but his translations of the component parts would render 'Tuaim Inbir' as 'the burial mound, hillock or dyke by the estuary'.[23] To what or where might this refer? The literary remains provide some clues. In *The Martyrology of Oengus the Culdee*, the saint celebrated on 2 December is glossed: 'Máelodran, i.e. Máel-odran of Túaim indbir or Druim Indbir in the west of Meath' (Stokes 1905: 257). In *The Annals of the Four Masters* it is noted that during the year 916 'Ceallachan

Ua Daint, Abbot of Tuaim-inbhir, died' (*AFM* II: 593); but O'Donovan annotates the entry thus: 'Tuaim-inbhir... where St. Mael-Odhrain was on that day venerated as the patron of that place. There is a Druim-inbhir, *anglicé* Drumineer, with the ruins of a very curious and ancient church in the barony of Lower Ormond, and county of Tipperary, about five miles north and by west of the town of Nenagh' (ibid.: 592). Although the modern counties of Tipperary and Westmeath are land-locked, they both have extensive lake and river systems which might support the water reference in 'inbir'; Drumineer, for example (latterly Dromineer) – 'the ridge of the river mouth' according to Joyce (*INP*: 414) – is situated where the River Nenagh enters Lough Derg.

In their *Medieval Religious Houses*, Aubrey Gwynn and Neville Hadcock cite Drumineer as an 'unclassified' monastic site 'said to have been intended for a foundation of monks from Inishcaltra which never materialized' (1988: 427). 'Tuaim-Inbhir', however, they list as an 'unidentified' early site, pointing out that although usually affiliated to larger settlements, many of the smaller early houses (often occupied only by a single anchorite or a few monks) developed independent religious practices and have never been traced (1988: 408). In the St Paul MS, however, the place-name itself is glossed with the words *barr edin* which 'seems to mean "crown of the ivy" (*edenn*), with which the abbey was covered' (Stokes and Strachan 1903: 294) – hence the titles 'The Ivied Summit' (Thurneysen 1949: 39–40), 'The Ivied Tree-top' (Jackson 1988: 72–3) and 'An Ivied Tree-Top' (Kinsella 1986: 23).[24]

As both Kenneth Jackson (1935: 122) and Gerard Murphy (1956: 224) suggest, the uncertainty of the place-name accounts for much of the scholarly debate regarding the fragment. The reference could be to an actual but unidentified monastic site located somewhere on an estuary in Co. Westmeath, or to a larger building at Dromineer on the shores of Lough Derg in Co. Tipperary, which has the ruins of an 'ancient and curious church' and which would be more likely to have ivy growing on it.

Jackson believed the fragment to have been originally a hermit poem referring to a real (though unidentified) site in 'Tuaim Inbir'. He points out that there had been 'a revival of ascetic monasticism and anchor-itism in the eighth century under Maelruain, founder and abbot of Tallaght', and that one of the effects of this – usually referred to as the Culdee movement (*Céile Dé*: Client of God) – was the production of a body of largely anonymous poetry by monks and hermits between the eighth and tenth centuries (Jackson 1935: 95; Flower 1947: 43–66; Hughes 1966: 185). Characteristic conceits of this genre were the iden-tification of Christ with nature, and the invocation of a little hut or cell 'in the woods and wilds, hidden away from all but God' (Jackson 1935: 96). The opening lines of this ninth-century 'Hermit's Song' are typical:

I wish, O Son of the living God, O ancient, eternal King
For a hidden little hut in the wilderness that it may be my dwelling.
(Meyer 1911: 31)

Jackson admitted that hermit verse and Wild Man verse are liable to blurring (1935: 121), but insisted that 'The Ivied Tree-top' – or 'The Ivy Bower' as his earlier translation has it (ibid.: 3) – is a typical product of ascetic religious practice, lacking 'anything which can properly belong to the Wild Man theme or is characteristic of the Suibhne story' (ibid.: 122). In this analysis, then, the Suibne connection would have been caused by scribal conflation of religious 'Wild Men', such as Máel-odrán, the (probable) anchorite of Túaim Indbir or Druim Indbir, with the Suibne Wild Man legend which we know to have been extant during the ninth century.

On the other hand, J.G. O'Keefe notes the 'striking resemblance in many respects to the poetry' (1913: xxxvii) between the ninth-century fragment and the twelfth-century text, thus suggesting that the '*Suibne Geilt*' gloss on the St Paul MS is not a mistake, but indicative of the fact that this fragment (like *Buile Suibne*) articulates a self-conscious metaphor designed to dramatise the confrontation between Christianity and an older dispensation. Jackson felt that the interpolated scholiasm *barr edin* 'must refer to the ivy which grew over the cell in question' (1935: 35). Ivy references recur throughout *Buile Suibne*, however, evidence on one level of a complex grammar of tree and animal references, but also of a possible connection between fragment and text. In each case, however, the possible reference to a building is conflated with Suibne's legendary arboreal domain. The tree in 'Tuaim Inbir' from which Suibne speaks merges with the image of the abbey with its ivy-covered walls or the little anchorite hut on a barrow on a river mouth somewhere in Westmeath. Following Heaney's suggestion, we may agree that the poem dramatises the confrontation between Christian and pagan world-views. But this confrontation – which is itself the root cause of Suibne's madness – is articulated in terms of a spatial metaphor in which culture (building, indoors) and nature (tree, outdoors) function in an ultimately undecidable exchange of priorities.

It is clear that the poem is structured around an elaborate spatial metaphor, specifically that of a built environment. The relevant term in the Codex, *Mairiuclán*, is translated as 'little hut' by Jackson (1988: 72);

'little lodge' by F.N. Robinson (in Hoagland 1947: 18); 'oratory' by
Stokes and Strachan (1903), O'Keefe (1913: xvii), Murphy (1956: 113),
Greene and O'Connor (1967: 101) and Williams and Ford (1992: 84);
and 'oratory' or 'chamber' by Thurneysen (1949: 60). Thomas Kinsella,
however, refers to it as a 'cell' (1986: 23), and this complicates the
matter even more. One of the principal Irish words for a church is *cell*,
adopted by early religious from the Latin *cella* as one of a number of
terms for a religious edifice (Ó Crónín 1995: 37). Its anglicisation as 'Kil'
came to constitute one of the most prolific Irish place name after *baile*
(*INP*: 288). But the 'cell' here is in fact one of the trees in which Suibne
was wont to take shelter from the elements as he endured his exile.[25]
And yet this use of a human structure as a metaphor betrays Suibne's
past as a member of a society which relied upon such buildings for
protection against both weather (rain) and human threat (spears).
Such edifices are in fact invoked throughout *Buile Suibne* – the tale to
which this fragment ostensibly belongs – in contradistinction to an
enforced outdoor existence (for example, O'Keefe 1913: 27, 37, 65).

The 'little hut' image is archetypal in so far as it creates the duality of
inside and outside, a duality which, as Edward Relph says, 'more than
anything else...sets places apart in space and defines a particular
system of physical features, activities, and meanings' (1976: 47). At
the same time it is a species of what Chris Fitter terms 'analogical
perception', a means of engaging with landscape which 'receives and
redacts the external world through the faculty of similitude'. Humans
perceive the landscape in this way because '[the] earth and its forms,
sounds and impressions exist for consciousness from the outset as a
great web of correspondences, types and oppositions' (1995: 21). Thus,
in the comparison between a simple, evidently poor dwelling and a
richer, more sophisticated or more capacious 'mansion' ('full house' in
Stokes and Strachan and O'Keefe; 'full household' in Thurneysen [91,
105], and in Greene and O'Connor; 'mansion' in Murphy; 'great house'
in both Kinsella and Robinson), the poem is still very much reliant
upon the 'cultural' even as it endorses the 'natural' (stars, sun and
moon) as a superior level of experience. It seems the 'natural' can be
expressed only in terms of different degrees of that to which it is ostensibly opposed: the 'cultural'. Which is to say: poetry is always linked
to the house, even when its ostensible location and/or theme is
outdoors.[26] In one sense this is indicative of Suibne's 'madness', caught
as he is between pagan Celtic and Christian world-views; as Heaney put
is, 'Sweeney was at once the enemy and the captive of the monastic
tradition' (1980: 187). In the present context, however, it goes to the

heart of modern environmentalist discourse, whether articulated in terms of a racial (Celtic) or party-political (Green) discourse.

It is possible to follow this 'madness' deeper still. 'Tuaim Inbhir', as we have seen, translates roughly as 'the burial mound, hillock or dyke by the river mouth or estuary'. Such 'hillocks' or 'dykes' could be the result of natural land morphology, but 'burial mound' definitely connotes human modification of the landscape, in this case for purposes of interment. The poetic voice locates itself in a specific place, which is also a description, so that all the historical and spatial connotations of that place are invoked to support and stand behind it. The formal naming of places in this manner indicates a social and cultural context (the one from which Suibne has supposedly been excluded) in which the place-name itself is thoroughly infused with particular associations, practices and meanings – in short, with considerations of power. As with the metaphor of the building and the invocation of the monastic site, however, the place-name Tuaim Inbir conflates the cultural (a burial mound) with the natural (an estuary). It is in this sense a trace of human landscape use, a record of the fact that space becomes meaningful for humans only when it is subjected to some degree of modification, even if that modification extends only so far as burial. Suibne's exile in the wilderness beyond the metaphorical walls of the dwelling is thus meaningful only in terms of the cultural boundaries that the walls themselves demarcate.

We could continue to trace the Celtic/Christian, natural/cultural division throughout the fragment, noting for example the opposition between Gobban (Gobán Saor, the mythological wright famed for the construction of monasteries) and God, the 'natural' artificer ('Creator') of heaven and earth. Much could also be made of the image of the 'fence', with its implications of protection and jeopardy – a 'good' or 'safe' nature subject to human modification on the inside as opposed to a 'bad' or 'dangerous' nature untouched by human endeavour on the outside. The point is this: the early literature is (as we have seen with *dinnshenchas*) one obvious source for the location of the 'special relationship' between place and identity in Irish cultural history. It would be a mistake, however, to expect this (or any other) discourse to produce pure or pristine forms of that relationship, as in every instance the text can be seen to operate on and across the boundaries which structure the human spatial (and hence ideological) imagination: home/away, identity/difference, built/natural environment. Rather than a spontaneous expression of the early Irish cultural imagination, the 'special relationship' is a construction of a later critical imagination intent on organising both the physical terrain *and* the idea of Ireland into the basis for a political ideology.

One of the traditions which the mainstream production of cultural space in Irish writing has tended to ignore is the topographical or loco-descriptive verse of the eighteenth and nineteenth centuries. Inspired in large part by Virgil's *Georgics*, this kind of poetry was first written in seventeenth-century England and had its heyday during the neoclassical period, although it continues to exercise both formal and thematic influences down to the present day. Loco-descriptive poetry is (as the generic name suggests) an overtly spatial discourse which uses actual topographical prospects or features to articulate particular political, moral or philosophical meanings. Typical of the age in which it enjoyed its greatest vogue, such meanings tended to emphasise issues of moderation, balance and harmony. In the poetry, the landscape becomes both a reflection and a model of a preferred socio-political dispensation in which there is a place for everyone and everyone is in their place. What such a poetic vision tended to ignore, however (a tendency that it shared with the closely related genre of landscape painting), was what John Barrell (1980) called 'the dark side of the landscape' – that is, the suppression and manipulation of certain elements which gave the lie to the image of particular landscapes as balanced, harmonic and moderate. John Wilson Foster concluded his survey of Anglo-Irish loco-descriptive poetry by noting that the conservative impulse underpinning the genre from the outset was in fact an attempt to find an artistic solution to the reality of 'discord, excess and imbalance' (1991: 27) which characterised Irish society during the eighteenth century and after.

Chris Fitter has charted the genealogy of what he calls 'landskip' in English poetry, seeing its emergence as characteristic of 'that increasingly metropolitan, secular and materialist relation to nature that encourages a personalized, empirical and affective engagement of landscape' (1995: 10). Although significantly shaped by English attitudes towards nature and space, Anglo-Irish topographical poetry developed through a number of discrete stages which were responsive to that community's changing attitudes towards the colonial landscape. Initially, the discourse developed with reference to the political dispensation of eighteenth-century Ireland, which saw a Protestant Ascendancy (in imitation of the mother country) discovering in the landscape a natural analogue for the contemporary distribution of power: orderly landscapes for an orderly society. Foster reckons that James Ward's 'Phoenix Park' (1718) introduced the genre into the country (1991: 12), after which time various local factors began to contribute to the emergence of a specifically

Anglo-Irish loco-descriptive tradition. One of the directions taken by this discourse (faciliated by both Irish social geography and topography) was *away* from the centres of civilisation and *back* towards nature, initially in terms of a 'tasteful' balance between the constituent elements of their own identity – Anglo art (reason) and Irish imagination (nature) – but increasingly as the century progressed in terms of a fully-fledged cult of the picturesque. The poet no longer looked to the landscape (only) for confirmation of a certain polity, but for the excitation of certain existential states unavailable in polite society (Copley and Garside 1994).

We have already noted one effect of this development by considering the growth of tourism and travel in eighteenth-century Ireland, and in this respect the rhetoric of topographical verse has had an enduring influence. Despite this, it is important not to confuse an Anglo-Irish penchant for the picturesque with the Romanticism which succeeded it, as the former never forsook the goal of an improved or cultivated nature – that is, nature as a model for the resolution of competing 'human' (in fact, racial) faculties. Seamus Deane points out that the work of figures such as Charlotte Brooke and Joseph Cooper Walker towards the end of the eighteenth century constituted an attempt 'to found a national consensus through the melding of the Gaelic- and English-language traditions in poetry' (1994: 120). As he goes on to explain, however, the vision of a 'cordial union' between different poetic traditions was overtaken by the very political discourses it sought to ameliorate. Indeed, in so far as amelioration was the dominant impulse of Anglo-Irish topographical poetry from its inception, its failure to develop an effective association with the native topographical tradition can be seen as a cultural echo of its inability (or unwillingness) to envisage a more equitable political settlement in the colonial territory.

Jonathan Bate has claimed that '[the] poet is as much geographer as historian' (1991: 85). No one is this more true of than Seamus Heaney, a poet whom we have already encountered in his roles as critic and translator. Especially in his early collections, Heaney revealed a deep concern with local place-names, landscape and memory, borders and boundaries, the location of art as a metaphor for the ability to speak, and so on. Now a Nobel Laureate, Heaney is widely considered the exemplary modern Irish *literatus*, in large part to the degree with which he appears to be focused upon issues of place and identity. His later work has shown evidence of a much more sophisticated awareness of the possibilities of space as both metaphor and subject (Picot 1997: 252ff); yet it seems as if his reputation as the most typical (if not the greatest) Irish writer of his generation was sealed during the period from *Death of a Naturalist* (1966) to *Field Work* (1979).

During this same period, Heaney produced many critical essays, lectures and talks which, although directed towards a variety of topics, actually functioned as a series of glosses on his own work. Quite a number of these critical endeavours take the relationship between place, art and identity as their specific subject. For example, recalling the countryside around Mossbawn, the farm in Co. Derry where he grew up, Heaney wrote:

> In the names of its fields and townlands, in their mixture of Scots and Irish and English etymologies, this side of the country was redolent of the histories of its owners. Broagh, The Long Rigs, Bell's Hill; Brian's Field, the Round Meadow, the Demesne; each name was a kind of love made to each acre. And saying the names like this distances the places, turns them into what Wordsworth once called a prospect of the mind. They lie deep, like some script indelibly written into the nervous system. (1980: 20)

Here may be found many of the issues with which our analysis of the Irish spatial imagination has thus far been concerned: territory division (fields, townland, acre), place-name (Brian's Field), cognitive mapping ('. . . a prospect of the mind . . .'), culture (script) and nature (the nervous system), and so on.[27] Much of Heaney's creative work comes into clearer focus after reading this and similar reflections. Culminating perhaps in the lectures collected as *The Place of Writing* (1989), such notions fuel the idea of Irish poetry as a discourse centred on issues of space and place.

Montague argued that 'the least Irish place-name can net a world with its associations' (1989: 43), and Heaney's early work appears to bear out this claim. In the poem entitled 'Toome' from the volume *Wintering Out* (1972), for example, he reflects upon both the physical and etymological properties of that particular word:

> My mouth holds round
> the soft blastings,
> *Toome, Toome,*
> as under the dislodged
>
> slab of the tongue
> I push a souterrain

This is one of a series of poems (including the more celebrated 'Anahorish', 'Gifts of Rain' and 'Broagh') in which Heaney employs place-names from his home locality in Co. Derry in an effort to locate both himself and his community in some kind of geographical and historical context.[28] It is immediately clear that, as with the St Paul fragment, spatial issues are being engaged at a number of levels. The poem's title, for example, signals a concern with issues of place and identity. 'Toome' refers to a place on the River Bann between Lough Neagh and Lough Beg, particularly noted for its eels. The AA map of 1963 refers to 'Toome' (Map 28, sub-zone H/99), whereas later maps tend to render the place 'Toomebridge' (*Bartholomew* 1994). The place-name 'Toome' is an English rendering of the Gaelic *Tuaim* which, to recall 'The Ivied Tree-top', means burial mound, hillock or dyke. Joyce refers to this particular place as 'Toome', but explains that '[there] must have been formerly at this place both a sandbank ford across the river, and a sepulchral mound near it, for in the Tripartite Life it is called Fearsat Tuama, the ford of the tumulus; but in the annals it is generally called Tuaim' (*INP*: 307–8).

In his *Topographical Dictionary of Ireland* (1849), Samuel Lewis notes the 'many sanguinary contests' that have taken place in and around the area over the centuries because of its strategic importance, including the dismantling of the Norman castle during the Cromwellian wars and the destruction of the bridge during the 1798 Rising. Lewis describes 'Toome' as a 'post-town or village', but remarks that it 'had at a very early period a ford or ferry across the river Bann, which formed the only pass from one part of Ulster to the other' (1849, II: 592).[29] It is worth noting that in an earlier map of 'County Londonderry' from his *Atlas of the Counties of Ireland* (1837), Lewis renders the place 'Toome B.' (Day and McWilliams 1995: viii). This is unfortunate in that the 'B' could refer to either 'bridge' (likely here) or 'bay', a sandbar on the nearby northern shore of Lough Neagh. 'Toome Bay' is in fact a noted archaeological location and has produced carbon-dated materials from the earliest detailed record of humans in Ireland – the 'Sandelian' (named after a major site at Mount Sandel near Coleraine) and the 'Larnian' (named after the Co. Antrim town of Larne) occupations, *c.* 9,000 and 8,000 years ago respectively (O'Kelly 1989: 15; Mitchell and Ryan 1997: 113–41; Waddell 1998: 21–2).

Many of these connotations are invoked in the poem – hence the references to 'loam [fertile soil], flints, musket-balls, fragmented ware, torcs [metal necklaces] and fish-bones'. As possible titles, 'Toome Bridge', 'Toome Bay' or even 'Toomebridge' (which Heaney had cited in 'Up the

Shore' from *Door into the Dark* [1969: 38]), are avoided because they are, with their English modifiers, at odds with the place-name connotations that the poet is attempting to energise here. The title 'Toome' encapsulates the different histories and geographies involved, as well as offering a more resonant, while at the same time more mysterious, enunciation – a 'vocable...wafted to us across centuries of speaking and writing' (Heaney 1985–86: 38). It is as if in 'summoning of the energies of words' (Heaney 1980: 36), the poet has summoned up himself as an effect of the (pre-) history encapsulated in the name. Indeed, in some senses the title is the 'real' poem to which the following 16 lines are but a glossary.

The English language has not been completely shed, however, as the place-name 'Toome' is a homophone of the English 'tomb', with which it is etymologically linked and which also signifies a place of marked interment.[30] Just as earlier meanings inhere in anglicised place-names, so a shared etymological root signals the exchange between Gaelic and Anglo-Saxon culture, especially in the context of that most universal of human experiences: death. Heaney himself has commented that writing the etymological poems from *Wintering Out* convinced him 'that one could be faithful to the nature of the English language – for in some senses these poems are erotic mouth-music by and out of the anglo-saxon tongue – and, at the same time, be faithful to one's own non-English origin, for me that is County Derry' (quoted in Mary Corcoran 1998: 43–4). And it is, of course, entirely appropriate that the word Heaney chooses in this instance to explore the continuity of the past into the present should in fact signify a place in which the living mark the passing of the dead.

In the poem itself, the mouth which must pronounce 'Toome' is invested with spatial dynamics, as Heaney uses one of his favourite early metaphors – digging – to excavate the meanings lying dormant in the utterance. The image of the bog, discovered at the end of his previous volume *Door into the Dark*, is also invoked in the image of an oozy, 'alluvial' substance through which the 'I' persona imagines moving as 'elvers [baby eels] tail my hair'. The mouth is imaged as a tomb which must be explored – hence the references to blastings, a dislodged slab, a souterrain (an underground chamber or passage) and prospecting – so that the 10,000 years of hominid experience encoded in the place-name may be made present. In formal terms the poem engages with *dinnshenchas* and other Gaelic poetic traditions (with faint echoes of Suibne in the final stanza, perhaps). 'Toome' exemplifies many of the technical features with which Heaney was engaged at the time: a complex rhyming structure, a deceptively simple verse schema and a delicate economy of vowels and consonants. Although supporting many clauses, the 16 lines comprise only one sentence, thus adding to the notion of continuity and connection. Note also the way in which the word 'Toome' (differentiated from the surrounding language by italics) booms out at the beginning of the poem and continues to sound through each verse (*tongue*, prospec*ting*, fragmen*ted*, *torc*, *till*, *tail*), like an echo resonating through a large underground chamber. The language of the poem thus supports the concept of an originary utterance – 'some ur-speech' (Heaney 1985–86: 38), perhaps the 'Word' itself – which persists into the present, and which may still be accessed. 'The poem,' as Neil Corcoran puts it, 'establishes a condition of primeval intimacy between poet and terrain, a sense that the existence of this "I" [as with 'I am sleeved in'] is coterminous with its knowledge of this place' (1998: 46).

If some found this a highly attractive poetic vision, others were less enthralled. Heaney's early writings, and especially the etymological explorations of *Wintering Out*, have been criticised as a thinly disguised revanchism, a poetics in which every word was a name, and every name came with an implicit claim to ownership, priority and a power irresistible by virtue of its 'primordial' status. 'At the heart of Heaney's early poetry about the Irish landscape is the myth of an Irish Eden,' writes Edward Picot, 'an undisturbed primitive state in which the Irish people and the Irish land were united by what he describes as "a feeling, assenting, equable marriage between the geographical country and the country of the mind"' (1997: 205). The rhetoric of 'digging' is predicated on the notion of a material goal, a layer of solid bedrock beneath the 'alluvial mud' that may still be accessed; 'those primary laws of our nature are still operative,' Heaney claimed at the end of his 1977 lecture on 'The Sense of Place', and 'it is to the stable element, the land itself, that we must look for continuity' (1980: 149).

Earlier in the same lecture, Heaney said that '[we] have to retrieve the underlay of Gaelic legend in order to read the full meaning of the name and to flesh out the topographical record with its human accretions' (1980: 132). To what 'full meaning' is he referring here? John Kerrigan points out that Heaney's place-name poems posit the existence of originary meanings where in fact such names (as Tim Robinson demonstrates with his maps, for example) 'are contingent, workaday, sometimes obscure, and misunderstood by local Irish speakers'. The criticism is that 'Heaney's poetic instincts are inseparable at this stage from a politics which wants to find, under layers of linguistic colonialism, a more authentic in-placeness in Gaelic than in a hybrid vocable' (1998: 148).

Most famously, perhaps, David Lloyd attacked what he understood as the trope of 'reterritorialisation' underpinning the sentiments in *Wintering Out* and other early volumes, the 'foreclosed surety of the subject's relation to place, mediated by a language which seeks to naturalize its appropriative function' (1993: 25). The mood in 'Toome' and similar texts is always redemptive, the movement always towards the restoration of something that has been lost without any questioning of the historicity (or indeed the 'geographicity') of the original state. Lloyd argues that such an aesthetic, no matter how complex its language or imagery, is in fact 'profoundly symptomatic of the continuing meshing of Irish cultural nationalism with the imperial ideology which frames it' (ibid.: 37).

From a less overtly political point of view, Heaney's early spatial imagination appeared to endorse a kind of 'habitat theory' in which there exists a primordial relationship between humans and environment. This itself is a remnant in the physical and psychic composition of *Homo sapiens* from an earlier point in that species' evolution (Fitter 1995: 6). Much green discourse argues, for example, that this relationship has been suppressed in the technologically advanced brave new world of the twenty-first century, yet it may still be tapped in certain circumstances and in certain societies which have not yet been fully alienated from their physical environments. The attraction of such a theory is understandable, as it offers a universal compensatory myth in which all merely historical differences may be collapsed into a sameness grounded (literally) 'in the stable element, the land itself'. What it misses, as Chris Fitter puts it, is 'the dialectical construction of environmental "reality" through the interplay of the physical with the psychical universe' (1995: 6). The meanings produced by specific environments are indissolubly contextual and determinate, whereas the tenor of Heaney's early writings, on the other hand, is idealist and essentialist. From this perspective one might argue that despite its invocation of history, 'Toome' is a poem in denial with regard to both the historical changes and the alternative interpretive practices which were always implicit in both the name and the place designated by the title.

Despite the ostensible attempt to 'map' himself in relation to a specific named landscape, then, Heaney's discourse would in fact appear to depend upon the notion of a pre-mapped terrain, or what J. Hillis Miller calls 'an encounter with the unmappable ... an unplaceable place'. As both topographical and toponymical reference, then, Toome 'was the locus of an event that never "took place" as a phenomenal happening located in some identifiable spot and therefore open to knowledge. This strange locus is another name for the ground of things, the preoriginal ground of the ground, something other to any activity of mapping' (1995: 7). In deconstructive terms, that is, 'Toome' is a species of performative speech act which attempts to create that in the name of which it speaks. Every 'event' – signified by the historical accumulation of 'loam, flints, musket-balls, / fragmented ware, / torcs and fish-bones' – is not a contribution to but a diminution of the original name, a sign of language's inability to name things and/or places. As Hillis Miller (and elsewhere Derrida) maintains, however, this is the unavoidable condition of language, and part of Heaney's appeal must derive from the manner in which his poetry speaks the absolute human necessity to return to something which is always already lost, to name something which is categorically unnameable. In this sense, the poem 'Toome' becomes the name upon the 'tomb' of language, a gesture of recognition dispatched from the land of the living to the city of the dead.

Territory, property, land, soil: always a significant factor in the discursive construction of the island, the question of the physical and mental spaces actually designated by these words took on greater significance after the Acts of Union of 1800 and the legalistic collapse of 'Irishness' into the Ukanian state. This is the motivation behind the enormous amounts of energy – exemplified by the Ordnance Survey – dedicated to 'knowing' and 'defining' Ireland during the nineteenth century. Physical space and ideological space are mutually reliant in so far as control of one is impossible without knowledge of the other. Literature was (and remains) a high-profile negotiation of ideological space, and it is in this context that Seamus Deane has claimed that '[the] reterritorialization of Ireland in the nineteenth century ultimately leads to a reterritorialization of the aesthetic category as well' (1994: 132). Thus, the Suibne poem and the tradition from which it emerges were employed as tactical weapons in the ideological war which waged throughout the nineteenth and early twentieth centuries for control of 'Ireland' as national signifier. During the same war, the Anglo-Irish loco-descriptive tradition was either ignored or condemned as evidence of an alien imposition possessing no 'natural' claim on, or mandate from, the Irish soil. The Heaney poem feeds out of those earlier struggles and is itself just one minor action in the ongoing battle for control of the 'space' of Ireland, a battle which is no less real for the fact that it is conducted in the virtual realm of language and literature.

The thing about 'wars', 'battles' and 'actions' is that they encourage us to consider the loudest conflict as the real or even the only conflict.

Eighteenth-century Anglo-Irish topographical poetry, for example, remains interesting in the context of this study in that it constitutes a spatial imagination which, unlike most other Irish poetic traditions before and since, was (in Foster's words) 'Protestant, unionist and conservative' (1991: 10). But were these, and do they remain, the only available choices: Protestant or Catholic? Unionist or Nationalist? Conservative or Radical? Just as perspective, experience and training can determine the meaning that a viewing subject will draw from a particular landscape, so perspective, experience and training may also determine what kinds of spatial practices are considered worthy of the subject's gaze in the first place – that is, what is inherently relevant and/ or meaningful and what, by virtue of its invisibility or incoherence, is 'obviously' neutral and/or existentially vacant. 'Space' in this sense is both the reality to be engaged (what kinds of space is the poet going to write about) and a metaphor for envisaging how the poetic subject locates itself in terms of an already inhabited poetic landscape.

Patricia Boyle Haberstroh has pointed to the fact that:

> images of farms, towns, counties, cities, streets, and museums figure prominently in the work of poets from both Northern Ireland and the Republic, illustrating the more 'public' life that men in Ireland have known. Their 'self' is often seen in terms of this history. Women poets, on the other hand, frequently circumscribe another kind of place: the predominance of internal spaces in rooms and houses clearly links them to one another ... another kind of history and geography surfaces, which validates their image of place as equally important as the more 'public' landscape Irish male poets often write about. (1996: 21–2)

Given the situation which has developed across the island throughout the twentieth century, the modern Irish women poet can either engage with dominant representations of public space (such as landscape), opening up what Catherine Nash has called 'possibilities for difference, subversion, resistance and reappropriation of visual traditions and visual pleasures' (1996: 149). On the other hand, she can attempt to politicise the 'neutral' spaces of domestic geography which history has enforced upon Irish women, exploring the ways in which the most intimate spaces are subject to disabling gender discourses which have been ratified by the state and the public sphere.

Eavan Boland's career encompasses both these projects. As its title suggests, her first volume of poetry *New Territory* (1967) was concerned with various aspects of the Irish spatial imagination. Many of the individual poems ('New Territory', 'The Flight of the Earls', 'Belfast vs Dublin', 'The Pilgrim', 'Migration') deal explicitly with issues of movement and place. Haberstroh has suggested that 'the central character in *New Territory* is a version of the epic wanderer who figures so prominently in Western literature' (1996: 60). 'Western literature' is not, of course, a naturally occurring phenomenon; it is, rather, the name given to an ongoing process in which certain interests and desires are accommodated and pursued while others are marginalised or demolished. It is not surprising, then, that the young Boland found the poetic terrain already mapped out in terms of certain 'significant' features and prospects with which she was obliged to engage: language, identity, nationality, landscape, tradition. Her early work demonstrates all the 'anxiety of influence' typical of any young Irish poet trying to find an original voice in a discourse dominated by the concerns of dead men.

By the time Boland came to publish her next volume, *The War Horse* (1975), however, a different awareness had started to register, one in which the accepted map of 'the Irish poetic tradition' would be challenged in the name of an alternative spatial imagination. Having made tactical and symbolic use of women during the long nineteenth century, patriarchal Irish nationalism had relocated the sex indoors, where they could 'support the...common good' and observe 'their duties in the home' (*Bunreacht na hÉireann* 1937: 138). Positioned as tenders of the national hearth, women were at the same time denied access to the public spaces in which the nation itself was effectively, materially engaged (Nash 1993; Martin 1997). The home was a womb in which the confessional state could be reproduced, but was itself off-limits as a subject for national-cultural discourse.

This situation was by and large still predominant across the island in the early 1970s. 'Ode to Suburbia' (1995: 44–5) initiates a recurring theme in Boland's poetry, one concerned to politicise the actual and metaphorical spaces into which Irish history has consigned women. The poem is a variation on the Cinderella myth, but it also employs a complex system of animal imagery – fish, rat, lion, zebra, mouse; the wild and the timid, hunters and prey – to dramatise the role of the Irish suburban woman, marooned in the half-world between 'the streets' and 'the shy countryside'. 'No magic here' is the verdict on a mode of life which has developed around the daily round of 'compromises' and 'claustrophobia'. At the same time, the 'power' and 'mystery' of those same 'housewives' – what in a later poem in the same volume ('Suburban Woman') is referred to as 'my craft' (1995: 52) – is invoked as a recoverable possibility, a way of being in the world which, in the face of alternative models possessed of great power and persuasiveness, has been temporarily excluded from the nation's cognitive maps.

In Her Own Image (1980) revealed the extent of Boland's dissatisfaction with her poetic inheritance, and her determination to unmask the links 'between the heterosexing of bodies and the heterosexing of space' (Martin 1997: 98) in Irish cultural history. Since then she has continued to engage with the economy of actual and metaphorical space negotiated by Irish women, in poems such as 'Woman in Kitchen' and 'Domestic Interior' from *Night Feed* (1982); 'Mise Eire' and 'Suburban Woman: a Detail' from *The Journey* (1987); and 'The Rooms of Other Women Poets' and 'Distances' from *Object Lessons* (1990). At the same time, essays such as 'The Woman, the Place, the Poet', which consider various historical and contemporary aspects of Irish women's experience of space, contribute to Boland's exploration of poetry as a passport to what she has called the 'country of the mind' (1995: 169).

As we saw in an earlier section, however, the processes of 'de-' and 'reterritorialisation' which accompany the 'deconstruction of the map' is a fraught process, involving all manner of risky manoeuvring and compromise in relation to the particular terrain at stake. Radical space remains an issue in the volume entitled *In a Time of Violence* (1994), but in that work Boland adopted a more liberal attitude towards the enmeshing of history and geography in Irish life. Her later poetry also shows evidence of a move away from suburban domesticity towards an engagement with 'the vexed relationship between poetic voice and public space' (Mahoney 1999: 145). The collection opens with the interestingly entitled 'That the Science of Cartography is Limited' (1995: 174–5). In this poem the absence of an unfinished famine road from the 'masterful', official map of Ireland symbolises the volume's main theme – a general decrease in human capacity for empathy (one of the 'dying arts' referred to in 'The Parcel' [1995: 194]) brought about by a general increase in instrumental discourse.

A later poem, 'The Huguenot Graveyard at the Heart of the City' (1995: 193–4), refers to a cemetery in Baggot Street, Dublin, a place (as with the place-names 'Tuaim Inbir' and 'Toome') in which the dead are ritually marked by the living.[31] That the Huguenots, who fled religious persecution in seventeenth-century France, should have a burial site in the capital city of a country so indelibly marked by religious strife and emigration is an irony that evades the modern-day Dubliners addressed in her poem. But the least reflection on their part would enable them to extend 'the least love asks of / the living. Say: *they had another life once.*'

'Dublin', which may be 'dear to us and particular', was also once 'Dooblan' for 'heart-broken' French exiles, and part of its identity relies on the survival of 'their' name for, and hence vision of, 'our' place. In short, the poem suggests that the onus is on 'us' – the living – to understand the language of the 'other' – the dead – for without such understanding, we are all diminished.[32]

Such a theme is not unfamiliar to the mainstream Irish (that is, male) tradition, of course, and it is capable of being troped in any number of ways: tradition and modernity, organic community and alienated individual, even (as in Heaney) the passive, female earth and the active, male sky.[33] The point here, however, is that it signals Boland's engagement (which was always implicit in her work in any case) with the established tradition of (male) Irish poetry and its range of formal, thematic and linguistic concerns. It also signals the poet's confidence to speak from the space she has created for herself *within* and *across* the established parameters of poetic discourse. Throughout her poetry, Boland asserts a peculiarly female viewing pleasure, thus disrupting and resisting (in Nash's words) 'both the idea of women as passive objects of the male gaze and hegemonic versions of what is an appropriate feminine viewing position and objects of view' (1996: 158). It is particularly significant that Boland's claims regarding the impact of women's engagement with 'the Irish poetic tradition' is expressed in terms of a spatial figure which is on one level obviously a metaphor, but which at the same time indicates the actual places and spaces necessarily negotiated by modern Irish women: '[When] the history of poetry in our time is written...women poets will be seen to have rewritten not just the poem, not just the image. They won't just have rebalanced elements within the poem. They will have altered the cartography of the poem. The map will look different' (quoted in Roche and Allen-Randolph 1993: 130).

'To a very significant extent,' Patrick J. Duffy writes, 'our past and present views of Ireland and Irishness have been shaped by readings of literature and art' (1997: 65). In this section I have invoked a number of representative examples from those traditions: a ninth-century fragment caught between built and natural environments; a genre determined by the desires of an eighteenth-century colonial community; an experiment with late twentieth-century *dinnshenchas*; a woman using the poetry of place to search for her own poetic space. Although ranging over more than a 1,000 years, all these texts and traditions are instances of what Seamus Deane has called 'the production of cultural space in Irish writing' (1994). By this Deane means the imaginative and cultural resources that have at different times undertaken the production of a range of literary images of Ireland. As well as the inevitable representation *of* different places, every poem is located *in* a place – the place of writing, which is also the place in which certain kinds of poetry are allowed, or not, to be written. These different kinds of place – the physical landscapes and names of the island on the one hand, and the virtual realm of writing on the other – are closely linked, so that the location of Irish poetry-writing from its earliest period to the present in part depends upon, in part determines, the different kinds of place available for representation in the poetic text. This is the enabling paradox from which the representation of space in Irish poetic discourse emerges.

The country and the city

The ideological division of physical space into an opposition organised around the concepts of 'city' and 'country' constitutes the major point of overlap between the disciplines of history and geography. Much of the respective literature of these disciplines is given over to the reciprocal relationship between the physical properties of these spaces and the ideologies which shape them. There is nothing natural about such a division; rather, modern notions of the urban and the rural have emerged in response to a number of specific historical factors, the most significant probably being (as Raymond Williams powerfully argued) the development of classical western capitalism.[34] The cultural force of these notions, however, is such that they structure much of our conscious and subconscious imagination of space, to the extent that it remains difficult to develop a sense of the significance of any place without reference to this by now core division between city and country.

Irish cultural history also bears witness to the ongoing debate between what still appears at the outset of the twenty-first century to be a 'natural' spatial division between the countryside and the city. Questions persist as to the provenance of Irish urban culture (Butlin 1977; Whelan 1992: 406–11), the evolution of Dublin from city to city-region towards the end of the twentieth century (Horner 1992; Killen 1992), and the impact of the notion of 'urban heritage' upon the image of the city (McDonald 1989; Lincoln 1993). There are also debates regarding the characteristic morphology of the Irish countryside (Aalen 1993; Mitchell and Ryan 1997), the ways in which rural landscapes are organised and managed (Lee 1985a; Gillmor 1993), and the continuing impact of a primarily pastoral or 'green' tourism upon postmodern Irish identity (Whelan 1992; O'Toole 1994). As most of these accounts stress, such places are simultaneously real and imagined; there *are* cities called

Dublin and Derry, but there is also a vast matrix of cultural and artistic representations of these places which interacts with the 'real' thing in complex ways. Likewise, there are areas throughout the island which would qualify for most definitions of 'countryside', but there has also been an enormous amount of cultural and political investment in the idea of rural Ireland throughout the modern period.

Pace Williams, this distribution of Irish space developed in ways which were themselves both responsive to, and determined by, the island's colonial experience. The values and meanings associated with cities such as Dublin and Derry, and also of abstract concepts such as 'the Irish countryside', have emerged in terms of a complex network of colonising and decolonising practices. Although 'new times' continue to be heralded at every turn, it would be a mistake to dismiss the continuing impact of these residual discourses upon the Irish spatial imagination. In this section I wish to outline some of the issues surrounding the urban/rural debate in Ireland by focusing on two initiatives that assumed high profile during the 1990s: the development of the Temple Bar area in the centre of Dublin as a permanent zone of carnival and bohemian culture; and the construction of an interpretative centre for the Burren at Mullaghmore in Co. Clare. After briefly introducing the issues, the analysis takes the form of extracts from two interviews with individuals involved in each project.

The Burren

The Burren is an area of carboniferous limestone located in the western counties of Clare and Galway. The wide range of burial monuments from various periods is an indication that this unusual landscape impressed itself upon pre-historic Irish communities. Likewise, the cultural and archaeological remains – including field boundaries, *dinnshenchas* and Christian architecture – reveal a rich heritage of human engagement with the area (O'Connell and Korff 1991). More recently, the Burren has become famous both as a site of 'authentic' Irish culture and as an area of special scientific interest. With features of outstanding natural beauty and a strong traditional music culture, the Burren remains a popular destination for tourists, especially 'green' tourists to whom this part of the island is often marketed at the point of purchase as the most traditional, the most Celtic, or simply the most 'Irish'. Furthermore, because of its unique geology and botany and the delicate ecosystem to which these have given rise, the Burren has attracted the interest of Ireland's scientific community since the eighteenth century.

It was perhaps inevitable that these two discourses – tourism and science – would clash sooner or later. Successive central administrations have stressed the importance of tourism for rural development. A strong conservation lobby, organised by, and composed mostly of, professionals, continues to oppose any initiative, no matter how 'soft', sensitive or sustainable, which might disturb local natural habitats or impinge in any way upon the landscape heritage. 'Development alongside conservation' has proved a difficult *via media* to find, especially in the Republic where both the institutions and the will to develop an integrated management policy appear to be absent (Gillmor 1993: 200–11). Caught in between these poles is an indigenous population increasingly resentful at the way in which its needs and desires have been coopted for one or another side of a debate which, whatever its focus, has its roots in non-local institutions and discourses.[35]

In April 1991, the government announced that an 'interpretative centre' would be built on the southern edge of the Burren near to the feature known as Mullagh More, in the area officially known as Gortlecka.[36] This decision was ratified in July 1992 by Clare County Council. Supporters of the project (from the local farming community as well as from the central institutions) accuse its opponents of elitism, scaremongering and greed (Deegan 1999). Less confrontationally, though no less insistently, the Office of Public Works consistently argued throughout the 1990s that some sort of centre or 'entry point' was needed to manage the large numbers of people who wished to visit the area each year, and that so far from it being a threat to local species and habitats, such a focal point was a necessary conservation measure. An Environmental Impact Statement commissioned by An Bord Pleanála in March 1999 suggested that the proposed centre would cause minimal impact, and that this would in any case be more than offset by the benefits to the local economy and the immediate environment (Cairns 1999).

Although such arguments have been rejected from the outset by bodies such as An Taisce, the World Wide Fund for Nature, the Conservation Foundation and Plantlife International, resistance to the interpretative centre was led by the Burren Action Group. This was an organisation of local people who refused to accept what they saw as imposition from a dictatorial central government. The group was not opposed to management as such, but rather to the insensitive ways in which it was being organised and focused. Although accepting the tactical assistance of green fellow travellers, the group's main argument (as their website puts it), was 'that visitor facilities should be sited in villages – where there are already existing services and economic benefits can accrue to the local populations – and not in the sensitive core area of the Burren National Park'.

Interview I: Joe Saunders, spokesperson for the Burren Action Group. Liverpool, 21 December 1999 [37]

GS: Two questions to begin with: What is the constituency of the Burren Action Group? What level of development at Mullaghmore would the group find acceptable?

JS: I've found that most people who approach this issue from the outside tend to be too focused on one particular direction. Much of the interest in the group and the issue is based on a media knowledge of the problem rather than seeing how things are actually played out on the ground locally. To elaborate, the media generally holds the dispute as one of being locals versus outsiders, or environmentalism versus development, and local pro-development and pro-Mullaghmore all being synonymous. In reality, with regard to the composition of the Burren Action Group, seven people risked their homes in court judgments, six of those are natives of north Clare, the other is a native of Galway, and the Burren actually does go into the Galway area.

Attendance at meetings would be 80–90 per cent local people. Very few of those people would have conceived of themselves as being environmentalists.

What a lot of people are concerned about, besides environmental issues, is local trade and traffic issues. For instance, one of the big honeypot tourism attractions in the area is the Cliffs of Moher which draws nearly 750,000 visitors per year now. A lot of those come in buses. The buses tend to over-night in Limerick or Ennis, before heading on to Galway the following evening. If they leave Ennis they generally have time for one stop before they hit the Cliffs of Moher. At the moment, that stop would tend to be in a locally developed facility, whether it be the Burren Display Centre in Kilfenora, Alwee Cave, or to do some shopping in some of the local villages. Now, if you build a stand-alone interpretive facility that has a marketing fund much higher than the facilities of local entrepreneurs and local community groups, you will tend to attract the package tours. And, therefore, the revenue to the area which accrues from locally developed initiatives is gone, and that account becomes one for the state which has a national-central agenda rather than a local one. The figures, sure, will contribute to

GNP, but they will be a distortion of the natural trade, traffic and tourism routes in the area. So, the idea of environmentalism versus development at two ends of a pole is probably mistaken in the first place.

It's quite a complicated issue. For instance, the creation of a national park in itself is problematic is an area where you have to see changes in agriculture as a response to the restructuring of the European economy. Europe doesn't really need the west of Ireland as a source of food any longer. To take land out of productive use and put it into conservation use is also something which has been problematic locally. Then you have competition between elites to deliver this project, and this also causes tension. We're just making a plea for recognition of the criss-crossing of a lot of different allegiance patterns when you take time to look at the issue.

As to what level of development of Mullaghmore will the Burren Action Group accept, we're looking for none at all. The reason for that is not because we've taken a philosophical decision as to what level of intrusion is acceptable; it's because if you are going to use taxpayers' money to build a facility, we believe that you should build it where there is a) value for money, and b) non-conflict with the practices of local people and local initiatives. With regard to planning policy throughout the country, if the state builds something at Mullaghmore, you or I will not get planning permission to build a craft centre or a tea-room next door, which is outside the area for development under the County Development Plan. Whereas if you build it elsewhere there is a possibility of spin-off, the more you concentrate visitor numbers into the shortest tourism season in the longest days of the year. It would be purely a June/July phenomenon. You're also denying the possibility of linkages with education facilities which are closed at that time. So, I think those are the considerations, not whether you can allow ten per cent or twenty per cent intrusion.

GS: The Department of Arts, Heritage, Gaeltacht and the Islands has a different name for what they want to construct; they call it an 'Entry Point'.

JS: You can imagine how much money the spin doctors got to think that one up. It's a 2,000-square foot building.

GS: That's a large 'Entry Point'!

JS: Ok, they've taken the tea-rooms out of it. They said they will engage in zero-marketing, but you cannot do that. The Burren National Park has global recognition. Wherever you go in the world on holidays there are some people who, if they stop in Ireland or in Swaziland, will look for a swimming pool, a casino, and some people who will look for national parks. It's not the administrator of the national park who decides on whether the national park is marketed or not. We set up a computer hooked up to the Internet during the hearing, we searched for 'national park' and hundreds of pages came out. Accommodation providers are the first people who, on their websites or any of their advertising, will advertise the facilities near them. The people who administer the Burren National Park have absolutely no control over the publicity for it, so 'Entry Point' or no 'Entry Point', it's the single stand-alone facility for entry into a park that has a globally unique ecology. As a tourist, would you want to go there if you're interested in that kind of thing? Yes, you would. And can you find out about it? Yes, you can.

GS: Do you think some kind of regional assembly would be more sympathetic to these kinds of considerations as opposed to the central administration?

JS: I think so. One of the problems in Irish politics that has led to a lack of resolution on this issue has been that the mediation mechanisms have been too confrontational. There's only two – An Bord Pleanála and the courts – and they're both adversarial. You have a political system that is based on proportional representation, but with multi-seat constituencies, and that leads to competition among representatives to deliver political goods, which leads to a lack of emphasis on the legislative role. Now, we have a system of social partnership in this country between the employers, the unions and the state, and there's various tiers off that, and over the last few years groups like the disabled and the unemployed have been able to tag on to one of those three legs and have representation at social partner level. The environment has not. The environment cannot get mediated at social partnership level because environmental issues seem to get agitated at a cross-constituency level – not within the boundaries of one single constituency – they're not plugged into any mediating system. I think that's why disputes like this have been left on the political agenda for ten years when under other systems they would probably be solved.

GS: Isn't this the case with government generally, that the sorts of issues which would bear upon environmental concerns are dispersed across so many different departments, and that the idea of trying to liaise between them is almost inconceivable? Roads, fisheries, planning, built environment – these are all environmental issues but because of the way they're organised it's very difficult to actually coordinate a coherent policy.

JS: Yes. One of the problems here is that originally this department was really the Office of Public Works, a satellite of the Department of Finance which was really the state stationery and building arm. But during the 1980s, successive governments built up its power and its revenue by channelling EU structural funds through the Office of Public Works. It was a way in which the successive Taoiseachs of the day, instead of kicking funds that were coming from Europe into various other Ministers' departments, would keep it in Finance. So the Office of Public Works moved from being quite a small, insignificant department into being quite a large one. The effects are being seen today.

GS: So what would you say is the overall philosophy or stance of the Burren Action Group?

JS: I can sum up the position by saying that there are environmental problems related to this project and they are purely site-specific; and there are no demonstrated or proven – despite four successive environmental impact statements – benefits to the project. We would welcome, and we believe that there would exist, economic and social benefits to locating the development in the centre of an existing infrastructure.

Temple Bar

Temple Bar is an area of Dublin's inner-city which after years of neglect was transformed into a centre of cultural and commercial activity during the 1990s. In 1966 the state transport company Córas Iompair Éireann (CIÉ) began to purchase local properties as part of a plan to construct a major new transportation centre on the site. While awaiting development, the company let its buildings on short-term leases and low rents to a variety of users. By the mid-1980s, when development was imminent, a significant community had emerged in Temple Bar. The Dublin City branch of An Taisce (a voluntary heritage body) also began to take an interest in these 28 acres of land on the Liffey's south bank. In 1991, a number of interested parties successfully lobbied for Temple Bar's conservation. A company called Temple Bar Properties was established under a government Act to administer an Urban Pilot Project, and subsequently to organise a Development Programme for the area.[38] Although the company's remit was primarily cultural, its two-phased plan (1991–96, 1996–99) also addressed residential, retail and environmental aspects (Temple Bar Properties 1996: 4). During this period, Temple Bar was converted from a series of run-down backstreets into a bustling commercial and cultural zone. Also during this time, the area became one of Dublin's major tourist attractions.

One of the new company's first actions was to set up a competition to develop a coordinated Architectural Framework Plan for the designated area. The competition was won by Group 91, a consortium of Irish practices possessed of a wide range of specialisms and skills. The eight firms which made up the group expressed their determination 'to release the dynamic potential of Temple Bar' through the deployment of 'a flexible series of integrated responses, while reinforcing its unique sense of place in our capital city' (Graeve 1991: 16). This could best be achieved, as the architect and competition assessor David Mackay suggested, by bringing a modern European urban sensibility to bear upon Dublin's own peculiar architectural heritage without compromising either:

> The object of the competition is revolutionary: it returns to a historical tradition of considering that the design of public space, streets, squares, and their sequence and proportions are a subject of cultural importance to the identity of the city and are therefore a public responsibility. That Dublin should be one of the first cities to regain this European tradition is particularly appropriate in this year that it is the European City of Culture. (in Graeve 1991: 11)

Group 91 took as its remit the entire 'atmosphere' of Temple Bar, covering aspects such as restoration, new-build, traffic management, pedestrianisation, permeability, streetscape, public and residential space (Cairns 1999: 16–31). The hope was that the area would provide a focus for urban renewal and (hence) cultural and architectural renaissance, forming what one commentator described as 'a kind of necessary heart to Dublin which it lacked and which it always needed if the city was to prosper' (McCullough 1996: 27). If Barcelona and Berlin had recently arisen from their own ashes, why not Dublin?

Renewal and renaissance have undoubtedly occurred. Temple Bar functions as a self-conscious urban landscape, cast against both the traditional image of a run-down, deprived, inner-city Dublin and also against the banalities of suburb and hinterland. Some critics have characterised the Temple Bar project as a typical example of 'gentrification', however – that is, the conversion of dilapidated vernacular cityscapes into playgrounds for professional urban elites. Focus on such relatively small honeypot projects does little, as Arnold Horner suggested, to alleviate Dublin's 'near-intractable general problems' (1992: 350). Mary Corcoran argued that the primarily symbolic changes associated with the area – renewal and renaissance – have been economically driven, and that the scheme 'reveals an inextricable linkage between culture and commerce played out in a discourse which privileges the powerful and margina- lises the vernacular in human terms, *and* in terms of the landscape'.[39] Colm Lincoln pointed out that '[the] continuing reference[s] to Temple Bar as Dublin's Left Bank are dangerously suggestive of a tourism prod- uct which could have a short shelf life.'[40] The project is also susceptible to the criticism that it attempts to manufacture in a controlled environ- ment an impression of random organic space, whereas in fact such spaces emerge, as Michel de Certeau explained with recourse to a linguistic metaphor, only as an ambiguous, vernacular response to the urban grammar constructed by planners and architects – 'a second, poetic geo- graphy on top of the geography of the literal, forbidden or permitted meaning' (1988: 105).

Interview II: Eve-Anne Cullinan, Head of Productions and a director of Temple Bar Properties. Dublin, 16 June 1999

GS: What kinds of criticism has Temple Bar Properties and the project in general been attracting in the past decade?

EC: There's been masses of controversy and debate and discussion. Even though I've been stuck in the middle of it lots of times it's actually really positive. It shows the organic nature of the project and the fact that so many different people had an opinion, they cared about the area and got actively involved. You had about 150 people who lived here in Crampton Buildings and now we have about 1,400 residents. That's a massive influx in a small area in an intense period. That has to give rise to conflict in terms of the mix of activities. We also had discussions about pedestrianisation, parking and how to live and work in the city.

Another controversial area was the actual cultural centres them- selves. People see them very positively now. Our events in Meeting House Square are always full, there's a great demand and we're getting huge audiences. There's a great sense of people using Temple Bar and people coming to free events, which are very accessible. But if you swing back five or six years there was lots of debate about the idea of having some of the smaller cultural concerns suddenly going into this purpose-built building. What does that do to your organisation and the way you work? And of course, there was also lots of discussion about 'Is this the right way to do culture?' It took a long time for people to realise that these centres weren't floated in from nowhere; there were actually people here in Temple Bar who had been doing these kinds of things already. These are the same people who championed the projects, saw them through the development and are still running them. We were only the facilitator to pull it all together. And I think that's the biggest positive factor for the cultural centres, that sense of ownership. Also, we were talking about a time when there wasn't the kind of money that's around today. I think there was resentment from some people, understandably maybe, saying why is Temple Bar getting so much money. I find it extraordinary that, at the time we're talking about, the cost of this project at IR£40 million for ten cultural centres, an archaeological project, two new open squares, a new street – that's a lot of activity to develop for what today seems a relatively small amount of money.

Another area of controversy involved the overall approach to the development of Temple Bar, because there were so many different opinions involved. We got into debate with An Taisce about our architectural plans. We stated in out policy that the Framework Plan was underpinning the entire project in our approach. The eight different architectural practices in Group 91 each got a commission for the major public buildings. There was a lot of discussion about what's conservation, what's refurbishment, what's restoration. 'Are we doing "façadism"', was one question. If you look at some of the buildings, what the architect proposed was to put back the spirit of how the building would have been used. So the Ark [a cultural centre for children] still has the Long Gallery which would have been there when it was a Presbyterian Meeting House; the round that is now a theatre space would have been similar to the main hall space. But it's absolutely a modern building from the back, and absolutely a restored façade from the front. We had expert craftsmen in, but that's controversial in itself because one man's demolition is another man's restoration.

I think now the area has settled down, but that period of change was really significant for many people. A lot of things happened in Temple Bar without people even noticing. It's important to remind everyone what it was like four years ago.

GS: Have there been any studies of the people who use Temple Bar?
EC: The Centre for Retail Studies did a really interesting study on people using the area and with that as our base line we've been

tracking it since. We do on-site consumer surveys on a continuous basis, questionaires to look at the usage patterns. In 1991 there would have been about 14,000 people going through a central point by day. Now it's more like 40,000. And the profile of people coming has changed dramatically. It used to be mostly teenage and early twenties who were the core group of people. And then there was thirty-something males – don't ask me why! The most recent study has seen a complete shift in which the middle ground – the people from 20 to 35 – is the main group of people, and there's an equal balance between the over-45s and the children and teenagers. I guess the Ark has helped that a lot. Also, we deliberately design our events to try to get a mix of people of all ages into the area. It's great that the shift has moved so that there's a much wider spread.

GS: Has there been any work on aspects of class? I'd be quite interested, for example, in who's going to the well-attended events in Meeting House Square.

EC: The CRS survey looked at income and employment, and that has been changing too. There's an increase of spending by people in the area which came out in the most recent statistics. I don't know if people are spending more, of if prices have gone up. The one that's really interesting is the ESB [Electricity Supply Board] Sunday Circus that started this year for the first time. That's a free entertainment from 2 to 4 every Sunday. What's fascinating about that is the spread. We do audience surveys at every one so we'll have a better idea of who's coming, but you can actually see there's a complete mix. I think the movies in themselves attract a kind of trendier crowd and then some older people, because the movie programme this year is on the theme of cities and some of the films are quite culty, so they generate their own kind of audience. Others are more classic and regular. The audience changes, depending on the movie. 'First Nights' which are on Friday nights is experimental new work from a whole variety of media – dance, music, comedy. Again, we're finding that each one of them brings in its own cross-section of audience.

I think it depends on the nature of the event. When we started doing 'First Night' we hoped to get an audience of between 150 and 200. We've been averaging between 350 and 400. So it just shows that when people don't have to go into a theatre or a gallery, when they can walk into a space and it's free, it creates a whole different dynamic and it breaks down a lot of barriers.

I think that's the most positive aspect. We send tickets directly to about 20 different groups with which we're linked, even though the tickets are free. We're also one of the inner-city employment contact points; we have three different projects going. One is a greening project, 'Greening Temple Bar' which is sponsored by FÁS [government employment and enterprise agency]. It's one of the community employment schemes, and it does planting, recycling and training for long-term unemployed people. Because it's manual work – planting and gardening – there aren't the kind of skills required that maybe you'd need in some of the cultural centres. But we've had a fantastic flow of people through that, and obviously they in turn go to the events and get involved as well.

On the cultural side of things we did a central training scheme in which people were placed in all the cultural centres. On the urban renewal front, we're also linked in to the Dubliner City Partnership with representatives from Smithfield and the Dockland. We've piloted a local labour incentive clause which provides apprenticeships and jobs for local inner-city people who are on the register with FÁS to work on our west-end project in construction. So they are the various pro-active side of things. I feel the easiest way to make Temple Bar accessible is through the free events. There's certainly a very local and loyal group of people who tend to come to the *Messiah* event, which we've run now for the seventh year. There's a really clear cross-section of age and background – or whatever way you want to describe it – at those events, which is great. It's hard work, though. I think you have to fight for audiences and to get that kind of cross-section as well.

GS: What's been happening on the residential front?

EC: First of all, we didn't set up with the ambition of only doing public housing. We set up to buy buildings, put apartments in them upstairs and then sell them. That was our mandate. Although we're not a housing authority, we always wanted to work with the housing authority to put in a mix of social housing as well. It constitutes about 30 per cent of the housing we're doing in the more residential quarter. The cultural quarter is in the middle. Things tend to be more business-led around the Fleet Street area. The other side of Parliament Street is where it's going to be mostly residential. We didn't do it as quickly as we thought we could because of trying to resolve the housing issues, capacity issues, and mainly because of the huge archaeological component on the other side of Parliament Street. Work only started on site after all the archaeological excavations were completed. But that's coming on stream now. It's all new-build, there's about five different architects involved, a new pedestrian street, a crèche, open green spaces and a mix of apartments. But the social housing aspect of it is already completed, and that's been occupied since last February.

GS: Was there a new competition for the job, or is it part of the masterplan?

EC: It was all part of the masterplan. Though for the private sector it's quite small, for us it was huge, close on 190 apartments in all. There was a substructure done first of all and then the architects were given commissions to do the superstructures. It was all integrated by coordinating architects, but the idea was to get a sense of interest and different styles in different buildings so it didn't become just this big block. The area is divided by a pedestrian street, and it's modelled on the original housing area, the Crampton Buildings here in Temple Bar. You've got a pedestrian street going up through the middle, a crust of retail on the outside, and the apartments are accessed from the inside where there's green courtyard space.

GS: Who lives in the apartments now, and who do you think is going to buy the new ones?

EC: If I was to be really honest I would say the people who can afford it. A few years ago, the apartments started at IR£40,000, 80,000 and 60,000. Because the tax incentives were designed to benefit owner-occupiers, it meant that people could afford to buy them. For the new apartments in the western sector we did a workshop to promote them specifically to owner-occupiers, and we set up a project with First Active whereby there was a special mortgage package put in place for those kind of buyers, as well as the normal tax incentives. We'll be trying to push for that again. But now, the starting price is IR£150,000 for the new apartments that are going up in the west end.

GS: What has been the impact of tourism on the area?

EC: Our opening marketing strategy was first of all to get Temple Bar developed into the kind of area we wanted it to be. We didn't go the mainstream route. We decided to promote Temple Bar through cultural events. That's why we started back in 1992 doing the Blues Festival. We needed to be a really good quality product, and to have a big sponsor to attract big headline acts. Guinness came in and sponsored it back in 1992. We stopped the Festival in 1996 because it was bursting at the seams and there was demand for it to be a Dublin-wide event. Although we're not involved in it anymore, some of the venues in Temple Bar are still used.

So, initially we didn't go the standard tourism route. We provided local information and we targeted specialist interest groups and the kind of short-break weekend traveller. We always felt that if we get Temple Bar right the tourists would find it, they would just come anyway. The area is not designed to cater for big groups; the hotels and streets are small, there isn't a coach set-down point. It's very much *not* about mass-market tourism. But what happened was that along with the popularity of Dublin, Temple Bar increased in popularity and again exceeded expectations. It's now almost like an international brand. There was a negative side to that last year where we conducted a study right through the summer, because there was this thing of stag parties coming to Dublin, and specifically to Temple Bar. Most of them were actually staying outside the area but they all seemed to end up here for night-time activity. There was a lot of anecdotal evidence about it and a lot of slagging off in the media. We wanted to get some hard facts on what was happening, so we commissioned a study and found that it was a tiny proportion of tourism into Dublin and into Temple Bar – only about 1 per cent – but it had a turn-off factor of about 13 per cent across the board. And that meant that for every one person on a stag party it was turning off 13 who wanted to do more things than come here and get drunk. It was a behaviour issue. The idea was starting to creep in that if you're in Temple Bar you can do whatever you want.

GS: And hen parties, of course!

EC: And hen parties, just as bad! Now, there are completely diverse businesses in the area but what they have in common is that they've invested in Temple Bar in the same way as we have. People loved coming down here, but this was always the one negative factor emerging in the surveys we did. It could be very intimidating. On Saturday afternoons you'd have kids at the family events, people going to the book market, the food market, or just hanging around shopping, and then you'd find these eejits coming across in the middle of the afternoon. So last November we met all 37 licence-holders, including restaurants and hotels, and they came together to confirm that they were here for the long haul. They decided not to cater for stag and hen parties. We also asked the Guards to come on board. Basically, the licence-holders agreed not to serve anybody who was dressed up for those kinds of thing.

We were really interested in what would be made of that, because we thought that people might think it was sending out a negative message, it was being unwelcoming, and that it was maybe making people think that Temple Bar was elitist or something. Ironically, when we did the survey there was a 78 per cent awareness of the change in attitude from the pubs, which was phenomenal because we were very clearly trying to get out the message at the time in the press conference that it was a behavioural issue, it had nothing to do with where anyone was from. About 24 per cent of people surveyed didn't agree with the move not to cater for stag and hen parties, but 76 per cent thought it was a really good idea. So there was none of that sense of it being anti-social or unfair or elitist.

GS: There seems to be a strong identification of Temple Bar as a public space.

EC: I was impressed that there was definitely a sense that people felt Temple Bar was theirs, they liked it, they wanted to keep it. Not elite or exclusive or anything like that, but those stag and hen parties were a negative aspect that they were sick of. The guys dressed up as Elvis four years ago were funny, but it became boring. From the surveys we did it wasn't so obvious at night-time, but during the daytime it was particularly annoying for people. We discovered that there were particular companies who were specifically targeting the area as a destination for these kinds of events. The local publicans, hoteliers and ourselves wanted to have a say in how Temple Bar was promoted and marketed, to take back control from those commercial tour operators, and to assure people that it was for everybody.

GS: Would you say that the piecemeal approach to urban renewal that appears to be happening in Dublin is better than an integrated city-wide plan?

EC: There are a few different issues to consider. I think that in order to try to get something done you have to have a focus and you have to have clear objectives, and that's what we had. We have very clear development, cultural and financial objectives. We had to make the project pay for itself. It's like a revolving fund in which the commercial aspects of the programme paid for us. So it is an integrated project in that sense. But quite clearly, the Framework Plan was designed to physically link the area to the rest of the city – things like the bridge to Jervis Street. Everything in the architectural plan was trying to delineate it differently, like the cobbles, but not set it apart, and not set it up as some kind of little ghetto. I think through the events and through links to other organisations you can try to bring people into the mix; but what's really important is that there is focused area-based planning within particular designated zones, but then some 'body' has to have the overview of how those area-based plans actually integrate into each other.

We were in a unique situation that won't happen again. When I started there was about eight of us, and then suddenly we mushroomed to this company of 30 – at one point we had 44 different design teams working in the area where we project-managed everything, and in a design team there would be an archaeologist, an artist, as well as architects and construction workers. It set up lots of connections that were extraordinary for people. Architects had to deal with artists, archaeologists, contractors, engineers on complex, purpose-built cultural centres. So: 44 projects, and only two project managers basically trying to coordinate all that. But things were made easier for us because it was a much more flexible organisation. You also had a group of people coming together from completely different disciplines – from event management, some of whom had worked in the Dublin Festival and Dublin carnivals, from absolutely down-the-line, straightforward property development, from CIÉ, the original landlord. It really was an unusual mix of people.

It's obviously the development section of Dublin Corporation which should be carrying out those other kind of urban renewal projects. I understand that's what's happening now with the Smithfield area. For us, there were benefits to not being a local authority in that you operate independently, you go through the planning process, you don't have those same bureaucratic issues. We only had to think about Temple Bar. If you're city manager back in 1991 and you want to develop Temple Bar, I imagine you would have so many other agendas from different parts of the city that it's very hard to prioritise one. Now the direction seems to be towards area-based planning. We only had one priority which made it much easier. But at the same time I think it should be integrated within the local authority system, because what happened was that Temple Bar rushed ahead but the services fell behind it. People didn't think we could do what we said we were going to do. It was built, it was done, the businesses came in. And then we needed more cleaning and more management, we needed the planning to change so that there won't be any more hotels or any more pubs.

I think everyone can find their niche in Temple Bar, and it's whatever you want it to be. If you want to be trendy and hang out you go to one kind of place, if you want to have a pint you go to another, another still if you want to be in a mad busy place. Whoever you are you'll find your place – but you have to find it. Finding a quiet pub that you can sit down in on a Saturday night in Dublin is something that I haven't cracked! Dublin has changed; it's not a place for people to hang out and have a quiet drink anymore. It's Partytown.

3
The Location of Criticism, or, Putting the 'I' into 'Ireland'

The material in this chapter arises from a concern with two related theoretical-methodological issues: 1) an emphasis on local and personal history in much late twentieth-century Irish culture; and 2) the possibility of developing new critical discourses.

One of the direct effects of rapid political and economic change in late twentieth-century Ireland was a focus on individual and community experience. The confidence resulting from successful material and cultural performance meant that in all sorts of contexts, the past was presented as something that was indeed truly 'past', sufficiently distant in time from the present to be examined in detail. At the same time, as life across the island became faster and more complex, as 'society' metamorphosed into 'economy', many people were led to consider the cultural and political systems within which they were caught up. This is one of the reasons why change in any form, even lifestyle improvement, is dangerous for the state: it encourages subjects to reflect on previous and present conditions from within the context of possible change and the factors bearing thereon. Some of this activity – for example, the local history movement – was already in place from earlier in the century. But such initiatives take on an added emphasis under pressure from insistent change, including the potentially radical alteration of established land-scapes and lifestyles. Ireland in the 1980s and 1990s witnessed various developments – such as a rise in the production and consumption of life-writing, and the exposure of a number of high-profile scandals from the recent past – which bespoke a deep concern with personal identity and the integrity of both local and national communities.

Some of the questions asked by people across the island at the end of the old millennium included: How did I get to be the person I believe myself to be? What political, sociological or historical factors influenced my development? What role did the state and official state ideology play? What life-style options were available and unavailable to me, and by virtue of whose decision was this so? In what kind of a place did I come to consciousness, and how did it get to be the way it was? Do I celebrate or regret its passing, and the passing of the way of life with which I associate it? Am I somebody?

One valid response to these questions might be: Get a life! To which the 'I' persona in the previous paragraph might equally validly reply: That is exactly what I am trying to do! The self-consciousness which animates autobiography is something that becomes particularly relevant at a certain stage of the individual's life. It might be described as a 40-something genre, and it is not difficult to appreciate how it could appear to be an embarrassing irrelevance to those possessed of different institutional circumstances and intellectual agendas. The categories of economics, class and gender, for example, remain heavyweight issues within Irish Studies, and they are invariably invoked in terms of generalised, impersonal models which militate against any turn towards the local and/or the personal.

I would like to suggest, however, that self-consciousness is also something that can attend political formations at particular stages in their history. It has long been recognised that because of the peculiar decolonising trajectory upon which the island was launched, Ireland was self-obsessed throughout the twentieth century. We also know that one of the signs regularly mooted by commentators is loss of self-consciousness as an indication of political and cultural maturity. Paradoxically, however, high-profile material success in the south and the prospect of political change in the north combined to increase the degree of self-consciousness which informed political and cultural discourse across the island. It was Ireland's fate to confront the modern world at a time when, as Alan Pred puts it, '[no] group or individual is immune from the unanchoring of identity elements, from the dissonance arising between deeply engrained experiences and meanings and startlingly new experiences and meanings' (1997: 129). Confessionalism was still part of the Catholic imagination, but during the 1990s it was employed to interrogate rather than bolster the state. At the same time, supposedly 'new times' raised old questions for all political affiliations in Northern Ireland.

This phenomenon permeated modern Irish culture towards the end of the century. A kind of fiction emerged, for example, which engaged quite deliberately with discourses of genealogy, local history and local geography. Thus, whereas Roddy Doyle explored the ways in which individual consciousness is indissolubly enmeshed with environment (the fictional Dublin suburb of Barrytown), Dermot Bolger used actual north-side locations (such as Finglas) to track both the persistence of the past into the present, and the impact of change on established practices and values. Novels such as *Paddy Clarke Ha Ha Ha* (1993) and *The Woman's Daughter* (1992) may be seen in part as attempts to address the questions regarding local history and personal experience posed above. I would contend that the same is true of the poetry of Paula Meehan, the drama of Billy Roche, the music of the Saw Doctors, the journalism of Nuala O'Faolain, the film-making of John T. Davids and the cultural produce of numerous other figures.

What does the cultural critic do when confronted with this phenomenon? I wished to include a cultural critic, theorist or scholar in the above list, but could think of none to whom issues of personal history would be of more than incidental significance.[1] While the renaissance of personal experience in Irish cultural history might be a legitimate subject for critical *debate*, it seems not to have impinged on critical *practice*. Like the western intellectual tradition from which it springs, in other words, Irish cultural criticism desires to be '*in* the world but not *of* it' (Birdsall 1996: 620, original emphases). The issue of personal experience is always *there* – anecdotally, in introductions, in reviews, the subject of conference gossip; it is even accepted (albeit reluctantly) as a semi-legitimate contribution to academic discourse in the form of the 'critical biography'. But the very notion of an academic 'discipline' seems to proscribe personal experience as a respectable level of critical discourse. From the established perspective, there appears to be something rather vulgar about it; it is a bad show, not the done thing.

This raises the second issue I wish to address here: the composition and function of criticism at the present time. Whereas certain economico-cultural developments induced Irish citizens and artists to address the background to their current circumstances, this is not an ability usually afforded the professional academic. There is a sense in which all criticism – indeed, all discourse – is self-constitutive in as much as it postulates an individual subject enunciating an intended message for other subjects. But this function has been routinely denied in the modern western academy. Instead, criticism (indeed, all kinds of academic commentary, including quite centrally philosophy and history) has been produced as a 'secondary' order of discourse which merely uncovers the meaning already embedded within 'primary' cultural phenomena; the critic, historian or philosopher is a conduit rather that an agent, rearticulating in 'real', less figurative language what the author had already said in the literary text, what is already 'there' in the historical artefact, or how the properties of certain given elements (human or otherwise) evolve and interact.

To some extent, the present study partakes of this elementary critical discourse, in so far as it is addressed to an implied interlocutor, and in so far as it shares certain findings and impressions that have developed in response to a range of primary materials. However, there have been alternatives to the dominant academic discourses since the notion of the 'discipline' was invented at the beginning of the nineteenth century.[2] 'History' has been haunted from the outset by the ghost of the 'story' embarrassingly encoded into its very name; if the historian *is* merely telling stories, using various rhetorical strategies and subject ultimately to the whims of narrative, where do the claims to truth and rigour lie? Likewise, the twentieth century has witnessed a bewildering array of critical paradigms, each attempting to produce the literary text in different ways, but each ultimately defeated by the postulation of literary criticism as a discourse paradoxically related to, yet divorced from, that self-same literary text. And what of those experiences and feelings that the 'discipline' simply cannot encompass? Madness, meaninglessness, luck, chance, passion, atmosphere, the body – phenomena described by Henri Lefebvre as 'the vast store of non-formal knowledge embedded in poetry, music, dance and theatre' (1991: 406). In their different ways and in different contexts, figures as diverse as Oscar Wilde, Friedrich Nietzsche and Walter Benjamin offered profound challenges to the dominant model of empirical humanism underpinning nineteenth-century 'discipline', and to the forms through which disciplinary knowledge is disseminated.[3]

The established humanistic notion of 'discipline' generated its own discourse of critical experimentation. The cross-fertilisation of traditional historiography with the discourses of fiction and autobiography by historians such as Norman Hampson (1974), Carolyn Steedman (1986) and Simon Schama (1991) are typical in this respect. More recently, however, the academy has been forced to confront (or ignore, as may be) what Denis Cosgrove and Mona Domosh refer to as 'a crisis in the production and representation of scientific knowledge which reflects a deeper postmodern crisis of ontology and epistemology' (1993: 28). Despite claims to empiricism and scientific truth, academic method has been exposed as a profoundly moralistic discourse, the principal concern of which is to reproduce the world and its meanings in certain privileged terms. Science itself emerges as 'one discourse among others, which constructs both the object of its enquiry and the modes of studying and representing that object' (ibid.).

Arguably, the most effective challenge to the notion of 'discipline' has emerged from a *fin-de-siècle* 'postal' complex, encompassing the holy trinity of poststructuralism, postmodernism and postcolonialism. Eclectic in inspiration and diffuse in application, such a complex may none the less be postulated in theoretical terms, and loosely defined as a critique (or deconstruction) of received binary thought coupled with an awareness of the dangers of converting the Other into the Same, even (or especially) in the name of radical criticism. One of the recurring motifs of 'postal' theory is the necessity to modify the forms through which disciplinary knowledge circulates so that the critic may continue to engage with 'reality' – which is to say, the phenomena traditionally addressed by disciplines such as geography and history – but in ways that expose the contingency of the disciplinary principle.

In this respect, one might mention the philosophical meanderings of Jacques Derrida in a text such as *Glas* (1986b), the intertextual montage constructed by the geographer Allan Pred (1997), or the anecdotal literary history of Stephen Greenblatt (1980, 1990). Each represents to some degree a 'criticism under erasure', that is, an attempt to place the critical voice inside rather than outwith the methodological framework. It is perhaps ultimately a question of authority, as Cosgrove and Domash point out:

> We somehow must let our readers know that what we are creating are themselves cultural, gendered and political products, that our writing is as much about ourselves and our conditions as it is about some purported geographic reality, and that our methodologies and techniques are not ways of establishing ground truth but rather are conventions devised to make our meaning intelligible. We are obliged to share authority with both subject and reader, but equally cannot evade the authority of authorship. . . . What we seek is a way of writing that is explicit about its political and moral nature, demystifies claims to scientific truth, shares authority with its audience and yet remains understandable. (1993: 36)

If the authors cited above are practitioners, there are many others who preach the gospel of critical innovation. Frustration with the limitations of established genres may be found in many places, as may calls for study which is openly grounded in a local, personal landscape: in Nicholas Thomas's perception that 'the modes of analysis that are typically employed often paradoxically characterize "colonial discourse" in unitary and essentialist terms, and frequently seem to do more to recapitulate than subvert the privileged status and presumed dominance of the discourses that are investigated' (1994: 3); in James Duncan and David Ley's identification of postmodernism as 'a radical attack upon the mimetic theory of representation [which interrogates] all metanarratives, including those of the researcher' (1993: 3); in Richard King's indictment of historiography's 'inability to represent the process of discovering and assessing evidence and then to construct a narrative which begins to convey the pain, joy, rage, audacity, even capriciousness of that process' (1991: 186); in Ciarán Brady's admission that '[the] open adoption of fictive modes in a manner that at once acknowledges history's impotence and attempts to transcend it is a strategy that has attracted some of the bolder scholars' (1994: 30). These concerns are addressed most radically in Jacques Derrida's perception, as described by Robert Smith, that

> [the] autobiographical detour which pure reason cannot but take and continue taking through the realm of the literary and the contingent, through the realm of what by compression will be called *writing*, suspends the autobiographical and the rational together in a synthesis both special and general, in a strange state chronically unsuited to rhetorical or philosophical classification. (1995: 6, original emphasis)

Of course, the 'postal' complex is susceptible to (for want of a better word) criticism, and there is no denying that significant problems attend the activation of autobiographical discourse as a resource within postmodern cultural studies. From a Foucauldian perspective, Jeremy Tambling has argued that confession may be seen as 'the production of the reactive spirit: focused on guilt, weakness and on the need for reparation', the function of which was 'to secure consent to the rule of a dominant ideology' (1990: 6–7). Rather than liberating the subject, confession is the ritual whereby the subject internalises contemporary power relations. Developing from this, it could be argued that postmodern academic confessionalism is a symptom of the 'Oprahfication' of society – the confirmation of identity through public revelation and confrontation.[4]

At the same time, it might be argued that the subjection of established genres to other kinds of knowledge in fact represents a mystification of practices which remain amenable to empirical analysis. For Marxists, an uncritical focus on micro-phenomena could be seen to divert attention from macro-patterns that have real consequences for subjects in every social and political sphere. In the 1980s and 1990s, Aijaz Ahmad was one of the most outspoken critics of postmodernist excesses with regard to supposedly 'authoritarian' notions of discipline and genre. The postmodernist critic's self-image as migrant or traveller, refusing to be housed in anything so constrictive as *a* theory, betrays him/her as an effect of reactionary, late capitalist culture, unable to grasp the very real institutional conditions of their own possibility. Ahmad argues that the supposedly 'liberating' exposure of truth as mere rhetorical effect has led in most instances to 'a very poststructuralist kind of ironic self-referentiality and self-pleasuring' (1992: 6–7) – critical onanism for the privileged. And yet he too insists on locating criticism in terms of 'the conditions of its production and the class location of its agents', whilst defining 'determination' as 'the givenness of the circumstances within which individuals *make* their choices, their lives, their histories' (1992: 6, original emphasis).

This chapter represents a critical engagement with both the new confessionalism I perceive to be animating modern Irish culture, and the challenge to received critical forms inspired by developments in literary theory, philosophy and a number of cognate fields. It represents a composite of some of the factors which have led to the present moment: an amateur interest in a professional context; an (ir)rational questioning of accepted regimes of (ir)rationality; a stand-off between history and memory. It also represents a search for home conducted in the knowledge that home was always slipping away and is now permanently lost. Such a study makes no claims to primacy, fidelity, originality or continuity. The 'memory' invoked here is set resolutely against a modal invocation of the remembered landscape in terms of loss and sorrow. I have no space for the exercise, but the study here undertaken might be productively compared with Foucault's notion of genealogy which 'seeks to make visible all of those discontinuities that cross us', and is 'opposed to "antiquarian" history, which seeks the continuities of soil, language, and urban life in which our present is rooted' (1984: 95). The goal, as with genealogy, would be the ultimately untenable position that works to reveal 'the heterogeneous systems which, masked by the self, inhibit the formation of any form of identity' (ibid.).

The material included in this chapter was selected and arranged to link with issues raised in other parts of the book. I have neither the space nor the desire to formalise such connections into an explicit narrative, but prefer to let them emerge (or not) as organically as possible.

This is the way of it, then. I was born in the Coombe hospital in Dublin and christened at Bohernabreena Church. I lived 10 km from the city, at the foot of Mount Pelier, in the barony of Uppercross, in the civil parish of Tallaght, in the Poor Law Union of South Dublin, in the Catholic parish of Rathfarnham, in the townland of Knocklyon, in the village of Firhouse, in a house facing onto a weir on the River Dodder. I served mass at the local Carmelite Convent between the ages of eight and twelve. This latter institution was established in 1827 in the house of the Fieragh family after whom Firhouse is reputedly named. The convent gave its name to the group of houses in which I lived: Mount Carmel Park. I drank in the Knocklyon Inn from the age of 16. My first gig was at St Columcille's Well in June 1977. I dropped out of University College Dublin after two terms. I lived in Firhouse until I was 20. I spent four years on and off in Spain as a professional musician. In January 1986 I returned penniless to Dublin and found a neighbourhood, a city and a country in a state of chronic economic depression. In February of the same year I travelled to England to play music in the pubs and clubs of Liverpool. I did not realise until quite recently that I had emigrated.

The River Dodder

The Dodder rises at 630 metres on Kippure in the Dublin mountains, just a short distance from the source of the county's more famous river, the Liffey. One of its four tributaries, Tromanallison, actually flows through Wicklow for nearly a kilometre, so the Dodder is not pure Dublin. Falling 451 metres in the first 5 kilometres, the river courses about 29 kilometres in total before it rejoins the Liffey at Ringsend, east of the city. The water emerges from Caledonian granite that is 400 million years old and part of the same chain that forms the Wicklow and Blackstairs mountains (Moriarty 1998: 20). Like the other Dublin and Wicklow valleys, the Dodder gorge assumed much of its present topography during the last Ice Age when the Midlandian ice field receded and powerful melt waters flooded down from the ice cap. The till and moraine deposited by glaciers has formed both the landscape over and through which the river has coursed for around 12,000 years.

On its journey to the sea, the Dodder flows through wilderness and suburbs, over rock and under bridges, between houses and down waterfalls, and finally (via the Liffey) into the sea. It passes through places that are now called Castlekelly, Glenasmole, Bohernabreena, Old Bawn, Firhouse, Templeogue, Rathfarnham, Rathgar, Rathmines, Ranelagh and Ballsbridge. The river and the surrounding Dublin mountains seem to have attracted settlers from an early period; as William Nolan noted, '[the] association between riverine sites and settlement forms a continuous theme in the historical geography of Ireland' (1982: 27). Geraldine Stout and Matthew Stout concur, pointing out that '[from] the first inland penetration in the Neolithic period, the southern uplands were the location favoured by all the pre-Viking peoples' (1992: 21). A number of axeheads dating from the Bronze Age were discovered in the Firhouse area (Ó Néill n.d.: 19), and cist tombs, passage tombs and major cemetery sites abound in the locality (Moody, Martin and Byrne 1984: 15). The existence of different burial practices seems to suggest a series of well-demarcated, coeval and overlapping cultures, but whether it would be possible to produce an accurate image of the prehistorical settlement patterns of the Dodder valley remains at issue. For millennia after the Ice Age, the area around the river was (like the rest of the island) part of 'a tribal nation barricaded behind a wilderness of forests and bog, divided into hundreds of tribal tuatha or petty kingdoms, each with its own royal forts and monasteries and mythological sites of timeless association' (Smyth 1982: 2).

Less contentious is the claim that local inhabitants would have had to cope with the Dodder's propensity for sudden, spectacular flooding. In his report for the 'Book of Reference' to the Down Survey Maps of 1655–56, Thomas Taylor described how

> the South East of this Barony [then Newcastle and Uppercross] is watered by the River Dogher which is a river that Descends by many branches from the Mountaines which being united doth after greate raines overflowe soe many times both man and beasts are cast away by the violence of the sudden flood but havi[n]ge the Sea to empty itselfe into is in a very Lytle time abated. (Simington 1945: 289)

The Dodder's reputation as a volatile and dangerous river is regularly borne out. The most spectacular flooding on record occurred when, following 'Hurricane Charlie' in August 1986, continuous heavy rain caused serious damage all along its course, but particularly around the Orwell Bridge area between Rathfarnham and Rathgar.

Although '*dothar*' is given as generic 'river' in Edward O'Reilly's dictionary of 1817 (1877: 198), there appears to be no satisfactory explanation as to the derivation of the name. Christopher Moriarty speculates that it could be pre-Celtic and therefore resistent to interpretation by Gaelic scholars (1998: 10). However, the Dodder provides the backdrop for a number of important stories and incidents from both Celtic legend and Irish history. The 'Dothra' is mentioned in the *dinnshenchas* poem 'Bend Etair' (Gwynn 1913: 105), while also meriting an obscure reference in the ninth-century *Martyrology of Oengus the Culdee* (Stokes 1905: 123, 131). More intriguingly, *The Annals of Ulster* refer to the 'killing of Dubhdoithre [the Black Man of the Dodder], King of the Uí Briuin' in 742 (Hennessy 1887: 205). Later, the area through which the Dodder flowed was ruled by a family rejoicing in the name MacGillamocholmog, renowned for their resistance to Danish expansion in that part of Leinster (O'Donovan 1862: xiii–xiv).

Perhaps its most significant role, however, was as backdrop to *Togail Bruidne Dá Derga*, or the *Destruction of Dá Derga's Hostel*, a ninth-century tale preserved in the twelfth-century *Lebor na hUidre*. One of the longest and most famous of early Irish sagas, it relates how Conaire Mór ruled the land from Tara but grew increasingly lax regarding the taboos or *gessa* whereby he was enabled to assume the kingship. Magically prevented from finding his way home from Munster, Conaire takes refuge in the house of Dá Derga, one of the six remaining great hostelries of Ireland. Apparently, *Bruidne* of this kind once proliferated in the island, with 93 in Leinster alone (Hegarty 1939–40: 71). Conaire suffers a supernatural thirst but '[the] cupbearers found no drink for him in the Dodder (a river), and the Dodder had flowed through the house' (Stokes 1902: 137). Despite valiant defence by the Ulster champion Conall Cernach, the hostel is attacked and destroyed, and Conaire is killed by his scheming foster-brothers and their British allies.[5]

Conaire is an historical figure, and there has been speculation that the ninth-century tale is based on actual political events preserved in memory and oral narrative. *The Annals of the Four Masters* record that in 'The Age of the World, 5160, Conaire, son of Ederscel, after having been seventy years in the sovereignty of Ireland, was slain at Bruighean-da-Dhearg, by insurgents' (*AFM* I: 91). According to this and other sources, the events took place any time between 33 BC and AD 43 (Stokes 1902: 4). It is significant, however, that the political machinations of 2,000 years ago, filtered through a number of interpretive lens at various points in history, remain imprinted in the place-name. Joyce explains that '[both] *brugh* and *bruighean* were often used to signify a house of public hospitality...No remains of [*Bruighean-Da-Derga*] can now be discovered, but it has left its name on the townland of Bohernabreena, which is the phonetic representative of *Bothar-na-Bruighne*, the road of the *bruighean* or mansion' (*INP*: 266–7).[6]

While the tale may preserve the memory of a significant political shift in ancient Irish history, however, Stewart MacAlister doubted the existence of an actual 'hostelry' as such, especially one with a volatile river like the Dodder flowing through or near it. Rather, he suggested, the tale should be understood as a ritual narrative inspired by Celtic religious practices, and the *bruighean* seen as a sort of 'worship-centre' or 'pantheon' (1939: 262). For Eugene O'Curry, the main interest of the tale was its style, structure and language, all of which indicated its great antiquity, 'more ancient even that the *Táin Bó Chuailgné*' (which immediately proceeds it in *Lebor na hUidre*). The principal value of *Togail Bruidne Dá Derga*, O'Curry maintained, was to provide 'the best and most copious illustrations . . . of the various ranks and classes of the officers that composed the king's household in ancient times, and of the arrangements of a regal feast – both social subjects of great historical interest' (*MM*: 259–60). For Whitley Stokes, likewise, 'the pathos and beauty' of this ancient narrative could not disguise the more significant anthropological and historical evidence it afforded, to wit, 'the primeval belief in the ruin wrought by the violation of tabus, [and] . . . the survival of totemism' (1902: 1). Eleanor Knott, finally, saw the tale as both a genuine 'native epic, uninfluenced in its general conception by foreign models', and also a partial vindication of Matthew Arnold's conception of romantic Celticism (1936: ix–x).

Whether oral or literary, narrative always plays on the interface between different kinds of evaluative discourse. Whereas MacAlister, O'Curry, Stokes and Knott subject *Togail Bruidne Dá Derga* to a primarily empiricist analysis, Samuel Ferguson found in the story of internal discord and foreign invasion an instructive allegory of Irish history. Like much of his creative work, the long epic poem 'Conary' was an attempt to wrest some measure of heroic compensation from what seemed an unfortunately congenital weakness in the Celtic psyche. Ferguson follows the Irish text quite closely in respect of the grandeur of Conaire's court and the complexity of the society he ruled (1880: 61–96). In this he was of a piece with nineteenth-century cultural nationalism's double programme: the confirmation of a discrete, ancient Irish culture, and the immorality of Britain's destruction of it. But the major tension underpinning this poem is a concern with 'order', or rather the breakdown of order with ensues from human weakness as manifested in political strife (Denman 1990: 157–8; Graham 1998: 73–122).

Like many of the great nineteenth-century Irish scholars, O'Curry worked for the Ordnance Survey collecting folklore and advising on local place-names. One of the parishes he covered was Tallaght, and although Firhouse – less than a blip on the map at this stage – merits no mention, O'Curry does describe a number of local landmarks, place-names and customs. These included an ancient mill on the Dodder at

Old Bawn, a holy well on the Balrothery Road, and the derivation of the place-name Killininny. In July and August 1837 he wrote a series of letters to the head of the survey, Thomas Larcom, describing his visit to *Gleann a Smoil*.[7] Joyce gives this place-name as *Glean-na-smól* and translates it as 'the valley of the thrushes' (*INP*: 437). Amongst many other things, O'Curry records the names of the four streams that feed the Dodder and the precise topography of the area in which it rises. He also makes reference to the valley's extensive Fenian and Ossianic associations.

The Fionn Cycle constitutes a large body of stories, with both literary and popular traditions, relating the exploits of the warrior band known as the Fianna.[8] Glenasmole is invoked a number of times in the Cycle, mostly in relation to its fauna and flora. Parts of the valley are still designated areas of 'National Importance' (Moriarty 1998: 65). In the archives of the Royal Irish Academy, William Wilde (Oscar's father) discovered a stray ninth-century Fenian poem in which Cailte Mac Ronain (one of the cycle's heroes) relates to St Patrick the story of how Fionn was placed under a *geis* to collect two of every wild animal in Ireland. Fionn found '[two] *Geilt Glinnes* from Glenn-a-Smoil' (1862: 190). '*Geilt*,' explains Wilde, 'means "a wild man or woman – one living in woods" – a maniac. It may, however, have been figuratively applied to some very fierce or untameable creature, either quadruped or bird, which inhabited the woods' (ibid.: 184). (*Geilt*, to recall, was the word used to describe Suibne.) Another poem, 'The Finnian Hunt of Sliabh Truim', describes Fionn's destruction of 'the *Arrach* [monster] of Gleann-an-Smoil' (O'Daly 1861: 121), while yet another (The Adventures of Amadan Mor') refers to a golden fort and describes Glenasmole as 'always full of witchcraft' (ibid.: 173).

More significant Ossianic references are recorded in 'The Chase of Gleann an Smóil' (O'Daly 1861: 75–87) and 'The Battle of Gabhra' (O'Kearney 1853). In the latter poem, Fionn's son, Oisín, returns from *Tír na nÓg* to visit his old companions, only to find Ireland occupied by a race of weaklings for whom the Fianna are just a distant memory. Riding through Glenasmole, he reaches from his horse to pick up a granite bounder that some locals are struggling to move, when his saddle strap breaks. On hitting the ground Oisín is transformed instantly into a feeble old man. He is brought to St Patrick, and in an encounter which echoes that between Suibne and St Moling, the two men argue as to the relative merits of pagan Ireland and a land tamed by the bells and cells of Christianity. At one point, Oisín returns to Glenasmole to find a rowan berry, an ivy leaf and a blackbird, all of giant size, so as to prove to Patrick the natural munificence of pre-Christian Ireland. Patrick's is the last word, however: 'Do you, now that you are here in your folly, turn your thoughts upon yourself: reflect on your own case, poor wretch: turn your thought now to your tomb' (Murphy 1933: 215).

Although at least two of the mountains on the valley's western flank, Seefin and Ballymorefinn, attest to a connection, O'Curry found no traditions concerning Fionn or Oisín in Glenasmole. A large granite 'erratic' (a boulder picked up and deposited some distance from its original location by ice flow) is referred to locally as 'Finn MacCool's Stone', and apparently once bore a plaque with the inscription: 'Finmakoom, one of the Irish giants, carried this stone on his shoulder from the opposite mountain on April 1st, 1444 – he was 9 feet 7 inches high, and weighed 44 stone' (Moriarty 1998: 36). If not a record of Finn, this at least provides evidence for the existence of someone with money, leisure and a sense of humour in the not too distant past.

Moving away from the realms of myth and legend, the Dodder tells a more elemental story of human modification and natural resistance. It seems reasonable to assume that the river would have been forded in pre-historical times, and also that because of the powerful floods to which it is prone, these structures would have been temporary. Well into recorded history we find evidence of increasingly sophisticated and stronger bridges intended, but invariably failing, to cope with the Dodder (Hegarty 1939–40: 59). It was only in the nineteenth century that engineering progressed to the point at which permanent structures could be designed, although this in turn proved to be a problem. Over the years, the bridge dedicated to Robert Emmet at Templeogue, for example, became a horrendous bottleneck for traffic flowing into the city from Firhouse and Tallaght, and a wider structure had to be built to accommodate a transport culture unimaginable in the nineteenth century. The present level of noise and fumes would not have been conducive to the nervous health of the poet Austen Clarke, after whom the new bridge is named, and who lived in a cottage named Bridge House beneath the older structure from 1937.

Before a road bridge was built a few metres to the east of Mount Carmel Park in 1986, the only means of crossing the Dodder between Old Bawn and Templeogue was a narrow lattice girder structure directly in front of Mount Carmel Park. It shook when you jumped on it. Built by British Army engineers in 1861, this footbridge remained in use until 1995 at which time it was replaced by a new metal one. In some ways, indeed, it might be said that Firhouse, like the concept of 'place' described by Heidegger, only came 'into existence because of the bridge' (1971: 154).

The 1986 bridge is itself defunct, now that a four-lane flyover, part of the M50 Southern Cross Motorway, is complete (Dun Laoghaire/ Rathdown County Council 1998). Built by EU funds to feed the Celtic Tiger, this road has already significantly altered the local perception of space. The completed portion, from Balrothery to Dublin Airport, affords rapid access to areas of the city and the hinterland which before demanded longer journeys on slower roads. Places such as the airport are potentially much nearer in time; the long trip into the city and back out the other side is no longer a necessity for travellers coming from or to Firhouse. The city has been shifted sideways on the cognitive map of that particular journey, although what this actually means in terms of the subject's relationship with the relevant spaces and places is difficult to assess. The motorway is certainly a more convenient option, if you happen to have IR£25 to spend on the taxi fare and do not wish to brave the inferno of Dublin city centre. On the other hand, the fabric of space has been materially altered with the provision of a new route which allows the traveller to bypass the city streets, offering instead to speed him to his destination without having to negotiate anything so bothersome as people. Even then, the promise of motorway speed can be illusionary, as peak-time jams of up to 40 minutes have been recorded for the motorway exit at Balrothery.

Besides fishing, there is a long history of attempts to harness the Dodder for material ends. Because of the river's swiftness and the steepness of its descent, a lot of gravel was washed down and deposited in lower-lying areas, such as Firhouse. One source reckons that '[in] the early nineteenth century, about 4,000 tons were removed each year', and this material (used mostly in road-building) was replenished by the annual floods (Ó Néill n.d.: 25). The Firhouse area in particular was renowned for its sand and gravel pits and block factories. A high-tech operation remains in place above Firhouse Weir. The other major industry developed along the Dodder was milling. South Dublin mills were 'a central feature of the manorial economy in the medieval period' (Stout and Stout 1992: 104), and the Dodder's vigorous flow made it suitable for exploitation. By 1844 the river fed 28 mills of various kinds between Kiltipper and Ringsend: parchment, paper, cardboard, glue, dye, flour, corn and woollen cloth. One of the suburban areas through which the Dodder flows is still called Milltown. There were besides a number of 'distilleries, breweries, malt houses, foundries, tanneries and a bacon curing factory' (Patrick Healy 1961: 113), all exploiting the river either for power or as a seemingly natural dump. The mills thrived until the late nineteenth century at which time, as the contemporary local historian William Handcock wrote, '[they] were unable to compete with foreign manufacture' and the place became 'a desert' (1991: 75). The fact that levels of pollution caused by all the industrial activity on the upper Dodder were much higher during Handcock's time than at the beginning of the twenty-first century provides a cautionary tale for environmentalists troubled by ecoguilt.

Ecocritical pessimism is also belied by the fact that much of the most beautiful scenery along the Dodder is the result of human activity. As Raymond Williams once pointed out, a considerable part of what we find attractive about 'natural' landscape is actually 'the product of human design and human labour' (1980: 78). In 1877 an engineer named Richard Hassard compiled a report for the Rathfarnham Township Commissioners in which he proposed the construction of two dams in Glenasmole to create a water supply for the Rathmines and Rathgar area of south Dublin (Durand 1992). The plan was adopted, and two reservoirs were built between 1883 and 1887. An artificial watercourse was also constructed to channel the Dodder in the direction and at the rate required by the engineers. If Glenasmole was a byword for bounteous and mysterious 'nature' amongst the Fenian poets, the Sunday trip out to the 'Bohernabreena Lakes' became a popular custom amongst south Dublin suburbanites throughout the twentieth century, and remains so into the present. Despite the 'artifice' of this latter landscape, however, it is no less 'natural' that the former, as in each case the relevant space is made a function of human – which is to say, cultural – desire.

Perhaps the most famous attempt to harness the Dodder was the construction of the City Weir at Firhouse during the thirteenth century. On 29 April 1244 Maurice Fitzgerald, Lord Justiciary of Ireland, issued a writ in the *White Book of Dublin* to find a suitable means of improving the water supply into Dublin (Gilbert 1889: 92). A team of twelve jurors decided that a weir should be built at Balrothery, now Firhouse, to construct an artificial channel from the Dodder that would enable it to augment the River Poddle which at that time still flowed above ground and provided the city's main water supply. The new 'City Watercourse' joined the Poddle in Kimmage, and the greater stream – known in medieval and early modern times as 'the Doder water' (O'Brennan 1940–41: 20) – flowed on through Dublin south-west before emptying into the city basin at St James Gate. The Firhouse Weir provided Dublin with its main water supply until the Liffey and the canals were adapted in the mid-eighteenth century (Jackson 1958–59: 33).

The structure testifies to the ambition and excellence of medieval engineering. The water descends over huge limestone slabs onto a concrete sill, before another drop takes it onto a verdant river valley below, an area known to generations of local children as 'The Jungle'. In terms of agriculture, industry and travel, the weir has obviously modified the surrounding landscape in a number of ways. But one of its most striking impacts has been the constant noise of thousands of cubic metres of falling water. To those unused to it, this sound can be as disturbing and intrusive as a pneumatic drill; to others it can seem an entirely natural presence, as familiar as the sky. This is not a silence-breaking sound, as for example in the manner of birdsong. In fact, there has not been silence in the immediate vicinity since the weir was constructed in the thirteenth century. Rather, the sound of falling water functions as part of the soundtrack to local everyday life. In this respect, it wards off the silence that, as the geographer and social psychologist Yi-Fu Tuan writes, has become a western signifier of 'isolation, death, indifference' (1993: 85). Firhouse Weir provides the sound of nature managed for cultural ends, a constant reminder that humankind is simultaneously of and in the world. On the other hand, its bleak unceasing monotone, lacking any of the dynamism or harmony of the city soundscape, can itself become a signifier of human absence and loneliness, what Edward Relph calls 'the drudgery of place' (1976: 39). The sound of the weir, in other words, functions as an index of those twin elements which delimit the human condition: fear and desire.

Tallaght

The general area through which the Dodder flows during the middle part of its journey to the sea is called Tallaght. This was not always the case. It is not that the river has changed its course, however, but that 'Tallaght' has come to designate areas that once had discrete place-names and identities. Located about 13 km from Dublin city centre, Tallaght in the 1960s was a one-street village with a small working-class estate called St Maelruans Park on one side, an area of middle-class bungalows on the other, and only a Dominican priory and an unreliable bus service to distinguish it from the other villages ringing the city. Towards the century's end, however, the name 'Tallaght' became synonymous with the massive housing programme undertaken by the County Council and the Corporation. In less than a generation, Tallaght grew into the largest town on the island, with a population (100,000 plus) greater than that of most Irish regional cities. There are parts of the conurbation that make Barrytown or Finglas look like quaint villages, and for every tale of community mobilisation and resistance there is another of alienation and breakdown. Tallaght is creeping, holding the mirror up to modern Ireland as it does so, and demanding that the gap between official ideology and the realities of those who continue to live and work that ideology be acknowledged.

There is another 'Tallaght', however, visible still beneath the developments of recent years. The backwards glance reveals a series of images which demand *the local* be located within a series of wider contexts: the 1867 'Battle of Tallaght' – a skirmish connected in some obscure way with the Fenian rising of that year; the medieval townland of Uppercross on the edge of the Pale, under constant threat from the O'Tooles and O'Byrnes in the Wicklow Mountains to the south; the monastery confirmed to the See of Dublin by Pope Alexander III in 1179 and subsequently the location of the country palace of the Archbishops of Dublin (Smith 1983; Handcock 1991). Tallaght was also close to the *Eiscer Riata*, the series of Ice Age ridges running from Dublin to Galway that served from the second century as the border between two loose political dispensations – the *Leth Cuinn* of the Úi Néill and the *Leth Moga* of the Eóganacht (Nolan 1982: 3). Tallaght provides a microcosm of the events and images that come to be known as Irish history, those same events and images that are used to negotiate a relationship with the otherwise intangible entity known as 'Ireland'.

'Tallaght' is not an auspicious place-name. The present version represents a gradual anglicisation of *Taimhleacht*, which itself is a composite of *tám*, meaning plague, pestilence or disease (*CDIL* 1943: 65), and *lecht*, meaning grave, tomb, sepulchral monument, resting place and/or, by transference, death (*CDIL* 1966: 70). In *The Annals of the Four Masters*, John O'Donovan glossed an entry for Tallaght with the explanation that it signified 'a place where a number of persons, cut off by the plague, were interred together' (*AFM* I: 9). Joyce translated it as 'plague monument – a place where people who died of an epidemic were buried', and noted that it 'is pretty common as a local appellative in various parts of Ireland, under different forms' (*INP*: 151). There is for example a 'Tamlaght' in Co. Londonderry, a few miles north of Toomebridge.

The origin of this particular place-name lies is Irish pre-history when the island was supposedly colonised by the followers of a Scythian named Parthalón. The eleventh-century *Lebor Gabála Érenn* (*The Book of the Taking of Ireland*) tells how this legendary figure, reputedly descended from Japhet, son of Noah, led the first influx of people after the Flood (MacAlister 1939: 253–73; 1940: 2–114). The colony occupied a stretch of land between Howth and the Dublin mountains called *Seanmhagh-Ealta-Edair*, which translates as 'Old Plain of the Flocks in Edar'.[9] In his seventeenth-century historical account, *Forus Feasa ar Éirinn*, Geoffrey Keating speculated that 'Old Plain of the Flocks' was so called '[because] that it is into it the birds of Erin used-to-come to bask-themselves-in-the-sun' (1880: 75). Parthalón is in fact noted as some-what of a plains-clearer himself, while the people accompanying him to Ireland are recorded as introducing various cultural innovations, among which were the brewing of fern-ale and the keeping of guest-houses. In some redactions Parthalón dies from wounds received in combat with a Fomorian enemy called Cicul or Cichol. In the more well-known story (perpetuated by the annalists and Keating amongst others) Parthalón's people, numbering 5,000 men and 4,000 women, died in one week from a plague and were buried at Tallaght; hence the name by which the area was known: *Taimhleacht Muintire Parthaloin*: the burial place of the people of Parthalón.

The Four Masters dates the death of Parthalón's people to 'The Age of the World, 2820' – that is, 2,374 years before Christ. Certainly, the surrounding area has produced plenty of archaeological evidence of human activity going back to the Neolithic including, as remarked above, a variety of burial cultures (Stout and Stout 1992). The remains of an important earlier Bronze Age cemetery, marked by a collection of ancient sepulchral tumuli, can still be seen on the nearby Hill of Tallaght, and this has lent weight to the Parthalón connection (P.W. Joyce 1869: 151; Hayward 1949: 76). According to this story, then, 'Tallaght' is a post-diluvian cemetery!

Lebor Gabála is not historiography, however, but the accumulated work of a number of imaginative story-tellers who combined biblical, first millennium and folkloristic sources with their own aspirations and persuasions. MacAlister, the editor of *Lebor Gabála*, rejects the plague story as so much 'editorial trimming' (1939: 266), simply a means of clearing the stage for the next invasion by the followers of Nemed. 'The Old Plain of Etar' or 'Edar' refers to a landscape near Howth, north of the Liffey; the association of the disaster with Tallaght to the south is, MacAlister avers, 'a mere unproved assumption or etymological guess, for which later writers like O'Clery and O'Flaherty are responsible. . . . The text before us gives us no evidence for the existence of a *place-name* based upon the catastrophe' (1940: 86, original emphasis). The 'apparent pointlessness' of the Parthalón story that eventually ended up in *Lebor Gabála* becomes apparent when it is understood that it is in fact 'a drastically artificial elaboration, by scholastic pedants, of primary folk traditions' (1939: 253). And this primary folk tradition, severely deformed but still recognisable, is an Irish rendering of the archetypal 'fertility-ritual drama' (ibid.: 264) in which the vegetation god must die at the onset of winter so that he may be reborn in springtime. This, for MacAlister, is the essence of the ritual combat with Cicul, echoes of which may be found in many primitive cultures.

The decision of the monk Máel Ruain to found a church at Tallaght in 769 may have been 'a conscious attempt to impose the Christian stamp on a site which had previously had strong pagan associations' (Flanagan and Flanagan 1994: 145). Howsoever, although only one of 67 pre-Norman ecclesiastical sites in the Dublin area (Stout and Stout 1992: 15), 'Tamhlacht Mailruain' (another early name) went on to become one of the most significant Irish religious sites of the late eighth and early ninth centuries. Indeed, 'had the course of events been favourable', one source speculates, the monastery of Tallaght 'might have become as famous in church history as Armagh or Clonmacnoise' (Hegarty 1939–40: 67).

Máel Ruain's monastery was an important centre of the 'Culdee' movement, this being an anglicised rendering of *Céle Dé*, meaning a serving companion, client or vassal of God. The Culdees were religious reformers occupying 'an intermediate position between the monks and the secular clergy' (Stokes 1905: xxviii), and Tallaght was from the outset one of the principal centres of ascetic revival (Hughes 1966: 173–84; Roy 1986: 167–9). Máel Ruain had links with like-minded religious throughout Leinster and Munster; indeed, one of the first men to have been called a *Céle Dé* was Suibne's interlocutor St Moling (Gwynn and Hadcock 1988: 43). Alarmed by what they considered to be the laxity and growing secularism of contemporary religious practices – exemplified 'by the proliferating involvement in business affairs by Armagh, Clonmacnoise, Durrow, Kildare and the rest' (Roy 1986: 168) – groups of men clustered together in an attempt to revive the spirit of the Irish church's golden age in the sixth and seventh centuries.

The emergence of the Culdees – described as 'puritanical' by one observer (Smyth 1982: 92) – appears to have been an effect of the cycle of modernisation and reform which attends any organised movement. Periods of development are followed by periods of back-to-basics austerity, and the Culdees were intent on being much more 'basic' than their worldly (as they saw them) contemporaries. Their observances are preserved in a number of documents, and what emerges from *The Teaching of Mael Ruain* and *The Rule of the Céli Dé* (both compiled in the ninth century) is an impression of a group of men who saw sin just about everywhere and were dedicated to its extirpation through prayer and penance. The monks of Tallaght observed a strict sabbatarianism, refusing even to eat windfalls on Sunday. Anything related to bodily appetites was especially suspect: women were fountains of pollution (Gwynn 1927: 37); music diverted attention from heaven (ibid.: 31); toilets were the abode of evil spirits (ibid.: 75). As the body was the primary source of evil, so it must be strictly controlled, through diet and mental discipline as far as possible, but when these failed through more pro-active methods such as flagellation and other mortifications of the flesh, including water-vigil and repeated genuflection.

Despite the attempt to formalise the movement through 'teaching' and 'rules', however, Culdee practice appears to have remained by and large attitudinal and improvised, never really defining a coherent philosophy nor a practical reform programme. Ascetic zeal stopped well short of fanaticism; adherents were advised but not constrained to follow the example of Máel Ruain and other reformers. It may in fact be erroneous to speak of a 'movement' as such, for '[each] reformed house determined its own standard of asceticism, and even within the same house there was no common level of discipline' (Hughes 1966: 183). The affiliated Culdee monasteries of Tallaght and Finglas (north of the Liffey) were known as the 'eyes of Ireland' (Somerville-Large 1979: 13), but theirs was not always a vision shared. Whereas Máel Ruain banned alcohol in Tallaght completely, it was accepted in Finglas where the abbot Dubliter sardonically commented to his counterpart: 'My monks drink ale ... and they shall be in the Kingdom of God along with thine.'[10]

Moreover, while they may have been admired and respected by their contemporaries, it would appear that the impact of the Culdees was limited to moral example and advice. Because they disdained institutional intervention – 'Meddle not with worldly disputes' advised Máel Ruain (Gwynn 1927: 11) – the Culdees made little lasting impression on Irish ecclesiastical organisation. The monks of Tallaght and the other Culdee centres constituted a 'folk' or a 'fraternity' rather than a *familia* in the Columban sense; they were tolerated and even encouraged by their non-ascetic contemporaries, yet possessed (and apparently desired) no executive or institutional power. Besides, Irish Christianity was becoming increasingly enmeshed with the world of politics from the eight century on; indeed, a secular dimension had been implicit from the beginning, as the careers of Patrick and Colum Cille reveal.

One result of the Culdee reform movement appears to have been a marked increase in the number of anchorites and hermits, a development which as we saw in the previous chapter may itself have been responsible for the emergence of the genre of 'hermit' poetry. Besides this rather nebulous literary influence and the documents already mentioned, however, there are a number of texts which directly relate to ascetic revival in general and to Tallaght in particular. The Culdees had a reputation for learning (Hughes 1966: 175; Smyth 1982: 92–4), and the scriptorium at Tallaght saw the composition and/or transcription of two important texts: the *Martyrology of Tallaght* and the *Félire* or *Martyrology of Oengus the Culdee*. Of the latter text Eugene O'Curry said: 'I almost think no other country in Europe possesses a national document of so important a character.'[11] O'Curry also recounts the legend – reproduced in a number of the medieval prefaces to the *Félire* (Stokes 1905: 7–11) – regarding the derivation of the martyrology as an Irish literary genre. On his way to Tallaght, Oengus visited the church of Cúl Bendchuir (Coolbanagher) where he had a vision of angels hovering above the grave of a man who, he was informed, had been in the habit of invoking as many saints as he could remember as part of his devotions. Impressed, Oengus determined to compose a metrical calendar so that everyone could follow this worthy example.

Modern scholars trace a different genealogy, however. Inspired in the first instance from the writings of St Jerome (*c.* 342–420), martyrologies providing a calendar of saints' days became a popular genre of the late first millennium. Besides redating the Tallaght martyrologies to a time (828–33) significantly later than the date traditionally ascribed to their composition (*c.* 800), Pádraig Ó Riain (1990) has provided a comprehensive schema of the interrelations between the *Martyrology of Tallaght*, *Féilire Oengusso* and a number of other texts, including the Stowe Missal and martyrologies associated with Knock (in Co. Louth), Glendalough and Turin. The *Martyrology of Tallaght* was written in prose, but *Félire Oengusso* (although based on the former) is comprised of metrical quatrains in a 337-verse 'Prologue' followed by a full calendar celebrating the lives and deeds of mostly Irish saints. These verses are, as Whitley Stokes wrote, 'of the most meagre description . . . [consisting] of the name of the Irish or foreign saint commemorated, with some stock epithet or standing phrase tacked on, so as to comply with the exigencies of metre, rhyme, and alliteration' (1905: xlv). This, however, seems to have been the point, especially of the verse texts: 'intended for private devotion rather than liturgical celebration' (Hughes 1966: 180), verse martyrologies were a particularly appropriate devotional form for the Culdees, allowing them to work and pray at the same time.

Oengus is an emblematic figure for the Culdee movement; he is, after all, generally known as 'Oengus Céli Dé', and his writings came to represent the ascetic spirit in a way that more important contemporary figures like Máel Ruain and Dubliter did not. It is doubtful if this would have pleased him, however; and it is only relatively late (the seventeenth century) that his sobriquet was formalised (Gwynn 1905: xxvii). Having been a monk at Cluain Eidnech (Clonenagh) in Co. Leix, Oengus founded his own monastery near the modern town of Port Laoise some time after 767 (Gwynn and Hadcock 1988: 383).[12] Dismayed by the attention his austere life-style attracted, he became a lay brother in Tallaght where he worked as a menial, grinding corn and cutting wood, for seven years before being discovered by Máel Ruain. The *Félire* he subsequently completed at Tallaght – having worked on it at the churches of Coolbanagher and Clonenagh (Stokes 1905: 7) – reveals 'a man deeply read in the Holy Scriptures, and in the civil and ecclesiastical history of the world' (*MM*: 370), even if much of this learning was circumscribed by limited sources (Gwynn 1905: xliv). At the same time, he appears to have identified closely with the Culdee life-style repeatedly opting for seclusion and austerity over company and comfort. There are references to self-inflicted flagellation and other bodily mortifications such as 300 successive genuflections (Gwynn 1905: xliv, xxvi).

Something of the complexity of Oengus and of the reforming spirit he represents can be traced through his reputed movements. Tallaght during the eight century was on the border between two of five natural Leinster regions identified by Alfred Smyth: the high mountain and peat covering the Dublin and Wicklow mountains, and the forest that still covered much of the lower-lying area of what would become Co. Dublin (1982: 141). The monastery's location was typical in so far as '[permanent] settlements of a Christian character,' as Ó Riain argued, 'were regularly established in boundary areas' (1972: 25). But Oengus was from a region to the west of the province designated 'Basin peat – Bog of Allen' by Smyth: 'In spite of his prominent contribution to the Tallaght scriptorium,' he concludes, 'Óengus was, from first to last, a saint and scholar of the boggy wilderness of his childhood' (1982: 92).

The use of the word 'wilderness' is interesting here. After he left Clonenagh but before he joined Tallaght, Oengus became associated with two other religious sites: Dísert Bethech and Dysart Enos. This latter is an anglicisation of *Disert-aengusa*. We recall from Chapter 2 that in many instances Latin words were adapted for use in early Irish Christian discourse. The Irish word *dísert* retained the meaning of the original Latin *desertum* which, as Joyce gives it, meant 'a desert, wilderness, or sequestered place' (*INP*: 298). *OED* gives 'desert' as '[an] uninhabited and cultivated tract of country; a wilderness . . . now conceived as a desolate, barren region, waterless and treeless, and with but scanty growth of herbage' (IV: 515).

These were the sorts of location sought out by the 'Desert Fathers', Christian ascetics who proliferated throughout Egypt and Palestine in the fourth and fifth centuries. So popular was this practice that one place in the inner Egyptian desert came to be called 'Cellia' for the great number of would-be anchorites who built their little huts there. Helen Waddell saw the development of desert monasticism at this time as one effect of the decline of civic Rome (1936: 17). She also pointed out the long quarrel between the philosophy of desert asceticism and what would come to be called humanist philosophy, which decried excessive asceticism. It may be that the first Irish Christians adopted the 'desert' in imitation of the spatial practices of these early monks; certainly, with their cells, 'Rules' and sayings there is more than a passing resemblance between the fourth-century *athletae Dei* (athletes of God) and the *céile Dé* of the eight and ninth centuries.[13] And it may be that the lukewarm response towards the Culdees on the part of mainstream Irish religious was of a piece with the disdain towards excessive asceticism professed by contemporary inheritors of classical urban philosophy, and also by those who maintained that charity rather than poverty was the Christian ideal.

In any event, ninth-century Ireland was notably lacking in 'deserts' in the sense employed in relation to the Desert Fathers. What it did possess in abundance, however, were topographical regions that might qualify to be described as 'wilderness' (a synonym for 'desert' in both *INP* and *OED*) – regions such as the Bog of Allen, or the mountains and forests which formed the backdrop for the Tallaght monastery. And in this respect, it is interesting to note the *OED*'s citation of an alternative usage of desert: 'formerly applied more widely to any wild, uninhabited region, including forest land.'[14] While both definitions connote a 'deserted' landscape – that is, an absence of human society – the former suggests heat, dryness and limited vegetation (from the Latin original), whereas the latter suggests a mixed landscape including possibly water, mountain and forest (the Irish adaptation). With just a slight shift in the spatial imagination, first millennium Irish Christians in pursuit of the ascetic life could still take to the 'desert', even if this meant forest, lakeside, estuary or mountain.

What happened next was even stranger, however. In a note to the use of the word *dísert* in *The Battle of Mag Rath*, John O'Donovan explains that '[it] originally meant desert or wilderness, but it was afterwards applied to a hermit's cell or habitation' (1842: 11). Mary E. Byrne and Maud Joynt trace a movement from 'solitary place' to 'retreat', 'asylum' and finally 'hermitage'; they also note that *dísertach*, meaning hermit or anchorite, was the 'title of a special office in the community of Iona' (*CDIL* 1959: 142). In his *Onomasticon Goedelicum* Edmund Hogan noted around '500 references to places of which [*disert*] forms part' (1910: 345); a well-known example would be 'Dysert O'Dea' in Co. Clare. There are moreover several places, as Joyce notes, 'where names have been changed by the substitution of the modern word *castle* for the ancient *disert*' (INP: 299); thus, 'Castledermot' in Co. Kildare (which also had an abbot named Máel Ruain) was formerly known as *Disert Diarmata*.[15] But what was the process whereby the description of an uninhabited landscape (desert or wilderness) came to signify its exact opposite – a habitation (O'Donovan's 'cell or habitation', or the many synonyms noted in respect of 'Suibne Geilt') within that landscape?

The desert signifies both the natural and built environments, thus revealing the extent to which the imagination of either is dependent upon the other. We have encountered variations on the natural/built environment theme in Chapter 2 when examining the Suibne fragment. As Kathleen Hughes explains:

> A man might come to such a cell after a long period of training in the monastic schools, so that a scholar sophisticated in taste and subtle in expression might enjoy without interruption the beauty of his surroundings at a time when his imagination, stirred by religious emotion, was peculiarly sensitive.[16]

Oengus may be imagined as one such man – a sophisticated scholar, learned in Christian history, striking off for some 'secluded spot' in order better to contemplate God's will as reflected in nature. In this, he was repeating an ancient religious pattern. 'The desert,' as Derrida, says, 'is one of the beautiful and difficult metaphors ... [representing] a paradoxical figure of the aporia' (1995: 53). Unmarked by frequent human passage, the desert path *might* take the traveller home, but it might take them further into the desert. It is thus a space 'of decision or event' (ibid.: 54), which is to say, an essentially religious space. This may be why desert imagery has figured so significantly in the systems developed by the Jews, Greeks and Christians. Impervious to objective spatial science, '[the] desert is ... a figure of the pure place' (ibid.: 57), the empty place where 'God' lives. Desert and language are linked as imaginary sites for the manifestation of, and the confrontation with, God. And like language, the desert is something that 'is found in us, whence the equivocal necessity of at once recognizing it and getting rid of it' (ibid.). Like all 'deserts', then, *Disert-aengusa* was *a* place that was *no* place, a place without a reliable map, a place where Oengus went to confront God and to map the desert inside himself.

Oengus forsook his 'desert' for the fraternity of Máel Ruain, however, before returning to Dysert Enos and eventually Clonenagh to die. Meanwhile, Tallaght itself proved unfortunately situated in so far as it was too close to the sea to escape the Viking raids which began (*c.* 795) just as the community was consolidating after the death of its founder. Curiously, around the time (810 or 811) the monastery was devastated by a Viking raid (D'Alton 1838: 382; Hegarty 1939–40: 69), it also received probably its most significant entry in the annals. After their 'termon' (a legally protected area surrounding the monastery) was violated by a member of the southern Uí Néill, the Tallaght monks organised a boycott of *Óenach Tailten*, the athletic assembly held annually at Teltown, Co. Meath. This event seems to have functioned primarily as an occasion for Uí Néill propaganda. The boycott was successful in so far as the offender, the High-King Áed Oirdnide mac Néill, 'afterwards gave their full demand to the family of Tamhlacht, together with many gifts' (*AFM*, I: 417); but such reports also reveal the extent to which Máel Ruain's plea to avoid worldly concerns had already been forsaken. The Tallaght monastery had always maintained a pastoral dimension to its mission, and as the ninth century advanced it became increasingly involved in church politics. Perhaps this does not represent so much a falling away from an ideal postulated by Máel Ruain and his associates, however, as the manifestation of a contradiction which had been at the heart of the *céile Dé* movement from the outset: the attempt to activate the anchorite's 'desert' values inside the monastery walls. And as with desert asceticism, such values may have carried their own deep contradiction: a human denial of humanity.

Firhouse

Long before it was 'Firhouse', the area now so named was owned by the O'Mothans, a sept of the MacGillamocholmog. After the Norman conquest the area between Knocklyon and Killininny, including the 'village' of Firhouse (never more than a few cabins), came under the control of a powerful baron named Walter de Ridelford. Thereafter it was held by numerous owners before coming into the hands of William

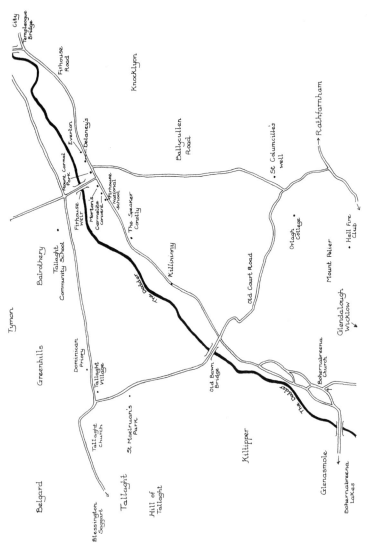

Tallaght and Environs

Firhouse

Conolly at the beginning of the eighteenth century. Conolly was known as 'the Speaker' because of his election to the office of Speaker of the Irish House of Commons in 1715 (Quane 1971–72). Besides owning the land for a number of years, Conolly made one enduring contribution to the local landscape. Around 1725 he commissioned a hunting lodge to be built on the site of a Neolithic passage tomb on the summit of a hill overlooking Firhouse. Apparently disliking its established Irish name (which has since been lost), Conolly decided to call the hill 'Mount Pelier' (Healy 1961: 124) and thus it has been ever since. When completed, the lodge became a clearly visible landmark from Firhouse, and indeed from much of south Dublin. After Conolly's death in 1729, the building became the property of a group of Anglo-Irish bucks led by the dissolute Lord Rosse. This group styled itself the 'Hellfire Club' a number of years before (*c.* 1720) the rather more celebrated society of that name founded in England by Sir Francis Dashwood (Byrne 1976–77: 29; Somerville-Large 1979: 156). The building itself came to be known as the Hell Fire Club from that time, and tales of hauntings, black masses and debauchery gave it a bad reputation which has endured to the present.

The origins of the place-name Firhouse are uncertain.[17] Because of a relatively low population until the 1970s, the area never warranted any official geographical designation. Except for a few families scraping a living in the local sand and gravel pits, Firhouse appears to have been mainly a space through which travellers such as Richard Pococke (McVeagh 1995: 131) moved from one place to another. The area may be named for a lumber-trading family named Fieragh which had roots in the area going back to at least 1474 – 'Firhouse' being a corruption of their family name and their profession (Ó Néill n.d.: 8). A tombstone in the graveyard adjoining Tallaght church is inscribed with a dedication to 'Patrick Fieragh of Furhouse' with an obituary of 2 April 1715.[18] Thereafter the area began to be generally referred to by some variant on 'Furhouse', as in John Rocque's map of 1760, in which it is 'The Fur House' (Firhouse C). It was only after the Ordnance Survey of the mid-nineteenth century that 'Firhouse' was established as the 'correct' name.

Firhouse was a genuinely rural community until well into the 1960s. Poor roads and a deplorable bus service made a trip to the city centre (or coming in the other direction, out to 'cowboy country' – Tallaght and environs) a serious undertaking. Apart from one or two developments, such as the construction of 28 houses called Mount Carmel Park in 1947, the area in the 1960s was much the same as that represented in the

Ordnance Survey map of 1867 (Ordnance Survey 1989), or in Handcock's 1876 description of what he called '[the] small, dirty village of Fir-House' (1991: 100). Extensive natural (that is, unplanned) greenbelt zones of pasture land existed between relatively small population centres such as Templeogue and Tallaght – the latter having a population of around 5,000 at the end of the 1960s. During the same decade, however, this area of south-west Dublin had been earmarked for massive housing development. In line with these plans, the population of Firhouse escalated in the last three decades of the century, and its official geographical designation has altered accordingly. Having been part of Rathfarnham Catholic parish since the Reformation, Firhouse was administered thereafter by the new entities of Tallaght-Bohernabreena (1968) and Bohernabreena-Firhouse (1972) until it was finally instituted as an independent parish in its own right on 1 November 1975 (Ó Néill n.d.: 43).[19] If these developments were an acknowledgement of the rise in population, they also reflected in part the views of many people for whom the connection with Tallaght had become invidious. This in turn reflected an older spatial issue.

Since the 1940s, Firhouse constituted not only a geographical but an ideological borderland between Tallaght and Templeogue, with the actual demarcation line itself located just north of the Knocklyon Inn. The address for Mount Carmel Park had always been 'Firhouse, Tallaght', but institutions such as the school and the convent – actually closer to Tallaght – retained close links with other parishes and communities.[20] Long before its explosion onto the national consciousness, Tallaght was generally considered to be working-class and rough. Templeogue, however, was middle-class and genteel. Firhouse National School, opened in 1954 to replace the old school beside the Carmelite convent, took the children of both and all places in between. Boys and girls from these latter areas – Knocklyon, Firhouse, Killininny, Old Bawn, Old Court, Bohernabreena – were obliged to locate themselves on a daily basis in relation to the factions and stereotypes that emerged not only in the playground but in the classroom. A troublemaker from Templeogue or a bright spark from Tallaght would be regarded as exceptions to the general rule that home-place was destiny, and the destiny of the Tallaght child was Tallaght Technical College or, after 1973, the newly opened Tallaght Community School, and a life of limited opportunities. A Templeogue address, on the other hand, more or less guaranteed a professional career after a 'proper' education in the prestigious Templeogue College or a similar institution, followed by one of the universities.

Because of its location on the 'wrong' side of the Knocklyon border line, Firhouse was generally regarded to be an outlier of Tallaght. This was understandable in so far as Mount Carmel Park, for example, was signally lacking in professionals: not a civil servant or banker in sight, but plenty of unskilled labourers and 'Corpo' (Dublin Corporation) men such as my father. Despite its relative proximity to Dublin, Firhouse in the nineteenth century was both officially and popularly regarded as beyond city limits, somewhat backward in the manner of rural or semi-rural communities. On 24 June 1880, for example, the *Irish Times* reported a faction fight at Firhouse in which 'five hundred combatants fell upon each other and fought desperate bouts'. The correspondent's major concern – that 'such things can still happen within a mile or two of the metropolis' (Firhouse A) – suggests a clear geographical demarcation between urbane metropolitan culture and a benighted hinterland which kicked in just over the city limits.

Well into the next century, Firhouse by and large maintained the traditions which fed the image of a pastoral community, an image no doubt enhanced by the backdrop of the Dublin mountains and the presence of the Dodder.[21] Although newly constructed in 1947, the houses of Mount Carmel Park were mostly occupied by local families, people who were aware of each other and the ways of the area. The neighbourhood surrounding the little estate quickly developed into a knowable community possessing well-established economic and cultural practices which were locked into the yearly cycle. An example would be the annual trip to St Columcille's Well, a long mile along the Bally-cullen Road. The saint's reputed association with a little spring at the foot of Mount Pelier was rediscovered in the early twentieth century, at which time monks from the nearby Augustinian Novitiate of Orlagh College instituted the practice of gathering there for devotions on the Sunday nearest the feast day of 9 June.[22] From 1970 the event developed into something like a village fête, combining prayer with other activities, such as entertainment and stalls. The short walk out and back from Firhouse provided an opportunity for play and gossip, while the event itself came to represent – despite its relative modernity – a ritual affirmation of community identity. St Columcille's Well thus became both the site of complex social processes and associations, a significant part of the community's cognitive map.

If Firhouse found it difficult to let go of rural roots and past times, however, from the mid-twentieth century Tallaght started to develop as a centre of suburban, working-class culture. Its rapid conversion from sleepy village into scandalously unplanned, unprovisioned suburban wasteland came as just as much of a shock to immediately neighbouring areas such as Firhouse as it did to the slightly more distant middle-class communities of Templeogue and Rathfarnham. It seemed that the building would never stop, and as Tallaght began to spread in all direc-tions, once discrete townlands and villages were swallowed up: Saggart, Greenhills, Belgard, Tymon, Old Bawn, Balrothery, Firhouse. No civic or cultural infrastructure was developed to support the occupants of the estates that continued to be thrown up year after year, however. Social malaise ensued, incorporating the inevitable elements of chronic unemployment, psychological distress and community demoralisation. Drugs and drug-related crime would come in the 1980s, but even then alcohol abuse and violence remained popular leisure pursuits for the burgeoning youth population of Tallaght. Rumours of disruption by gangs of Tallaght skinheads or boot boys threatened more than one St Columcille's fête during the early 1970s.

One problem facing Firhouse children at the local National School, then, was that they were not tough enough for Tallaght, nor yet well off or cultured enough for Templeogue. While this had tactical advantages in the playground or on the football field, the general identification of Firhouse with Tallaght could have unfortunate consequences in the classroom, especially in the hands of an insensitive teacher, or outside the school when individuals struggled to modify their behaviour so as to identify with one or other of the stereotypes. A 'bad' Firhouse youth would have to be pretty bad to cut it in Tallaght, and some of them were very bad indeed. On the other hand, the 'good' Firhouse child, although born to labour, had to reject – at least to some degree – the values of youth before he could embrace the middle-class values from down the road. The stress created by such spatial affiliations is what makes humans who and what they are, colouring their lives at every possible level from the most public enunciation to the most private desire. Space determines identity, in other words, where 'determines' signifies not a loss of agency but rather, to reprise Aijaz Ahmad, 'the givenness of the circumstances within which individuals *make* their choices, their lives, their histories'.

A version of this same dilemma emerged in a somewhat different con-text during the late 1970s and 1980s, specifically in relation to what remains the favoured leisure locale of the majority of Irish people: the pub. Both the brewing reputedly introduced by Parthalón's people and the hostelry of Dá Derga provide dubious antecedents for public houses in the Firhouse/Tallaght area. It is more usual to trace such institutions to the medieval period when the brewing and selling of ale developed into a recognisable economic activity, generating as it did so an array of related cultural and social practices. A series of Licensing Acts beginning in 1635 attempted to regulate both the brewing industry and its attendant social activities. The wisdom of having one or more houses in which people could gather for the consumption of intoxicating liquor in every village in a fragile political state must have been questioned by more than one imperial legislator. Nevertheless, the public house became the centre of Irish life during the eighteenth and nineteenth centuries, becoming (as John Urry writes of the English counterpart) 'a major centre for public life in the community, providing light, heat, cooking facilities, furniture, news, banking and travel facilities, entertainment, and sociability' (1990: 5). Although its functions may have changed, the pub's role as a centre of Irish life has been maintained into the twenty-first century, sustained by a peculiar social culture and an expanding tourist industry, and sustaining in turn an image of the Irish as a nation of heavy drinkers.

'The Speaker Conolly' was opened at the end of the 1980s specifically to cater for the new estates on the Firhouse Road, south-west of Mount Carmel Park. It is typical of a new generation of pubs that sprang up on the outskirts of cities and towns all over Ireland during the last decades of the twentieth century. It has a huge bar area, 'authentic' decor of doubtful vintage, and close connections with the local soccer team.[23] Before 'The Speaker' was built, however, Firhouse had two pubs: the Firhouse Inn and the Knocklyon Inn. Known locally as Morton's and Delany's after the families who owned them, these establishments were less than half a kilometre apart along the Firhouse Road on either side of Mount Carmel Park. In 1842, after the main road was moved 100 metres or so north from an earlier inn at Delaford House, the latter was bought by the Delany family and run as a public house and general grocery store. One of the pub's many old photographs, subsequently turned into a postcard and beer-mat logo, shows a group of locals sitting outside around 1900 enjoying a drink; in the centre, relaxing on a barstool beside the aproned proprietor, is the local postman, my paternal grandfather. Hounded out of Co. Carlow with his Catholic wife, this well-to-do Protestant had come down in the world but nevertheless managed to secure a job with the Post Office. They moved to a cottage named 'Everton', a few hundred metres along the Firhouse Road towards Templeogue, where in 1917, as my other grandfather was being wounded on the Western front, my father was born.

Well into the twentieth century, the South Dublin Harriers would assemble outside the pub before heading off to terrorise the countryside all around the Hell Fire Club. The road fork opposite was also a favourite meeting place for the local Blue Shirts and Republicans during the 1930s. The Dublin city limit crossed Firhouse Road just on the Templeogue side of the Knocklyon Inn, and this made it useful for those city drinkers looking to avail themselves of the country's rather bizarre *bona fide* laws, which stated that alcohol would be served after 10.00 pm on weekdays only to genuine travellers not living within a 5-mile radius of the pub. Before the law was revoked in 1960, some of these 'travellers' included the Behan family, Patrick Kavanagh, Flann O'Brien, John Ryan, Austen Clarke, Christy Brown, Augustine Martin and Jack Doyle (Delany II and Delany III, n.d.). According to the recently retired Michael Delany II, other famous guests over the years have included Pandit Nehru, Christine Keeler and François Mitterrand.

For a short period during the late 1970s and early 1980s Delany's became the pub of choice for the local teenage population. Thursday, Friday and Saturday nights were given over to serious drinking. Sunday morning and particularly heavy Sunday evening sessions were a popular way of seeing off the weekend. Especially during summer, a genuine party atmosphere reigned within the building for much of the time. Like most contemporary Irish pubs, Delany's tended to be unofficially zoned in terms of different age groups and activities. The two small, dark bars at the front were the preferred areas of older men who wished to talk, drink and smoke without distraction. Musicians and singers would gather in the parlour at the back when Delany's began to develop a short-lived reputation as a traditional music venue. Twenty- and thirty-something couples favoured the main part of the lounge, while the local teenage and under-age clientele gathered in an architecturally demarcated area known as the 'snug' at the back of the lounge. Joints were in continuous circulation. Drink could be ordered from cruising lounge boys or by struggling up to the tiny bar. The ritual lining up three or four drinks as last orders are being called may still be observed in Irish pubs. An official closing time of 11.30 pm never saw anyone who wished to continue drinking leave the premises until well after midnight, and there was always a party.

Individuals could move between these zones over the course of an evening, buzzing off the friction between their 'home' patch and an artificially exotic elsewhere located somewhere else in the building. At the same time, Delany's was (like thousands of similar pubs around the country before and since) a home away from home for many of its clients, or as Luke Gibbons has described it, 'a space that hovers between the private and the public spheres in Ireland' (1996b: 268).

Therein lay both its charm and its limitations. The pub is a location where one is 'licensed' to behave differently from the way one would 'at home', yet it had many of the physical and cognitive attributes – architecture, acquaintances, protocols – of the house/home. Many of Delany's younger patrons quickly came to realise that the attraction of the local pub was restricted to the pleasures of the knowable community and the ability to move about its spaces with comfort and security. Much art, Irish and otherwise, dramatises the fact that the latter are necessary but ultimately unsatisfactory emotional properties for the average teenager. Meanwhile, a few miles along the road was the big, bad city, not half as big nor as bad as it would become a few years later, but even at the end of the 1970s a more physically and conceptually complex prospect than that offered by the relatively unsophisticated pleasures of the home town.

I do not wish to overstate the case; trips to the city for purposes of leisure (cinema or rock gigs, for example) and shopping were routine practices for youthful generations up to and including the late 1970s.[24] The Saturday morning bus ride (anywhere between 25 and 50 minutes depending on traffic) and subsequent stroll through the city streets was an especially familiar ritual of early teenage years. But the imaginative geography of the community was constructed in terms of specific coordinates in which 'Firhouse' and 'Dublin' signified different, perhaps even mutually exclusive, orders of experience. As with its location relative to Tallaght and Templeogue, Firhouse was a borderland, the geographical articulation of a choice – encountered and negotiated afresh by each generation – between an intimately familiar local place and an undoubtedly more dangerous yet potentially more rewarding city space.

Unique to my generation was the fact that one element of this opposition was in the process of dissolving, as Firhouse rapidly lost its semi-rural identity from the early 1970s. More and more green landscape disappeared beneath the rows of houses, more and more unfamiliar faces vied for space within 'our' places – schools, shops, roads, churches and, of course, pubs. By the middle of the 1980s, Firhouse had metamorphosed subtly yet irreversibly into a suburb, and the spatial relationship with Dublin city had evolved into a recognisable urban/ suburban one, although not without some residual peculiarities. The Dodder and the relative proximity of the mountains continue to complicate the relationship, but there is no doubt that infrastructural changes precipitated changes in the imaginative geography of the present generation. Dublin is no less distant, but its cognitive location – which is to say, its *meaning* as a function of its relationship with Firhouse – has altered as a consequence of changes in transport and the physical environment.

While the spatial history of Firhouse is unique, there is nothing unusual about its status as a place subject to a number of coterminous, cross-referenced geographical systems. At any one time, people are obliged to negotiate these systems, using the spaces and making them 'mean' in terms of different cognitive maps. Maps which were just emerging at the beginning of the 1980s have moved into a position of dominance at the time of writing, while once dominant systems are by now residual, the stuff of reunions or memories that flash across the brain for reasons we do not as yet understand. As for Delany's, like Mount Carmel Park it has at the time of writing been temporarily marooned in a sea of concrete and mud by the construction of the motorway flyover almost directly overhead. The noise of this twenty-first-century transport technology will soon compete with the noise of Firhouse Weir's thirteenth-century water management technology in the area's soundscape, providing an aural history of the desire to mod-ify the landscape for human ends. In the meanwhile, a new generation took over Delany's in 1989, the pub was expanded and its target audience changed. The building itself may now be seen on some flight paths into Dublin Airport as a large, pink landmark on the south Dublin landscape. Naturally, the pint is not as good as it used to be.

Conclusion: homework

Traditional anthropology classifies fieldwork into three levels of assimilation: 1) behavioural – in which the fieldworker engages with the activities of the culture while remaining a dispassionate observer; 2) empathetic – which involves emotional as well as behavioural partici-pation, while retaining an awareness of not being a full member of the culture; and 3) cognitive or 'going native', in which case it ceases to be possible to do cultural anthropology (after Relph 1976: 48). According to this tripartite model, too close an identification with the object of study obviates a properly 'disciplinary' discourse, and any conclusions reached from within this context would be compromised. The under-lying premise of the model, moreover, is that the fieldworker is never a 'native', but may come to identify with the native in certain conditions and to different degrees. But what happens when the fieldworker *is* a native, and when the subject/object dyad that structures disciplinary knowledge is blurred?

In the introduction to their edited collection entitled *Displacement, Diaspora, and Geographies of Identity*, Smadar Lavie and Ted Swedenburg describe a kind of ethnographic method that must be responsive to the conditions under study:

> [Many] essays blur the boundaries that are expected to distinguish authors from their subjects of research, turning authors into subjects or semi-subjects of study. Such insertions of the author as subject are not just pretexts to occupy center stage in narcissistic self-displays or as omniscient self-controllers. . . . In many instances, the interjection of the autobiographical is also concerned with the authors' own engagement and/or belonging or partial belonging to the community under study, which produces a kind of lovingness towards the embattled groups. (1996: 22)

Lavie and Swedenburg produce a self-consciously spatial metaphor to refer to this kind of research: 'homework'. This is distinguished from traditional 'fieldwork' in so far as it refuses the methodological bound-aries (which are themselves, as we have seen, founded on deeper philo-sophical and political discourses) between 'home' and 'away', between the place of 'legitimate' study – Out There – and the privileged locations – In Here – wherein 'legitimate' study may be undertaken.

This chapter has been a kind of 'homework' for me, simultaneously Out There in the field of cultural historical research and In Here in the storehouse of memory, association and experience. The concept of home encoded into 'homework' remains central as Edward Relph says: 'To have roots in a place is to have a secure point from which to look out on the world, a firm grasp of one's own position in the order of things, and a significant spiritual and psychological attachment to somewhere in particular' (1976: 36). The researcher undertakes 'home-work' to discover where and what 'home' is, to secure its coordinates on her/his own cognitive maps, and to plot its position in relation to the changing circumstances which have allowed such privileged work to be undertaken in the first place. These are the contradictory motives which have animated my own brief engagement with Firhouse, Tallaght and the Dodder Valley.

One further contradiction remains, however. Writing, Derrida teaches us, is both the beginning and the end of everything. The landscapes and place-names broached in this chapter have been cognitively mapped but at the same time foreclosed, finished, 'covered' in terms the institutional and personal agenda for which they were ever only 'fieldwork'. In their remembering lie the seeds of their forgetting. The 'same' has become 'other', 'home' has been rendered 'homeless'. It would be paradoxical indeed if a supposedly 'radical' methodology, conceived as a means to reinsert the researcher as a figure within the academic landscape, should contribute to the final 'un-remembering' of the home in whose name it was undertaken.

4
Big Mistakes in Small Places: Exterior and Interior Space in Seamus Deane's *Reading in the Dark*

At its most general level, natural selection favors mechanisms which induce the individual members of a species to frequent those types of environment which best suit their life-styles. Whatever we call such mechanisms, they must be capable of establishing an attractive bond between creature and place. At a more particular level, each individual or mating pair of individuals of most species will also be motivated to select a special place, conveniently accessible to the food supply, which can be adapted, with varying degrees of modification, for the purpose of raising a family. (Appleton 1990: 7)

The critical systems through which a spatial analysis of the modern novel might be attempted are many and various. For convenience, however, they may be organised into three main groups: those that focus on the built environment, those emphasising apparently 'natural' outdoor environments, and those engaging with issues of aesthetic spatiality. This latter, most fully expounded by Joseph Frank in his book *The Widening Gyre* (1963), concerns what he termed 'spatial form in modern literature'.[1] While not denying the potential for an analysis of Seamus Deane's celebrated debut *Reading in the Dark* in terms of 'spatial form', in this chapter I intend to focus upon this text in terms of the first two groups – that is, theories which have addressed themselves to the novelistic representation of built and natural environments.

Before beginning such a reading, it is important to acknowledge the existence of a significant critical literature dedicated to the analysis of different kinds of space. In general terms, *Reading in the Dark* might be considered a 'regional' novel or an 'urban' novel, although in each case such an analysis would confront major difficulties.[2] More specifically, the text engages with an established Irish critical tradition focused on aesthetic representations of a variety of spatial images derived from the island's history of landscape and built environment.[3] Mostly, this critical discourse functions to show how such images come laden with ambiguous political baggage, in so far as each represents a site of contention between various historical endeavours to capture Irish space and make it 'mean' one thing or another. This applies equally to 'natural' and 'cultural' landscapes, which becomes clear if we consider the political investment in places such as the field, the mountain and the bog on the one hand, or the Big House, the cabin and the tenement on the other. As Deane and others have argued, the Irish novel is also frequently held to resist a deeply ingrained 'European' (or often simply 'English') ideology, which holds the cultural traditions of more modern-ised formations in its sway, and which allows only certain limited ways of engaging with space (Deane 1986: 90–118; 1994: 119–20; Leerssen 1996: 192–5, 226).

Reading in the Dark is in implicit dialogue with all these theories and critical traditions. Without anticipating analysis proper, I wish at this early stage to announce what I consider to be the major issue raised by novelistic representations of space, be they interior or exterior, Irish, English or whatever. In his study of Hardy's *The Return of the Native*, J. Hillis Miller argues that:

> [The] landscape in a novel is not just an indifferent background within which the action takes place. The landscape is an essential determinant of that action. No account of a novel would be complete without a careful interpretation of the function of landscape (or cityscape) within it. (1995: 16)

Most modern literary critics would accept this statement, I think. It is sympathetic to a radical geographical emphasis upon 'situated human-ity' (Oelschlaeger 1997: 384), and forms one of the twin points around which this chapter is organised. But Hillis Miller refines the point by arguing that:

> [Novels] do not simply ground themselves on landscapes that are already there, made by prior activities of building, dwelling, and think-ing. The writing of a novel, and the reading of it, participate in those activities. Novels themselves aid in making the landscapes that they

apparently presuppose as already made and finished. ... This making is, however, ambiguous. It is both a making and a discovering. ... There is no way to decide which of these it is. Yet nothing could be more important for thinking and action than to decide. (ibid.: 16–17)

The novel, he argues, both creates new landscapes and reflects existing ones, and it is the readers' role to locate themselves in relation to these spaces.[4] In the text, 'imaginary' space confronts 'real' space (no matter whether indoors or outdoors at this stage), and the anxiety resulting from this confrontation is both symbolic of, and contributive to, the reader's wider fate as language-using subject. Every text is an act *in* space (for example, a 'real' Northern Irish city we know from personal experience and/or representation through other media); at the same time every text *makes* space (the city represented in *Reading in the Dark*). The reading subject's necessary engagement with what remains an irresolvable choice, and the various social and political regimes through which subjects have been encouraged or forced to choose one or the other, constitutes the other major point I wish to explore in this chapter.

Having raised the issue of critical methodology, something also needs to be said regarding the profile of Seamus Deane, one of the most influential and controversial of contemporary Irish critical figures. As a poet, literary historian and Field Day director, Deane has been at the forefront of most of the major issues and debates which have animated Irish cultural criticism since the 1970s. It would not be overstating the case to say that he has been responsible in large part for setting the agenda of the latter discourse as it is currently practised. Some of the more prominent items on that agenda have been: a) the appropriateness of (post-)colonialism as a theoretical paradigm for island history; b) the confrontation between tradition and modernity in modern Ireland; and c) the function of revisionism at the present time.

As a prominent figure within Irish Studies worldwide, Deane is as subject to what Foucault (1988), terms the 'author function' or what Derrida (1977) understands as the crisis of the signature, as any other cultural producer. Which is to say: certain connotations and expectations, elicited from prior enunciations and alternative contexts, attend upon any text published under the authorship of 'Seamus Deane'. *Reading in the Dark* could thus be read as an engagement with the issues associated with that name – that is, as an apology for postcolonialism, as a dramatisation of the confrontation between tradition and modernity, or as a refutation of revisionism. From the author's perspective, this is inevitable; books, like children, must make their way in the world, irrespective of authors'/parents' desires or pronouncements. From the critic's perspective, however, the use of the name as a critical key to the text is a perfectly valid exercise. Indeed, name-based analysis remains a crucial aspect of contemporary critical discourse, even for those who subscribe to the postmodern notion of an absent, functional or frankly 'dead' author.

Within the fairly limited pool that is Irish Studies, the temptation would be to address any text produced by a fish as big as Deane in terms of the (obviously disputed) issues and attitudes – often reducible to a few adjectives or nouns – with which he has associated himself in previous works. Such an undertaking could no doubt generate a useful and interesting analysis. It seems clear, for example, that Deane has developed the hybrid genre of *Reading in the Dark* the more effectively to dramatise the confrontation between official narratives in Northern Ireland and a range of silenced voices capable only of being represented through the medium of imaginative writing. I have decided to take as read the existence of certain disputed meanings attached to the author's name, however, and to bypass the well-documented controversies with which that name is associated. Instead, I wish to focus on various aspects of Irish spatial history as they are engaged in this high-profile text.[5] This is complicated by the fact that Deane has written suggestively about spatial matters in both his poetry and his criticism, as a glance at the index and the bibliography of this book will confirm. But in what follows I have attempted as far as possible to resist addressing *Reading in the Dark* through the prism of the author's public persona, and to differentiate between the real 'Seamus Deane' and the fictional characters he has created – in short, to register the space between the writing 'I' and the 'I' that is written.

Reading in the Dark

The photograph on the first edition cover of *Reading in the Dark* is of the author and his brother celebrating their First Holy Communion in Londonderry just after the Second World War. Deane's debut 'novel' is set in Derry City and its environs between February 1945 and July 1971, and tells a story loosely based on the experiences of Deane's own family. In interview he has admitted that '[most] of it is actually based on events that really did happen' (Davidson 1998). This text was in fact one of a number of high-profile autobiographical or semi-autobiographical Irish texts to appear during the 1990s. *Reading in the Dark* was published in the same year as three particularly successful examples: Frank McCourt's

Angela's Ashes, Nuala O'Faolain's *Are You Somebody?* and Dermot Healy's *The Bend for Home*. Introducing the section on 'Autobiography and Memoirs 1890–1988' in the *Field Day Anthology of Irish Writing*, Deane signalled the significance of life-writing in Irish literary history, observing (in terms reminiscent of Joyce's famous words from *A Portrait of the Artist as a Young Man*) that it is 'one of the obsessive marks of cultures that have been compelled to inquire into the legitimacy of their own existence by the presence of another culture that is forever foreign and forever intimate' (1991, III: 380).

The more recent success of this genre, however, was consequent upon the rapid changes overtaking life in Ireland north and south towards the century's end. Events in different spheres combined to reveal the partiality of the dominant narratives through which people in all parts of the island were invited to make sense of themselves and their experiences. Much emotional and intellectual energy was dedicated to reflecting upon the recent past, and to reviewing the practices and beliefs which had shaped modern Irish life, but which seemed to be on the point of extinction. In particular, the category of memory – official, secret, repressed – came under intense scrutiny. In this sense, (semi-) autobiography represents a desire to relate a range of previously unspoken (or only whispered) stories from the margins, or more accurately the interstices, of official island culture.[6] Deane's profile as an established poet, critic and literary historian meant that he was particularly sensitive to the concerns of a society in flux, and also to the ways in which these concerns could be effectively represented.

Reading in the Dark is constructed of a series of interrelated vignettes possessing incremental and reflexive weight throughout the text. Both the structure and the language could be described as 'poetic', as certain images and words accumulate complex symbolic resonances over the course of the narration. At the same time, the story itself is 'lifelike' in its intricacy and ultimate irresolution. If, on one level, Deane appears to disdain 'official' narratives and to insist on the existence of alternative temporalities, he also remains acutely aware of 'real' time issues such as order and duration. After several readings, I am still not *exactly* sure what happens to whom, in what order, and what the implications of every event and exchange are for the overall 'meaning' of the book. Behind the attractive *sjuzet* (the representation of the story in narrative form), in other words, is a concrete *fabula* (the story as a sequence of events in real time), although whether the latter can ever be grasped by means of the former is one of the text's major themes. In any event, the form of *Reading in the Dark* – a convoluted family saga emerging from a sequence of minor epiphanies – is an important clue as to Deane's intentions. The form offers a textual analogue of the relationship between part and whole, individual and community, past (the narrated 'I') and present (the narrating 'I').

Other generic echoes resonate throughout *Reading in the Dark*. The dates at the beginning of each section render it a sort of diary or journal, adding to the impression of the text as autobiography or memoir. At the same time, it is in one sense a failed *bildungsroman*, representing the progress of an individual who must overcome certain problems and obstacles so as to realise his true self. The failure is caused by the narrator's inability to overcome the problems and obstacles which have arisen in a colonial context. The text also bears traces of detective fiction, in so far as there is a series of deaths and betrayals at the heart of the story which the reader, along with the narrator, wishes to solve. Thus, while there is a developmental trajectory to the story, as we move forward in time towards 1971 when the *book* will end, there is also a retrograde movement as both reader and narrator try to grasp the series of related and ongoing *stories* into which he has been born. *Reading in the Dark* also bears traces of an older discourse of oral story-telling, a narrative genre focused on characters, references and anecdotes from the local community.

So: history, date, memory, event, chronology, causation, effect – all these temporal concepts are at the heart of *Reading in the Dark*. The text is a testament to the survival of alternative rhythms and narratives alongside those officially recognised and accepted as 'real'. One valid interpretation of the text might be that it is by tapping into these alternative rhythms and narratives, and by becoming sensitised to the complex dialectic of past and present, that previously marginalised or silenced meanings are made available (Harte 2000).

If *Reading in the Dark* is a novel about time, however, it is also most certainly a novel about space; as Stephen Regan puts it, the text's 'hybrid realism ... is founded not just on intersecting temporal dimensions but on intersecting spatial dimensions as well' (1997: 38). With specific reference to Irish fiction, John Wilson Foster has argued that 'preoccupation with place is a preoccupation with past without which Irish selfhood is apparently inconceivable. The past is constantly made contemporary through an obsession with remembered place' (1991: 30). What Foster is referring to here is the fundamental dialectic of time and space manifested in Irish fiction, the sense in which neither category is existentially practicable without the other. As Deane engages with the intrusions of the past upon the present, he also engages with the spaces and places wherein those intrusions occur. I suggested above that all novels develop over the course of their narration a complex set of spatial coordinates, an imaginary map within which the action is set. In the case of *Reading in the Dark* these coordinates comprise house, garden, neighbourhood, city, hinterland, hill, horizon and wider world. I want to spend the remainder of this chapter examining a selection of these images in detail.

Derry

Reading in the Dark is obviously 'about' Northern Ireland, dealing with life in the place which bears that name, and more specifically with an earlier phase in the sectarian history which became so familiar towards the latter end of the twentieth century. In this sense it belongs to the established genre of 'Troubles' fiction. Rather unusually, however, the novel is set in Derry rather than Belfast, which has traditionally been the focus for artistic (especially novelistic and cinematic) engagements with the 'Troubles' (Smyth 1997: 113–43). Besides the autobiographical dimension (Deane is from Derry) this is an acknowledgement of the importance of the city as both name and location in Northern Irish history. In a review of *Reading in the Dark*, Eamonn Hughes classified it as a 'Derry book' (1997: 152), pointing out that '[the] divisions between nationalist and unionist, Catholic and Protestant, Irish and British, in the North tend to obscure other, potentially more interesting, though still largely unexpressed divisions such as that between Belfast and Derry' (ibid.: 151).

'Derry' is an anglicisation of *doire* or *daire*, the Gaelic word for an oak wood (*INP*: 445). In pre-Christian times, the place was known as Daire-Calgaich – the oak wood of Calgach. The latter words means 'fierce warrior' and was a common name amongst the ancient Irish. Although 'derry' is incorporated into many place-names in Ireland, at least in this case the oak tree references seems merited. *The Annals of the Four Masters* refers to a 'violent wind-storm' in the year 1178 which 'prostrated one hundred and twenty [oak] trees in Derry-Columbkille' (*AFM* III: 39). The latter name refers to a monastery founded in the area in 546 by Colum Cille, a leading member of the Cenél Conaill branch of the Northern Uí Néill clan (of which more presently). Along with Columban sites at Iona and Kells, the Derry abbey emerged as one of the principal centres of the *familia* of Colum Cille, and played an important part in church-state politics, especially during the twelfth century (Herbert 1988: 109–23).

Some might see these words – Calgaich and Colum Cille: fierceness and saintliness – as premonitory of the place's history. But the most radical and contentious modifier was added during the reign of James I when, under a charter granted to London companies in 1613, the place-name was changed to 'Londonderry'. The walled city itself was under construction at this time, and it is to this relatively modern place incorporating the imperial capital in its name that the local unionist population give allegiance. The identity of this population as a loyal Protestant community was confirmed during the Williamite war when the city held out for 105 days (between 18 April and 31 July 1689) against Jacobite forces. That same identity was consolidated during the Second World War when the local port became an important centre for Allied activities in the North Atlantic. Londonderry, Derry: if *Reading in the Dark* is on one level about the apprehension of different temporalities at the same moment, it is also about the coexistence of two places in the same space and both the provenance and the consequences of such a challenge to geographical normality.

It should come as no surprise that in such a relatively small province there should be rivalry between the two major population and administrative centres. That relationship is the result not of natural geographical proximity, however, but of specific developments in the historical *and* geographical manipulation of the relevant spaces and places. Derry is not 'naturally' the second city of Northern Ireland, for example; it is only so because of certain negotiations and decisions taken by and about a Boundary Commission set up under the terms of the 1921 Anglo-Irish agreement to oversee the drawing up of a border between the new Irish Free State and the province of Northern Ireland. The latter administrative area was itself only set up by the Government of Ireland Act 1920. Because the remit of this Commission was to consider both economic viability *and* the wishes of the affected people, Arthur Griffith and Michael Collins (the chief Irish negotiators) reckoned they had a good opportunity to wrest certain border areas where Catholic-nationalist opinion was strong away from unionist control (Foster 1988: 527; de Paor 1986: 301). In the event, the Commission was abandoned and 'Londonderry' became part of Northern Ireland. 'This was border country', the narrator of *Reading in the Dark* says of the countryside outside the city: 'Less than a mile beyond, a stream, crossed by a hump-back bridge, marked part of the red line that wriggled around the city on the map and hemmed it in to the waters of Lough Foyle' (1997: 49). Together, physical topography and imaginative geography – hump-back bridge, stream and red line – form the limits around which social and individual identities are obliged to organise themselves. But it is not too difficult to appreciate how different the political and ideological landscape of the entire island might look if Derry City had ended up on one side of that red line rather than the other.

After 1920, the city's Catholic population (a majority throughout the twentieth century) came to see Londonderry as the centre of a corrupt administration. Although 'Belfast' has in many ways become a synonym for 'Northern Ireland' (if not indeed for 'Troubles'), it was in Derry on 30 January 1972 that the world was forced to acknowledge the extent and the complexity of the divisions in that part of the island, with the televising of the events that came to be known as 'Bloody Sunday'. It was out of a sense of political grievance and cultural disinheritance that Brian Friel and Stephen Rea launched the Field Day theatre company in the city in 1980 with Friel's play *Translations*. With the recruitment of figures such as Seamus Heaney, Tom Paulin and Deane himself to the board, Field Day broadened not only its functional remit, to include translations of 'relevant' classics, a pamphlet series, the *Field Day Anthology of Irish Writing*, and a series of scholarly titles published in association with Cork University Press. It also broadened its ideological remit, becoming the site of a putative 'fifth province'. This was an attempt to institute a new 'Irish' space, located outwith the island's overburdened geohistory, yet still engaged with those discourses; a space in which to discuss alternative ways to view the past and new ways to imagine the future. The fate of this initiative remains undecided – the geographical metaphors (fifth *province*, *field* day) leaves it particularly susceptible to deconstruction. Nevertheless, since its inception Field Day has been at the centre of Irish cultural debate, and the image of Derry as a divided city which must be reconciled has remained at the heart of the Field Day enterprise. Indeed, one might argue that although geographically marginal, Derry was for a number of years the cultural-critical capital of the island.[7]

At one point in *Reading in the Dark* the narrator walks with 'a group through the Protestant area that lay between the school and our streets' (1997: 157); there are numerous further references to 'our streets' and 'their territory'. Throughout the text, in fact, the entire city is shown to be subject to a precise sectarian geography upon which safety (and later survival) depends:

> There were two open spaces near our house. Behind our row of houses, the back field sloped up towards the Lone Moor Road; it

ended in a roadway that curved down towards Blucher Street and then straightened towards the police barracks, three hundred yards away. The roadway was flanked by a stone wall, with a flat parapet, only five feet high on our side, twelve feet high on the other. On the other side was Meenan's Park, although the older people still called it Watt's Field, after the owner of the distillery. We could climb the wall and drop down on the other side; but the wall ran past the foot of the streets – Limewood, Tyrconnell, Beechwood and Elmwood – pierced by a rectangular opening that led to a flight of railed steps down to the park. (ibid.: 34–5)

This is the beginning of a finely triangulated map of the neighbourhood that develops over the course of the narrative; but even in these few sentences we are provided with a super-sensitive impression of the various 'scapes' in which the story is set. The narrator's house, the police barracks and the distillery all carry intense emotional and political charges, and these charges are in turn realised in the architectural form of the different buildings. In this passage we have reference to official measurement and 'cultural' shape (three hundred yards, five feet, twelve feet, a straight road, a rectangular opening, a flight) as well as unofficial, impressionistic measurement (open spaces, a row of houses, a back field, a curved roadway); official routes (Lone Moor Road) and clandestine routes (the other side); official spaces (the park) and unofficial negotiation of space (climbing); official names (Meenan's Park) and unofficial names (Watt's Field); English place-names (Limewood, etc.) and Gaelic place-names (Tyrconnell).

Engagement with *Reading in the Dark* depends as much upon these spatial discourses as it does upon an historical appreciation of sectarianism in Derry. More importantly perhaps, 'real' places in Derry and the surrounding countryside are transformed into an imaginary landscape which provides the setting but also the meaning of the story. As Hillis Miller writes:

[The] landscape around, behind, or beneath the novel must both pre-exist the novel as what is outside it, prior to it, giving it solidity, and be incorporated within it. . . . If the landscape is not prior to the novel and outside it, then it cannot be an extratextual ground giving the novel referential reality. If it is not part of the novel, in some way inside it as well as outside, then it is irrelevant to it. But if the landscape is inside the novel, then it is determined by it and so cannot constitute its ground. (1995: 21)

Which is to say: *Reading in the Dark* would appear to be based on the author's experience of certain identifiable places in Derry – there really is a 'Lone Moor Road', a 'Craigavon Bridge', and so on; but at the same time, those places exist only as an index of human activity, as manifested in cultural texts such as *Reading in the Dark*. Deane's book in this sense bears out Gregory's insight that '[the] trope of tracking "roots" and "routes" [which] has become an established genre of intellectual inquiry – and of contemporary writing more generally . . . does not so much redraw our maps of the intellectual landscape as call the very principles of mapping into question' (1994: 12). The text offers a 'manipulated' geography, meshing 'landscape and memory within the contested areas of cultural identity and nation-building' (Graham 1997: 183). Derry is simultaneously real and represented, the space that allows writing to take place, and the place that writing brings into existence. A particular feature of this text, however, is that unlike most other 'novels' (and probably because of its semi-autobiographical status), it makes a virtue of necessity, working to show that the text's spatial crisis – reality *and* representation – is the community's crisis: Catholic *and* Protestant, nationalist *and* unionist, Derry *and* Londonderry.

Oak wood, monastic site, siege-city, border-town, cradle of civil rights, womb of Field Day, 'city of bonfires' (Deane 1996: 33), imaginary landscape – Derry is all these and more. *Reading in the Dark* offers a depiction, in the words of the narrator's mother, of a small place in which people make big mistakes: 'Not bigger than the mistakes of other people. But then there is less room for big mistakes in small places' (1997: 211). In many ways this is what the novel is about. The events that lie at the heart of the story take place in 1922 when the 'meaning' of the city in geo-political terms was being contested. But those events are already part of larger historical and geographical narratives of which the human actors are – can only ever be – partially aware. Subsequently, large parts of the action, and of the narrator's understanding of events, are based on the existence of that expeditious map line that came into being during the revolutionary period and the emplacement of Derry as a Northern Irish city rather than a city within the Irish Free State, Éire or the Republic of Ireland.

Aileach

One of the most important places in the text is a circular hillfort a few miles outside Derry City. Like 'Toome' in Heaney's poem, Grianán of Aileach conjures up a host of historical and political associations.[8]

Most of these were explored by John O'Donovan in his field report for the Ordnance Survey in 1837 (compiled about the same that Eugene O'Curry was recording his notes on Glenasmole in Dublin). 'Grianán of Aileach' is a large, multivallate site on Greenan Mountain (*c.* 260 m) in the townland of Carrowreagh, about 10 km from Derry City. Situated at the approach to the Inishowen (*Inis Eógain*: 'Eógan's island') peninsula, the site in the modern-day county of Donegal, traditionally part of Ulster but sequestered (along with Cavan and Monaghan) from the six-county political unit set up by the 1920 Government of Ireland Act. 'Greenan' is a common name throughout the island, and there are several instances in the north-west in particular (Flanagan and Flanagan 1994: 96–7).

This particular site, however, is widely held to be the ancient seat of the Cenél nEógain, a branch of the northern Uí Néill claiming descent from Eógan, eldest son of the tribe's progenitor, Niall Noígiallach, or Niall of the Nine Hostages (de Paor 1986: 63–4). Grianán of Aileach was a sub-kingdom of the one established at Tara by the descendants of Conn Céad Catharc (Conn of the Hundred Battles) in the second century (Nolan 1982: 3). The two political centres were linked by the *Slige Midluachra*, one of five principal roads radiating out from Tara. Along with their fellow Northern Uí Néill kinsmen the Cenél Conaill (from *Tír Chonaill*, 'Conaill's country', named for another of Niall's son's), the Cenél nEógain were overlords of an area covering the modern counties of Donegal, Derry and Tyrone (*Tír Eóghain* – 'Eógan's country') between the fifth and the twelfth centuries.[9] Along with their kinsmen in the south, the Uí Néill may be justly considered '[the] chief family of Ireland for over a thousand years' (Dudley Edwards 1973: 81), descendants of whom remained dominant in central Ulster until the surrender of Hugh O'Neill in 1603.

Grianán of Aileach has been described as 'Ulster's best known antiquity' (AA 1963: 181). The original stone complex was quite extensive, and possessed of a number of defensive outer ramparts as well as a central circular cashel (O'Donovan 1837: 217). The building was about 5.5 m high and 25 m in diameter, although from the number of fallen stones found during his survey, O'Donovan concluded that it must 'have been at least twice, and was possibly four times, its present attitude' (ibid.: 217). From early in the fifth century Aileach was the 'capital' of the Kings of Aileach, such as Murchadh mac Máele Dúin who defeated a Viking force at Derry-Chalgaigh in 832; and Niall Glúndub mac Áedo, a Cenél nEógain leader who also held the title *rí Érenn* (king of Ireland) between 916 and 919, and was claimed as the progenitor of the medieval and early modern O'Neill family. In fact, 16 of the 50 High-Kings between Niall Noígiallach and Brian Bóruma mac Cennétig (Brian Boru, d. 1014) were also Kings of Aileach.

The hillfort was destroyed in 1101 by Muirchertach O'Brien, King of Munster, in a campaign to establish his claim to the high-kingship of Ireland and in retaliation for the destruction of Ceann-coradt (Kincora) during an earlier invasion of his Munster kingdom by a combined force of O'Connors from Connaught and Cenél nEógain (*AFM*, II: 967–9). Although defeating Muirchertach the following year, the Uí Néill – dominated between 1083 and 1170 by the Lochlainn or O'Loughlin sept, principally associated with the Inishowen peninsula (Herbert 1988: 110) – relocated to Tullaghoge near Lough Neagh in Co. Tyrone, with which place the dynasty henceforth became associated (*INP*: 195). Despite this, Cenél nEógain leaders such as Muirchertach Mac Lochlainn continued to use the title 'King of Aileach' as part of their claim for the high-kingship.[10]

The peak of Aileach's power and influence was during the sixth and seventh centuries, and the cashel itself probably dates from this period (Evans 1966: 88). But the site certainly pre-dates the coming of the Cenél nEógain. Aileach is mentioned in the *Book of Genealogies* of Dubhaltach Mac Firbisigh, compiled between 1650 and 1666 from a number of lost sources, as having being built by Ringín and Gabhlan, the son of Ua Gairbh; as Eugene O'Curry pointed out, such claims were part of a strategy 'to show the fidelity of the historians and the error of those who make such assertions as . . . that there were no stone buildings in Erinn until the coming of the Danes and Anglo-Normans into it' (*MM*: 222). O'Donovan notes that Ringín (Rigriu or Frigriu) is celebrated in numerous early sources as a Fomorian master-builder, and this he adduces as evidence for the site's pre-Milesian origins (1837: 229). He also points out that Aileach may have been rendered as 'Regia' in Ptolemy's second-century map (ibid.: 232) (although this is disputed in the Ptolemaic maps reproduced in de Paor [1986: 35] and Moody, Martin and Byrne [1984: 16] amongst others). Indeed, although the central cashel was rather aggressively renovated between 1874 and 1878 by one Dr Bernard, there is archaeological evidence to suggest that it is in fact a multi-period site, and that the Cenél nEógain stone fortress was built upon an earlier pre-Christian hillfort (Mitchell and Ryan 1997: 239; Waddell 1998: 356).

These pre-Christian and pre-Celtic connections are supported by the 'historical' references included in the three *dinnshenchas* poems associated with the place-name. Written over the course of the eleventh and twelfth centuries, these stories relate a journey from Tara (in modern-day Co. Meath) to Aileach by a legendary figure named Corrgend of Cruach. Corrgend killed Aed son of the Dagda, a magical king of the Tuatha de Danann and a figure who recurs throughout the mythological cycle (*MD*, IV: 93–121). The murderer is doomed to carry the dead man's body on his back along the Slige Midluachra (an ancient road running north from Tara) until he can find a worthy grave stone for the corpse. 'From the stone shall be the place's name', says the Dagda (ibid.: 113) – hence Aileach from *ail*, a stone. Having found a suitable stone on the shores of Lough Foyle, Corrgend struggles up the slopes of Greenan where he expires after burying Aed:

> This is what he said as he bore the burden over road after road, 'Ach! ach! the stone! 'tis by it my heart is bursting!' ''Tis right that Ail-ach should cleave to it,' said the Dagda; so that was the name of the height, in the spot where this befell. (ibid.: 103)

The Dagda references form part of O'Donovan's claim that Aileach was in fact a 'Danann' site 'from a period considerably antecedent to the introduction of Christianity'.[11] Speculations as to the pre-Celtic peoples of Ireland abounded throughout the late eighteenth and early nineteenth centuries, with the 1830s being a particularly contentious period (Leerssen 1996: 91ff). But despite his wariness and formidable erudition, O'Donovan may have been too credible when it came to the *dinnshenchas* texts upon which he based many of his claims. Stewart MacAlister pointed out that references to 'Ailech Néit', for example, probably arise from one of the 'pseudo-learned artificial [manipulations]' (1939: 254) that punctuate *Lebor Gabala Érenn* (*The Book of the Taking of Ireland*). In certain redactions, 'Ailech Neit' is cited as a place inherited by Er, eldest son of Parthalón (1939: 273; 1940: 23). MacAlister argued convincingly that the reference to 'Ailech Neit' has strayed in from Section Four on 'Nemed' which follows that on Parthalón in *Lebor Gabala* (1940: 87), and that it offers a good illustration 'of the desperate straits of the would-be harmonizers' (ibid.: 94) who sought to bring 'history' into line with contemporary politics. The principal aim of the Aileach poems may not have been the vindication of Ireland's antiquity, but the provision of an illustrious and highly imaginative pedigree for the Cenél nEógain who were highly active in the state–church politics of the eleventh and twelfth centuries.

This notwithstanding, it is still possible to agree with O'Donovan's estimation of Aileach as 'one of the most remarkable and important

works, of its kind, ever erected by the ancient Irish' (1837: 221). It was
a place and a name at the centre of Irish history for possibly 2000
years. If Derry assumed a profile beyond its geographical status
towards the end of the twentieth century, this was a repeat of a first
millennium and early medieval situation in which nearby Aileach was
at the centre of Irish political affairs. In *Reading in the Dark*, the fort's
liminal status as a place caught between different times and spaces is
encapsulated in the description of its disappearance and reappearance
as the narrator and his brother approach it through a mist. There is no
account of the actual moment of arrival, the narrator merely says: 'At
the top, we looked into the gathering darkness that welled up towards
the Donegal mountains beyond, where the horizon light still survived
among streaked clouds' (1997: 50). Focus is on the bats hunting, the
view and (for the remainder of the section) the feud in his father's
family. The effect is to introduce the fort into the imaginative
geography of the narrative, establishing it as a recognisable place,
without at this stage giving any hint of its role in the story that will
unfold.

In etymological terms, *Grianán* is derived from *grian*, the sun, and
has a number of possible meanings, many of which O'Donovan traces
and rejects (1837: 221–3). A modern authority suggests that '"[import-
ant] place" would seem a most fitting title for this imposing structure'
(Flanagan and Flanagan 1994: 96). Joyce translates *grianán* as 'a sunny
spot, for it is derived from *grian*, the sun; and the Irish-Latin writers
often translate it *solarium*, and *terra solaris*'; in 'the best Irish writers',
however, it is used to signify 'a royal palace' or 'a palace on a hill' (*INP*:
269).[12] As noted above, however, Aileach means 'a stone house or
stone fort, being derived from *ail*, a stone' (*INP*: 270).[13] So, 'Grianán of
Aileach' could be translated as 'stone palace on the hill' or 'sun palace
of stone'. The narrator of *Reading in the Dark* translates it as 'the Fort of
Light, the Sun Fort', although his information that 'it had been there
for a thousand years' (1997: 50) is a significant underestimation.

In each case, two different elements are conjoined in the one name:
sky (sun, light) and earth (stone, fort). This accords with the narrator's
experience, for if on the one hand the fort's elevated position affords
open views across Lough Swilly and the surrounding landscape, on the
other it becomes for him the site of an alternative power, which is
confined, subterranean and earth-based. Stone galleries run about half
the circumference of the fort's inside wall. These are about 75 cm at the
bottom, about 60 cm at the top, and are about 1.5 m high (O'Donovan
1837: 218). Although not underground as such, the Grianan galleries

offer an impression of enclosed space which is in stark contrast to the openness outside:

> At the base of one inside wall, there was a secret passage, tight and black as you crawled in and then briefly higher at the end where there was a wishing-chair of slabbed stone.... Once, my friends – Moran, Harkin, Toland – locked me in the secret passage.... If I were out and on the circular parapet again, I would see Inch island and the wide flat estuaries of the dark-soiled coast and hear the distant war noise of the sea grumbling beyond. But here, inside the thick-walled secret passage which ended in this chair-shaped niche, there was nothing but the groan of the light breeze in that bronchial space, and the sound of the water slitting into rivulets on the sharp rock face.... Later, when we climbed to the parapet again and scrambled down the wall to the road that took us home, the sky and the hills around seemed so wide and high that the dark passageway felt even worse in retrospect, more chilled and enclosed. (1997: 56–8)

If the narrator is intent on 'unearthing' the family secrets, this is where he must start. Locked within the secret passage, the narrator experiences the enclosed space not as the abode of a mysterious yet on the whole benign earth goddess as in Heaney's 'Toome', but as a 'bronchial space', minatory and claustrophobic.[14] It carries resonances of the 'tomb' and, in its description of a higher space at the end of a dark corridor, of famous neolithic 'passage graves' such as the ones at Newgrange and Knowth. This dark, secret space might also be instructively compared with the cellar about which Gaston Bachelard wrote so suggestively in *The Poetics of Space*. Although tending to avoid what he referred to as 'hostile space' (1994: xxxvi), in relation to the other floors of a house Bachelard describes the cellar as a place of 'buried madness, walled-in tragedy ... the cellar dreamer knows that the walls of the cellar are buried walls, that they are walls with a single casing, walls that have the entire earth behind them' (ibid.: 20). The cellar is a locus of fear for two possible reasons: a human fear of 'the sinister projects of diabolical men' (ibid.: 22), or 'an anthropo-cosmic fear that echoes the great legend of man cast back into primitive situations' (ibid.: 23). In *Reading in the Dark*, the latter is encapsulated in the image of the 'the sound of the water slitting into rivulets on the sharp rock face'. Here, Deane brings his poetic skills to bear to render an archetypally soft, fluid and healing substance – water – in terms of a hard, abrasive confrontation between elements. This image speaks to the fear of human impotence in the face of a relentlessly and impersonally hostile earth. It is this fear which, in the story related by one of the narrator's friends, deranges the customs officer enclosed in Grianan's secret passage (1997: 58).

Although neither exactly souterrain, grave nor cellar, the secret passage has also been a locus of death and 'the sinister projects of diabolical men', for it was here that the narrator's Uncle Eddie was shot by Larry McLaughlin. The boy senses the danger in the place as he listens to 'the groan of the light breeze' and remembers the 'chilled and enclosed' place, but the full extent of the 'madness' and 'tragedy' associated with the passage beneath the walls of Grianan only emerges as the narrative unfolds. Although a place of death, the passage is not silent like the tomb; it may be a 'dead' space yet it retains a power to affect the living.[15] As he smells the heather and gorse wafting in from outside and listens to the wind and the underground streams, the young boy imagines that these are the signs of the dead – Druid spells, breathing warriors, sighing women – coming back to intervene in the 'real' world outside. In this way, the secret passage is revealed as an essentially gothic space, symbolic of the betrayal and guilt that have infected the narrator's family like a virus.[16] The texts works to suggest that the family tragedy, however, was created by the exigencies of a political struggle, which itself was a response to what Deane has called 'the corrupt Unionist system' (Davidson 1998). In this sense, and despite the 'tragedy' associated with the place, Grianan has an uncanny attraction for the narrator; for the same forces that turned the once central hillfort into a marginal political space will also eventually alienate him from his family.

Borders and bridges

As noted above, by the twelfth century the Cenél nEógain had become dominated by the Mac Lochlainns, a branch of the Uí Néill (or increasingly after 1022, O'Neill) deeply embroiled in medieval Irish politics. Brian de Breffney writes that '[the] families descended from that sept will be found mostly still in Co. Donegal and Co. Derry' (1982: 149). Uncoincidentally, MacLoughlin is the name of a family whose fate is entwined with that of the narrator's in *Reading in the Dark*. In the story told by his Aunt Katie, Brigid McLaughlin goes insane after the children in her care are stolen away by supernatural forces in a remote part of Donegal just after the Famine. This story introduces many of the themes that will resonate throughout the text – madness, the impact of other worlds upon 'reality', the ambivalent space of the house. If

Donegal represents an imaginary homeland – that is, 'real', Catholic Ireland – it is also the location of insanity and betrayal, such as the events leading to the family feud. But the ghost story has another function is so far as Brigid is a relative of Neil McLaughlin, the IRA man murdered by Billy Mahon in 1922, who is in turn murdered by the narrator's grandfather. Larry McLaughlin is the name of the man who executed the narrator's Uncle Eddie, and subsequently also goes mad.

It is the character named Crazy Joe who first hints at the role played by Larry McLaughlin in the story:

> 'Now, when he [Larry] was a young man, within a week of getting married, off he goes one day up Bligh's Lane towards Holywell Hill or Sheriff's Mountain. Is it not strange that the same bump of heather has two names? Have you been there?'
> 'Yes, often.'
> The hill beyond that was the hill where Grianan stood. (ibid.: 85)

Joe is licensed to soothsay because he is 'crazy' and thus capable of making the hazardous journey between different 'states' – that is, between life in contemporary Derry and its others: the past (as opposed to the present) and fantasy (as opposed to reality). The theme of migration between different 'states' is supported by the fact that 'the same bump of heather has two names', thus attesting to the survival of (at least) two different and competing mapping/naming regimes into the present. It is further borne out when, a little later in Joe's story, he tells how Larry crossed a bridge over a stream on his way back to the city at dusk, an act which is 'bad luck' (ibid.: 86) according to local folklore. The same stream, moreover, marks the border between Donegal and Derry, between the Republic of Ireland (as it would have been by August 1951 when this scene is set) and Northern Ireland.

The stream is thus the 'natural' analogue of a 'cultural' ideology, a topographical manifestation of the imaginary borderline between different political dispensations. In Heidegger's terms, the stream is a 'rift' dividing one place from another: '[the rift]', as Hillis Miller describes it, 'sets one bank against the other in antagonistic opposition' (1995: 13), offering apparently physical evidence of the human concept of division.[17] At the same time, the rift marks 'the intimacy with which opponents belong to each other. . . . This rift does not let opponents break apart; it brings the opposition of measure and boundary into their common outline' (Heidegger 1971: 63). In other words, the rift – in this case, both a 'natural' stream and a 'cultural' border – both divides and unites those lined up on either bank. It is a mark *in* the ground which creates division, and a mark *on* the ground which results from division; in each case, however, the divided are united in a 'common outline'.

The deep impact of topography on the human psyche no doubt accounts in some measure for the social prescriptions (such as the one cited by Joe) that attach to prominent geographical rifts such as the stream. There is also the consideration that Ireland's territorial development tended to 'coincide with either physical or man made features. Running water and hill crests were widely used as were roads' (Nolan 1982: 20). As Hillis Miller goes on to argue, however, the novel formalises the paradox whereby landscape is both prior to, *and* an effect of, the text; as such, it is an entirely suitable medium for the realisation of the paradox whereby the rift is both prior to, *and* an effect of, the political ideologies for which it is recruited. In this sense, the rift marks not a natural frontier between various different (political and mental) states, but a perpetual moment of crisis in which the subject is forced to confront his fractured status as that (first, causer) which calls the landscape into existence and that (second, caused) which comes upon an already existent, already meaningful landscape.

Although Joe names 'Holywell Hill or Sheriff's Mountain' as the relevant places in this context, these English place-names are immediately located by the narrator in relation to Grianan, a topographical feature with which he (and by this stage the reader) is more familiar. The effect is not only to dramatise the conflict between different mapping/naming systems, but to associate Larry (the subject of the story) with the dwelling of his patronymic ancestors. Larry is also associated (like Crazy Joe himself) with 'migration' from one series of states to another – Republic to Province, past to present, speech to silence. But it is neither a happy association nor a felicitous journey. And just as the journey from the Donegal to Derry proves perilous for Larry's identity, so the interpretive journey which moves from topographical feature to politico-cultural value is revealed as one fraught with danger. The story in which Larry is seduced by a fairy on a road outside the city and struck dumb for the remainder of his life is an allegory of the 'real' story in which, seduced by the myths of his ancestors, he consummates his attraction to an imaginary past by the execution of the narrator's Uncle Eddie. But the Druids, Fianna warriors and women sensed by the narrator in his adventure beneath the walls of Grianan combine to rob Larry of both his voice and his ability to function within the spaces of present reality. Unable to resolve the crisis embodied in the landscape, he spends his waking hours standing on a street corner on the edge of the city, looking up the road that leads out towards Grianan some 9.5 km distant, where his fate was sealed. This liminal location (on a corner, on the *edge*) between city and country symbolises his liminal existence between different temporal and spatial regimes.

If the stream itself represents the frontier between various different mental and political states, then the bridge Larry uses to cross the stream on that fateful night becomes a significant building. For Michel de Certeau:

> Stories are actuated by a contradiction between the frontier and the bridge, that is, between a (legitimate) space and its (alien) exteriority. . . . The bridge is ambiguous everywhere: it alternately welds together and opposes insularities. As a trangression of the limit, a disobedience of the law of place, it represents a departure, an attack on a state, the ambition of a conquering power, or the flight of an exile; in any case, the 'betrayal' of an order. (1988: 126–8)

In this reading, the bridge is a necessary yet dangerous space, simultaneously holding together and keeping apart the opposites on either side of the rift. If all stories are love stories, then de Certeau suggests that they are all also travel stories, structured at every level by the meanings consequent upon the border and the bridge. The latter speaks the inadequacy of legitimate place, marking as it does the route desire takes away from home towards an alien 'state'. At the same time, recrossing the bridge back towards home dramatises the inherence of the alien within the legitimate, and of the Other within the Self.

No less poetically than de Certeau, Heidegger saw the bridge as an ambivalent place, a 'building' capable of serving humankind's proper dwelling on earth but just as likely to function as an agent of homelessness and alienation. This is because landscape functions undecidably as that which pre-exists humankind and that which is made by humankind in its pursuit of proper dwelling. The bridge simultaneously *admits* (in the sense 'reflects') and *installs* (in the sense 'institutes') a spatial awareness. But in this double action – reflection/institution – lies the possibility of unhomeliness (and this is also where Derrida's interest in Heidegger arises). The bridge will always be an ambivalent space, capable of reflecting unalienated dwelling while at the same time announcing the possibility of creating dwelling *ex nihilo*. Every gathering is thus also a dispersal; with reference to the bridge in particular, every conjoining is also a potential sundering. Yet it remains the human fate to search out a home in the universe which will bring earth and sky, divinities and mortals into a relationship for which the proper word is 'dwelling'.

Whether one favours de Certeau or Heidegger, however, it seems clear that popular culture makes use of the bridge as an architectural metaphor for healing and rapprochement between opposed phenomena on the one hand, and estrangement and enmity on the other. *Across the Bridge of Hope* was the optimistic title of one post-Omagh cultural initiative (Various Artists 1998). And there is no doubting where the emphasis lies in the geography of *Reading in the Dark*. Bridges in the text are associated with danger and death: 'When [Father's] parents became ill, they were taken away immediately to the Fever Hospital in the Waterside, across the Foyle, on the other side of the Craigavon Bridge, and he never saw them again, not even at the wake, for the coffins were closed' (1997: 46). Larry crossed the bridge in the first place not in pursuit of alterity or in the service of dwelling, but in the name of an identity denied him at 'home'. Recrossing the bridge after his foray across the border brings Larry not to an acceptance of alterity or an acknowledgement of dwelling, but to an accentuation of the bridge's divisive function. His silence is a fitting symbol for a community that cannot speak to the Other within itself.[18]

Another character who might want to dispute any positive archetypal interpretation of the bridge is Billy Mahon, the policeman thrown off Craigavon Bridge by the narrator's grandfather in retaliation for the death of Neil McLaughlin. As Brother Regan relates the story:

> 'They lifted him to the parapet and held him there for a minute like a log and let him stare down at the water – seventy, eighty feet below. Then they pushed him over and he fell, with the street lights shining on his wet coat until he disappeared into the shadows with a splash. They heard him thrashing, and he shouted once. Then he went under. His body was washed up three days later. No one saw his assailants.' (1997: 23)

There are more efficient ways to liquidate political enemies (although this particular murder smacks of authenticity – improvised, speculative, no danger from an unanticipated search before the deed and no weapon to be traced afterwards). More significantly, Mahon's fate is an important symbol within the text's geographical imagination. It seems that all communities develop detailed maps of 'home' and 'away', and it is with reference to these maps that both imagined (such as the border) and real (such as the bridge and the stream) places are negotiated. But the discursive figures (healing and enmity, for example) through which these spaces and places are invoked are themselves ambivalent and contested, nowhere more so than in a community divided along sectarian lines. The city is 'home' for both Larry McLaughlin and Billy Mahon, but in different ways, as their respective experiences with bridges attest. For the latter, the bridge is the space where a repressed Other violently surfaces to exert its own topographical consciousness. For the former, crossing the bridge is a physical enactment of the movement from crisis to breakdown. In this respect, Larry (along with Mother) is the most representative figure of Derry's Catholic community, 'utterly immobile' (ibid.: 170), shocked into silence by the exigencies of nationalist geography.

House

If *Reading in the Dark* engages with some of the larger spaces wherein Irish identities are contested, it also focuses upon the phenomenon of intimate human space, namely, the house. Besides Bachelard, whose work will be considered presently, a number of theories have focused on the relationship between fiction and the built (particularly the domestic) environment. In *Living Space in Fact and Fiction*, Philippa Tristram traces the emergence of the English novel in terms of its representation of interior or 'living' space. She argues that 'the novel is invincibly domestic', and that '[from] the beginning the house and the novel are interconnected' (1989: 2). Because it evolved during a period when, and in a geographical location where, the concept of domestic dwelling was undergoing rapid change – that is, eighteenth-century England – it is little wonder, she suggests, that the fates of the novel and the house should be intertwined. The connection between fiction and domestic architecture may be observed in the very language criticism has developed to engage with the novel: 'structure', 'aspect', 'outlook', 'perspective', 'character'. The house may be either the specific subject of the text (Tristram points out the long tradition of English novels named after houses or buildings), or a significant factor, almost an additional character, in the setting of the narrative. In any event, critical analysis which ignores the impact of the domestic environment upon novelistic discourse is necessarily incomplete.[19]

In *Desire and Domestic Fiction*, Nancy Armstrong adapts Foucauldian discourse theory to trace the interrelationship between the rise of the English novel and the emergence of an English middle class. Central to both, she argues, was the development of a gender discourse which functioned to produce male and female as both producers of certain kinds of knowledge and natural inhabitants of certain kinds of space. 'My point,' she writes, 'is that language, which once represented the history of the individual as well as the history of the state in terms of kinship relations, was dismantled to form the masculine and feminine spheres that characterize modern culture' (1987: 14). Thus, the tradition of English domestic fiction that emerged from the example of Samuel Richardson sees both family and house becoming the material bearers of bourgeois values – in short, 'a private domain of the individual outside and apart from social history' (ibid.: 10).

Tristram and Armstrong produce powerful accounts of both the emergence and the characteristic forms and themes of English fiction. In many ways these theories are borne out in *Reading in the Dark*, a text in which houses are important both as sites of action and as volatile symbols. The narrator's mother occupies an interior domestic realm, whereas his father moves and works in the public world of men. Women, such as the narrator's maternal and paternal aunts and Brigid McLaughlin, are associated with houses throughout the text, and especially with kitchens in which 'the lids of the saucepans trembled on the range and the bubbling water gargled' (1997: 128). Crazy Joe, on the other hand, can fulfil his role as ambassador between reality and fantasy, symbolised by his peripatetic presence throughout the narrative, because as a man (even one who is crazy) he is licensed to engage in outdoor pursuits. Other men, such as Tony McIlhenny and the narrator himself, are associated with travel and the outdoor world of streets and fields.[20]

Movement beyond these apparently 'natural' environments signifies danger within the text. A 'devil woman' (1997: 185) seduces Larry McLaughlin on the road outside the city. The feud in his father's family is caused by the exclusion of his sisters from the farmhouse where they have been resentfully adopted, and their emplacement in a shed, removed from the house proper, instead. And it is only when Grandfather is incapacitated by age that he becomes a bitter figure within the domestic landscape. The twice-told tale (ibid.: 10, 162–5) in which a couple is haunted to death by a usurped husband living across the street is a parable of the dangers of disrupting the socially accepted domestic order. In the story, the houses themselves appear locked in struggle, and thereafter every house belonging to the guilty parties was haunted: '[some] days you couldn't go up the stairs to the bedrooms, or you couldn't get down the stairs from them. No one saw anything – there was just this force that blocked and stopped all movement, that made the house shudder' (ibid.: 165).

On the other hand, Father plays a significant domestic role. The narrator's assault upon Father's authority takes the form of his destruction of the 'feminine' space of the rose garden – which had been Father's joy – after which it is rendered 'masculine' by being concreted over. (It is significant that Mother's madness is manifested when she steps out into the backyard, leaving the shelter of the house for this new 'unnatural' space.) The female workforce at Derry's famous shirt factories points to the possibilities of a woman's role beyond the home. Likewise, 'the woman in the house' can signify an assault upon the family rather than its succour, when the house in question is a brothel and the woman a prostitute (ibid.: 169–71).

This is not just a class issue, as the social milieu described in *Reading the Dark* is some way removed from the middle- and working-class traditions described by Armstrong and Tristram. It is, rather, indicative of the fact that the use of such theories in an Irish context is limited because of the difference in social and political development between Ireland and England. There is a range of domestic spaces represented in Irish fiction since the eighteenth century, but these spaces follow a markedly different ideological trajectory from the ones represented in the coeval English tradition. No systematic study exists of what John Wilson Foster calls 'the rhetoric of place in Irish fiction' (1976: 33), however; in so far as space is an issue at all, most accounts tend to focus on aspects such as landscape and 'home', where the latter signifies less the built than the topographical environment – the neighbourhood, village or farm. While remaining alert to similarities and differences in the English tradition, therefore, an engagement with the representation of domestic space in *Reading in the Dark* must proceed speculatively from hints in previous Irish critical studies and from the text itself.

There remains one theoretical resource we must acknowledge when considering the representation of the house in novelistic discourse, however. *The Poetics of Space* was introduced in Chapter 1 as an increasingly influential study of intimate domestic space by the French phenomenologist Gaston Bachelard.[21] *Reading in the Dark* strikes me as particularly amenable to a reading informed by Bachelard's thought. The novel opens on the stairway of the narrator's house, where a ghostly presence, manifested in the form of 'a clear, plain silence' (1997: 5), is making itself felt:

It was a short staircase, fourteen steps in all, covered in lino from which the original pattern had been polished away to the point where it had the look of a faint memory. Eleven steps took you to the turn of the stairs where the cathedral and the sky always hung in the window frame. Three more steps took you on to the landing, about six feet. (ibid.)

This opening scene illustrates the otherwise commonsensical point made by the geographer Edward Relph that 'the places of childhood constitute vital reference points for many individuals' (1976: 35). The space described is clearly not that of a machine for living in, but a space gravid with human emotions of desire, fear and regret. This remarkable opening, as Stephen Regan suggests, 'establishes a strange and uneasy conjunction between exactness and ineffability, between that which can be physically measured or registered by the senses and that which lies beyond recovery or comprehension' (1997: 36). The landing, the stairway, the corner of the stairs and the kitchen are immediately invested with symbolic resonances that will accrue over the course of the text. The 'clear, plain silence' is on one level an obvious reference to the silences at the heart of the family, silences which are themselves examples of those missing narratives haunting contemporary Northern Ireland. Likewise, the 'faint memory' of the lino's 'original pattern' is a symbol of one of the text's major themes – the persistence of the past into the present. At the same time, however, the domestic space in which this incident takes place is rendered in strikingly precise detail. We are given the number of steps on the stairway, the point at which it turns, the length of the landing. The emotional gulf that will emerge between mother and son is presaged by a physical gulf, capable of being crossed – 'I could have touched her' – but foiled because of the way space has been warped by an unquiet, unresolved past.

After some persuasion, the boy retreats to the 'female' space of the kitchen: 'I went down excited, and sat at the range with its red heart fire and black lead dust. . . . The house was all cobweb tremors. No matter where I walked, it yielded before me and settled behind me' (1997: 6). The boy's emotional state is manifested in terms of his relationship with and movement through the living space of the house. The hearth constitutes the heart of the dwelling, the still centre around which both movement and emotion is organised.[22] In a typical patriarchal society such as Northern Ireland in the 1940s, the male's life is measured in terms of the increasing distance from the hearth he shared in childhood with mother. *Reading in the Dark* maps the narrator's journey away from a secure emotional terrain, which is both mirrored and supported by a familiar domestic terrain. A portent of this is provided by the boy's departure – unremarked in the narrative – from his seat by the hearth so that he may walk through the house. But the domestic space through which he moves is not empty; 'the neutral glimmer on the banister' noted later in the scene gives a false impression, for directly after this description the boy feels the ghost behind him on the stairs. The 'cobweb tremors' provide an image of the disturbance of settled space by incursions (the presence of the ghost) from the past. 'Atmosphere' or 'ambience' are inadequate words to describe the vaporous yet tangible substance which has been formed from the family's established spatial practices, but which now is literally displaced ('yielded . . . and settled') in response to the boy's excited movements.

The ghost is felt by both characters in this scene in the window at the corner of the stairwell. Each of these features (window, corner, stairwell) represents a familiar aspect of domestic architecture which is at the same time highly ambivalent within the space of the house. Even more than the door, the window functions as a classic architectural metaphor for what Bachelard calls 'the dialectics of inside and outside' (1994: 211). Like the door, the window is a threshold between inside and outside. It can be opened or closed; but each condition is predicated on its alternative, for every opening assumes a prior closing, and every closing announces a prior opening. 'If one were to give an account of all the doors one has closed and opened, of all the doors that one would like to re-open,' Bachelard muses, 'one would have to tell the story of one's entire life' (ibid.: 224). In some ways, that is exactly what the narrator of *Reading in the Dark* is doing – telling the story of all the thresholds (doors and windows) that have impacted upon his life, and trying to make sense of the ambivalent values attached to the crossing of such thresholds.

The window is different from the door in so far as one may gaze *on* the outside (in this case, the cathedral and the sky) *from* the inside, and a number of things are apparently confirmed as a result: the relative location of outside and inside, the nature of the relationship between these locations, and the subject's location in terms of the values and meanings associated with this relationship – security, danger, freedom, repression, welcome, aggression, culture, nature, etc. As Bachelard argues, however, 'inside' and 'outside' are essentially geometrical terms, and '[metaphysics] should beware the privileges of evidence that are the property of geometrical intuition' (1994: 214–15). He continues: '[if] there exists a border-line surface between such an inside and outside, this surface is painful on both sides' (ibid.: 218); as a consequence it is necessary to '[demolish] the lazy certainties of the geometrical intuitions by means of which psychologists sought to govern the space of intimacy' (ibid.: 220).

For Bachelard, art and daydreams are the principal means by which geometry is refused and the threshold (such as a window or door) is recognised for what it truly is: not the architectural arbiter between inside and outside, or open and closed, but the physical manifestation of a fundamental 'hesitation of being' (ibid.: 214). The window is particularly revealing in this sense, for in certain circumstances (darkness) it can function as a mirror, reflecting the gazer back to himself. As the story progresses, the narrator of *Reading in the Dark* finds himself increasingly caught between discourses of openness and closure, interiority and exteriority. Just as the supposed security of the community is compromised by the existence of an 'open secret' – rife sectarianism – so the safety of the house is compromised by the return of the repressed – that is, secrets and lies from the recent past. If the window allows the subject to gaze out, it also enables the subject to be gazed upon. *Reading in the Dark* is a testament to Bachelard's assertion that 'man is half-open being' (ibid.: 222); and with its demarcational, reflective and transparent properties, the window offers a suitable space for a ghostly presence caught between past and present, between openness and closure.

Bachelard also maintained that 'every corner in a house, every angle in a room, every inch of secluded space in which we like to hide, or withdraw into ourselves, is a symbol of solitude for the imagination; that is to say, it is the germ of a room, or of a house' (ibid.: 136). But the corner on a stairwell is not the same as a corner in a room. It may retain the impression of privacy and seclusion associated with corners, but it is actually located on the well-trodden route between different floors and different functions. And if the corner of the stairs is an ambivalent space, then so too is the stairwell itself. In *Reading in the Dark* this is partly to do with its location in the house of a family (and a community) only a generation or two removed from predominantly single-storey dwelling (Gailey 1984: 40–1). But the more general thing about stairs is that they are *used* every day but nothing is actually *done* there. It is a familiar yet dynamic space, living yet dead; for Bachelard, its main purpose is to provide a route from 'the rationality of the roof to the irrationality of the cellar' (ibid.: 18). The stairwell serves as a spatial symbol of the fear associated with descent to the irrational and the desire associated with ascent towards the rational. It comes into its own as a radical and dangerous space (as in this scene), however, when community-regulated discourses of fear and desire, ascent and descent, rationality and irrationality, are disrupted. For what the remainder of the text is largely concerned with, as we have seen, is the confrontation between different spatial practices as a physical and mental manifestation of the confrontation between opposed political ideologies and conflicting personal convictions.

For these reasons, then, the window above a stairwell corner functions as a highly resonant place in a story about the discrepancy between official discourses and lived experience. Where else but in the most ambivalent, most erratic space in the house should the established dialectics of past and present, inside and outside, open and closed come under pressure? And as all these examples demonstrate, the house does not provide a passive backdrop for the dramatisation of human emotion, but an active, formative influence upon experience and identity. At the same time, remembering these intimate places and the movement between them is part of the process whereby the narrator, removed in time and space from the house, learns to 'abide' within himself.

Conclusion

The opening scene of *The Shan Van Vocht*, the novel 'read in the dark' by the narrator, depicts a number of people 'talking in whispers about the dangers of the rebellion as they sat around a great open-hearth fire on a wild night of winter rain and squall...Outside was the bad weather; inside was the fire, implied danger, a love relationship. There was something exquisite in this blend' (1997: 19). This imaginative construction of the world, 'reading' in the book's dominant metaphor, proceeds with reference to a complex geography of 'outside' and 'inside' which appears to be deeply embedded in the human psyche. *Reading in the Dark* rehearses this geography at a number of levels, and part of its impact as a narrative lies in its own exquisite blend of the fears and desires associated with these imaginative locations.

In its own distinctive way, *Reading in the Dark* replays a familiar trope from Irish fiction, what Foster calls '[the] strategy of escape from place and past' (1976: 33). Indeed, for all its generic hybridity and originality, Deane has written what is in many ways a very traditional Irish novel. Having become a problem within the local community, the narrator undergoes a form of voluntary exile, a fall into knowledge which is also a fall away from the blessed ignorance of youth. This leaves him seemingly doomed to spend the remainder of his life caught between resentment towards a history that has forced knowledge upon him, and an attempt to avoid idealising the home he knew before the truth made it impossible for him to dwell there. Variations on this pattern may be found throughout the canon of Irish fiction. Although the text functions primarily as a complex rendering of this archetype, however, it would be a mistake to underestimate the existence of a specific sectarian history underpinning and penetrating the narrative at every stage. *Reading in the Dark* may offer an intense analysis of the dangers attending both the deprivation and the pursuit of 'homeliness', but it conducts this analysis from within an historical context which is itself in dispute.

Perhaps the principal achievement of this text, however, is that it challenges received spatial discourses, showing that familiar places may possess alternative meanings or functions, while places apparently absent through ignorance or preterition may in fact be present all along, modifying in many different ways the cognitive maps we use to negotiate 'reality'. The 'clear, plain silence' invoked in the opening line of *Reading in the Dark* is paradoxically there and not there, 'clear' and 'plain', yet silent and obtuse. The family secret (which is also the text's secret) is, like Derrida's crypt, *there* – in the past, in the text, 'motivating everything, but you cannot get there from here' (Hillis Miller 1995: 305). If there is a secret at the heart of the family (or at the heart of the text), why should we expect to be able to access it through 'reading', that is, through the tactical deployment of knowledge, truth, narrative, imaginative cartography or language? Yet we are apparently both naturally and culturally obliged to pursue that secret, to search out the way home, and these are the devices and mechanisms that we invariably use. The best available option, the text seems to say, is to insist upon the existence of secrecy without trying to violate the integrity of *the* secret. As so many commentators and theorists argue, this is what literature is for, after all: to map the invisible route home, to keep the secret.

5

'Show Me the Way to Go Home': Space and Place in the Music of U2

Introduction: mapping the beat

This chapter offers an analysis of Irish rock supergroup U2 in terms of certain spatial practices and motifs that recur throughout their music. Before going on to look in some detail at these issues, I want to consider the theoretical and methodological contexts in which such an analysis might be undertaken.

One fundamental premise must be that music, more than any other artform (including literature and painting), is capable of creating imaginary landscapes. This capability emerges from its basic function as 'sound'. In sensory terms, it is clear, as Yi-Fu Tuan puts it, that 'sound itself can evoke spatial impressions' (1977: 15). Elsewhere he writes that '[a] feeling for distance, which we tend to think of as an exclusive effect of visual-kinesthetic experience, is powerfully enhanced by sound' (1993: 92). Touch, smell and especially vision are capable of conveying spatial relations in terms of distance and size. But sound, John Shepherd argues, 'evokes a sense of space very different from that evoked by other phenomena' (1991: 20). One of the earliest human skills developed during infancy is the ability to orient oneself in relation to the soundscape, be this urban or rural, industrial or agrarian, human or animal, or (as is more usual) some specific combination of these. Sound is dynamic, suggestive of movement and energy by virtue of its fundamental properties – loudness, softness, depth, distance, proximity – and the manner in which these are perceived by the hearing subject. Put simply, the ability to hear is always already a spatial ability.

Moving beyond this elemental capacity, we find that the question of the relationship between music and space may be addressed with reference to a familiar methodology encompassing institutional, textual and consumption issues. Like the sociology and (more recently) the cultural studies from which it sprang, the relatively new discipline of rock music studies is for the most part dispersed across these three areas of inquiry. The internecine squabbles which already attend the nascent discipline tend to concern the precise economy of analytical approach adopted in any given instance. Lack of an institutional dimension is condemned by those coming from a social-scientific background, while those possessing specialist musicological training decry 'lay' ignorance of formal effects in the musical text. Both are suspected by ethnographers and anthro-pologists whose primary concern is with the ways (and the locations) in which music is consumed.

The fact is that music is imbued with spatial connotations at every level, from its institutional determination, through its technological manipulation and formal properties, and on to its performance and consumption contexts. Each of these aspects has a history, moreover, which has impacted on the making of music and which as a consequence continues to feed, however remotely, into every possible listening event in the present. Tuan has pointed out, for example, that the European sense of time and of space was significantly expanded during and after the seventeenth century as a result of specific institutional, techno-logical and conceptual changes in the production of sound (1993: 91). When the quality of 'loudness' became capable of being artificially manipulated, the human significance of that quality was altered, as were related concepts such as 'quietness' and 'silence'. Musical history is part of everybody, in other words, constituting an important aspect of our shared and personal identities.

Spatial issues also impact on both the technological production and the formal structure of music. Music might be defined as the conven-tional organisation of noise. And if Bachelard could imagine the house as an elaborate metaphor for the human adventure, the same is no less true of the musical scale which, with its intervals, progressions and modulations, is capable of creating impressions of home, travel, danger and safety as surely as any topographical or architectural phenomenon. Sheila Whiteley explains that '[the] key note, or first note of the scale, has strong connotations of home-centredness' (1992: 125). The vast majority of western music genres from both the art and the popular traditions are organised around this notion of 'home-centredness', which is to say, the music has a key which constitutes its 'home'. It will modulate away from 'home' along various related pathways, sometimes far away, but without ever losing the sense of where 'home' is and how the music might return there. Music in this form offers the listener a narrative which is securely grounded in the real world. To employ another metaphor perhaps more appropriate here, music is a map that guides the listener on a journey through a sonic landscape. Like all traditional journeys there is a point of departure which functions as an image of home. 'Narrative' tension and colour are added by the manipulation of various sonic properties such as tempo, harmony, counterpoint, phrasing and volume. But after the problems have been addressed and the obstacles overcome, the map leads us home again towards resolution and closure.

It was this general model with its inherent sense of a knowable reality against which western art music rebelled towards the end of the nineteenth century. As in literature and fine art, modernism rejected the notion of the musical text as a map that confirmed the listener's sense of reality by leading them 'home'. Such a notion was merely the reflection of a Eurocentric, bourgeois worldview which excluded the cultural experiences of large sections of the globe, and which was in any case collapsing all around. As the twentieth century progressed, while popular idioms such as rock 'n' roll remained in thrall to the notion of music as a reflection of a stable reality, modernism was taking music on a journey without maps to a place where home, although perhaps still alive in memory, was accessible only through self-conscious irony or authoritarian imposition. Interestingly, the 'progressive rock' which emerged in the late 1960s in the wake of the Beatles' *Sgt. Pepper's Lonely Hearts Club Band* (1967) took its inspiration from neither African-American blues nor European tonal music (widely considered to be the traditional source materials for rock'n'roll) but from modernism and its determination to 'leave home' (Whiteley 1992; Macan 1997). Progressive rock came in turn to constitute the target for a supposedly more 'authentic' punk rock, the popular musical context from which U2 emerged.

The previous paragraph engages with another significant dimension of the formal analysis of music: a supposed difference in the quality and range of spatial effect afforded by the art, popular and folk traditions. Whereas late twentieth-century popular music tends to be considered (even by those who value it) primarily corporeal in effect because of its sheer volume and its derivation in dance-oriented sites, art music – no matter how far removed from high classicism nor how engaged with technological and/or formal innovation – is widely believed to evoke qualitatively different (that is, more rewarding, more sophisticated or simply more interesting) spatial connotations. Thus Tuan again: 'whereas certain kinds of music produce almost tactile sensations (for example, the loud and deep boom of rock), others open up spaces "out there" and invite a more contemplative frame of mind' (1993: 95). With its roots in the cultural pessimism of Theodor Adorno, such an attitude represents an impoverishment of the radical eclecticism of contemporary popular music. At the same time, it promotes a sterile formalism aganist which institutional analysis and ethnography so justly rebelled aganist in the latter decades of the twentieth century.

The unique thing about modern popular music is not that it is primarily body-oriented, but that it developed in a climate of increasing technological sophistication. The manipulation of sound through instrumental innovation and recording technology is an important consideration for any analysis of popular music and space. Mostly, such an analysis would concern itself with the 'texture' of the sound produced. Texture, explains Allan F. Moore,

> refers to the presence of and relationships between identifiable strands of sound in a music. . . . It can best be conceived with reference to a 'virtual textural space', envisaged as an empty cube of finite dimensions, changing with respect to real time (almost like an abstract, three-dimensional television screen). . . . All rock has strands at different vertical locations, where this represents their register. Most rock also attempts a sense of music 'depth' (the illusory sense that some sounds originate at a greater distance than others), giving a sense of textural foreground, middleground and background. Much rock also has a sense of horizontal location, provided by the construction of the stereo image. The most important features of the use of this space are the types and degrees of density filling it (whether thin stands or 'blocks'), and the presence of 'holes' in this space, i.e. potential areas left unused. In this respect, earlier styles can seem almost one-dimensional, while more recent styles can make fuller use of the potential, which, of course, has to be set up by and for each individual style. (1993: 106)

What Moore is referring to here is the sense of space produced by the modern rock song, irrespective (although that is strictly impossible) of factors such as production location or listening context. The difference between an early Beatles song such as 'Love Me Do', with its primitive stereo mix, and the rich stereophonic soundscape of a later track such as 'Penny Lane' is an indication of how rapidly compositional and instrumental techniques were developing in relation to the available technology.[1] As Moore goes on to point out (and as we shall be examining in greater detail shortly), U2 was one of the most interesting rock bands in the 1980s in terms of its regard for texture and the spatial connotations afforded by specific manipulations of sound. This was obviously impressionistic to a large extent, as when the band's singer imagined the recording of a vocal track in terms of '[making] a map' (Flanagan 1995: 332). But U2 were fortunate in that their musical instincts were consistently supported by a series of brilliant producers and technicians, of whom the most celebrated have been Brian Eno and Daniel Lanois. I believe that the concern with texture has been maintained throughout the band's career, and that this consistent interest renders U2 one of the most interesting purveyors of popular music in terms of space.

Space as a significant analytical category clearly emerges from institutional, technological and formal considerations, then. But music is also widely invoked (both popularly and professionally) in relation to the notion of 'identity' made fashionable in end-of-century theoretical debates. And this notion is itself heavily overdetermined by questions of space. 'Amongst the countless ways in which we "relocate" ourselves,' writes Martin Stokes,

> music undoubtedly has a vital role to play. The musical event, from collective dances to the act of putting a cassette or CD into a machine, evokes and organises collective memories and present experiences of place with an intensity, power and simplicity unmatched by any other social activity. The 'places' constructed through music involve notions of difference and social boundary. They also organise hierarchies of a moral and political order. People can . . . use music to locate themselves in quite idiosyncratic and plural ways. (1994: 3)

Despite the 'idiosyncratic and plural ways' in which people use music to locate themselves, however, music tends to be invoked in relation to certain salient socio-political spaces within which its 'meaning' may be determined and delimited with greater or lesser degrees of violence. One such space is that occupied by the 'ethnic' or 'national' subject, and it is in relation to this subject that concepts such as 'Irish traditional music', 'the European tradition' or 'American rock' may be posited as relevant analytical criteria. The supposed 'purity' and 'authenticity' of these traditions can politicise even the most recreational of contexts, as Stokes argues in relation to the use of 'foreign' instruments at traditional Irish music sessions (ibid.: 9–10). As he goes on to point out, however, ethnicity and nationality are not resident 'in' the music, but are 'achieved' or 'constructed' by the subject through musical performance and consumption. Thus, '"Celtic music" is . . . something which has been created by certain ways of classifying musical experience, and is certainly not a residue of authentic "Celtness" waiting to be discovered in the many and various musical styles and genres played in the Celtic world' (ibid.: 6).

To take a more recent and relevant example, we find that much is made at the beginning of a new century of the fact that culture, like capital, is multinational. Popular music is considered particularly mobile in terms of aspects such as production, recording, performance, broadcasting and consumption. Thus, a great variety of institutional and consumption considerations bear upon the music of U2 at any one time: Where is the music being recorded and packaged? Where is it being mixed, remixed and sampled? Where – geographically, institutionally, architecturally – is it being broadcast and listened to? All this before we consider the ideological construction of Ireland as a 'land of music' from Giraldus Cambrensis to *Riverdance*. All this before we consider genre, lyrics, image, video, touring and a host of related issues which bear on the 'meaning' of the postmodern rock song. And yet it is difficult to read or hear anything relating to U2 without confronting sooner or later the fact that they are an 'Irish' band (Cloonan 1999: 202). If individual members do not raise the issue, commentators, journalists or fans feel compelled to.[2] Although it is impossible to define the category of 'Irishness', a large part of the band's significance and impact depends specifically upon its national status in an increasingly multinational world, and particularly on the great variety of connotations which trail that identity into the twenty-first century.

Despite the blunt fact of the band's 'Irishness', however, the meaning of a U2 song at any one time over the past 20 years has depended on a wide range of spatial factors which has little or nothing to do with the band's ethnic or national status. The fact is that, despite the best efforts of those with an investment in the concept of an authentic national or ethnic, musical tradition, 'sounds migrate'.[3] And nowhere more so than in rock music which, as a technologically complex yet highly populist cultural practice, manages to resist the powerful mystique of 'authenticity' by adumbrating the 'constructivist' dimension to music at each of its key stages, from production through formal structure and on to consumption context. Modern rock music reflects the process whereby older spatial paradigms begin to unravel under pressure from changes in the political and economic organisation of the world. At the same time, it facilitates the imagination of new maps which cut across what have become increasingly defunct institutional boundaries.

So far, then, I have broached issues of form, technology and identity. The production–text–consumption model which enables this sort of analysis remains the basis of modern critical discourse, and I shall return to each of these issues in due course. In the meantime, we should not be surprised that, given the implicit spatial dimension to traditional analyses of music, 'space' should have emerged as an integral part of what might be termed the 'cultural studies' approach to rock music. In the introduction to their edited collection *Mapping the Beat*, Thomas Swiss, John Sloop and Andrew Herman discuss what they term 'spaces of noise and places of music' (1998: 6), while also calling for '[a] spatial-ized analysis of popular music, an analysis that explores the promises and possibilities of a cartography of sound as a territory of power' (ibid.: 17). Rock music, they assert, dramatises space in a number of popularly accessible ways; as a result, during its brief history the genre has developed into one of the principal means for the imagination of global 'countermappings ... spatial practices through which space is lived in and used in ways quite different from those imagined and desired by the powerful' (ibid.: 8). It does this by concretising an enduring political stand-off between 'music' – the formal and institutional manipulation of sound in the service of certain ideological narratives – and 'noise', the fundamentally unmanageable effects caused by the conglomeration of sounds in postmodern society. Paraphrasing the French music critic Jacques Attali, Swiss, Sloop and Herman claim that:

> Music is tamed noise, a structural code that defines and maps positions of power and difference that are located in the aural land-scape of sound ... noise is 'unlistenable' static and interference, a cacophonous anarchy of sound. Thus noise, as an element of the aural landscape of society, can challenge positions of power and difference that are assumed to be 'natural'. (ibid.: 19–20)

Although rooted in music's traditional interpretative contexts, the project of 'mapping the beat' refers to the ambiguous and essentially unmappable locations (with streets, carnivals, festivals and concerts providing key sites) when properly 'musical' considerations – institution, form, consumption – are suspended in favour of a primarily 'noisy' analysis. Making a related point, George Lipsitz writes that music exceeds the established spatial coordinates (such as nation-states) through which we are encouraged to make sense of the world: rather than think-ing about traditional spatial units such as 'the country' or 'the nation-state', we should think about 'ethnoscapes, mediascapes, technoscapes, finanscapes, ideoscapes, through which we can all inhabit many different "places" at once' (1994: 5).

All in all, emphasis in these cultural studies models tends to be on the ways in which music is endowed with the capacity to problematise received spatial discourses, and to extend the realm of the affective, and thus the 'political'. My purpose here is not to engage self-consciously with these approaches, but to indicate the extent to which space (rather than, as might be expected, time) has emerged as the principal critical category for the analysis of modern rock music. The point is that whether it be its basic sonic properties, its formal organisation, its location in a national or international framework, its technological manipulation, or its ability to chart relations of social and political power, music is a cultural practice which is spatially engaged in a number of complex and overlapping ways.

U2: space and place

'Music is located in relation to an imagined geography,' writes Andrew Blake, 'and often expresses that geography' (1997: 171). In what 'imagined geography' are U2 located, and how did the band set about expressing those spaces and places in musical form?

All over Dublin after the summer of 1977, groups of teenage boys were energised in the wake of the punk rock explosion into playing guitar-based popular music. U2 emerged from one such matrix on the city's northside. This particular band was atypical from the beginning, however, in that only one of its members (the drummer, Larry Mullen) came from what might be termed a conventional Irish background – that is, two Irish Catholic parents. The others, singer and lyricist Paul Hewson (Bono), guitarist Dave Evans (the Edge) and bassist Adam Clayton, all had British and/or Protestant elements to their upbringing. Many commentators have speculated that these differences contributed to the band's sense of alienation from, and identification with, their youthful milieu; as Bono was to say in 1992: 'I didn't know whether I was working class, middle class, Protestant, Catholic, English, American or Irish' (Waters 1994: 71). It was this confusion, indeed, which infused U2's music from the beginning and which in time metamorphosed through a number of increasingly sophisticated forms.

One manifestation of Bono's alienation from 1970s Ireland, and more particularly from northside Dublin, was his membership of 'Lypton Village', a loose affiliation of friends which formed into a kind of unofficial opposition to contemporary Irish attitudes and mores (Dunphy

1988: 85–106). That a 'village' should be cast against a city and a nation in this way indicates a significant (albeit unconscious) spatial imagination at work; 'we do not acknowledge your space', the implicit message is, 'therefore we shall create a place, with its own language, practices and priorities, wherein we can feel at home'. Yet in many ways it was precisely a kind of 'village' mentality which still dominated Irish life up to and including 1970s against which 'Lypton Village' was rebelling. This may indicate that, typically of subcultural discourse, resistance was constructed in terms of an ironic, playful redeployment of currently dominant terms of engagement; this is certainly in keeping with the other famous artistic endeavour to emerge from 'Lypton Village': the Virgin Prunes. But it also shows that U2's relationship with the culture in which the band had evolved – including quite crucially its spatial aspects – was always more than simple rejection, and certainly a more complex prospect that the punk ideology which constituted the band's immediate musical context.[4]

One of the reasons Bono in particular was attracted to the idea of touring was a deep sense of alienation from 'home', or more particularly the house he shared with his father and brother after the death of his mother in 1974 (Waters 1994: 68). A more mundane reason was the fact that Dublin had few serious rock venues in the late 1970s, and U2 either quickly exhausted the potential of those that did exist, or were obliged to invent new ones, such as the by now legendary Saturday afternoon gigs at the Dandelion Market off St Stephen's Green near the city centre. In any event, Bono's antipathy for home did have a positive outcome in so far as U2's early success was in fact developed in large part through a strategy of constant, extensive touring. This was all the more remarkable in that it occurred during a period when most popular musicians were in search of a fast track to the top through chart success and media hype. In retrospect Adam Clayton could say that 'U2 were never any good in clubs, in small places' (Flanagan 1995: 65); yet, in tour after tour of Britain, Europe and the United States, the band won an enormous and loyal fan base which has remained at the core of their success ever since.[5]

During this time, the success or failure of a show depended, at least for the band, on the creation of what the Edge called a 'feeling of intimacy' (Gardner 1994: 126) between performers and audience. This in turn depended in large part upon the energy and charisma of Bono. From the outset, he and the rest of the band took the matter of performance very seriously: 'I'm frightened of the responsibility of standing in that space,' Bono told Paul Morley of the *New Musical Express* in February

1980 after a gig at the Cork Country Club; 'Sometimes I don't want to be on that stage . . . I haven't got complete control of myself but I do want some sort of discipline' (cited in de la Parra 1994: 11). From the band's earliest performances, Bono's strategy was to collapse the gap between stage and audience so that, in the words of one of their most famous songs ('Sunday, Bloody Sunday', from *War*, 1983), 'we can be as one'. His stage antics, which frequently included climbing on sets and interacting with members of the audience, amounted to an assault on the artificial space of the stage so that concert-goers would feel they had been a part of, rather than merely witness to, an event.

Also at this time, the kind of music that U2 produced seemed especially geared to work in the context of live performance. As their popularity grew and the venues got larger, so the music itself seemed to grow in terms of the sonic evocation of space and the characteristic themes of the lyrics, so that by the time of *The Joshua Tree* tour it was difficult to know if the venues were expanding to fit the sound, or vice versa. In a 1988 *Rolling Stone* interview, the Edge discussed his discovery of echo, speculating that 'the use of treatments and effects is one reason why U2 works so well outdoors and in these big arenas. The sound just seems to resonate. . . . We've never had any problem making our music work in a big space. In fact, I think I feel more at home in a big space than I do in a small club or theater now' (Gardner 1994: 126).

The greater the band's success and the larger the shows they played, however, the more difficult it was to achieve the desired 'oneness'. Such was their reputation as premier live rock act (especially after Live Aid in June 1985 and the mainstream success of *The Joshua Tree*), and such was the ticket demand, that the band were obliged to move from small clubs and theatres to arenas and finally into stadia. Although the music remained 'big' in terms of sound and atmosphere on 'The Joshua Tree' (1987) and 'Love Town' (1989) tours, there was a lapse between the inception of U2's stadium career and the realisation that what had worked for an indoor audience of 3,000 or less would not necessarily work for an outdoor audience of 40,000 or more. As a consequence, the band and its management was obliged to extend significantly the concept of live rock performance in the 'Zoo TV' (1992–93) and 'Pop Mart' (1997) tours. These tours were ground-breaking in terms of the number of people played to, the amounts of money and equipment involved, and the quality (sound, vision and incalculables such as atmosphere) of the product (Cunningham 1999: 147–90; Flanagan 1995: 149).

Bono has admitted that such has been the band's investment in touring, and such was the length and intensity of the 'Zoo TV' and

'Pop' tours, that his sense of 'home' has been seriously compromised (Flanagan 1995: 185). This is all the more interesting in that, although U2's reputation was forged for the most part in the United States, Europe and Britain, the band opted to maintain their base in Ireland. In a 1980 interview Bono said: 'U2 is an Irish expression, so we don't want to leave. Obviously, we will have to go away for long periods but our home is here' (Prendergast 1987: 177). This decision became more all the more significant as U2 progressed during the 1980s from impressive underground band to biggest cult band in the world, and on to simply the planet's 'best' rock band.[6] In Irish rock tradition, local success to any degree was usually followed by swift relocation to London which, in terms of European rock music, had been where it was 'at' since the early 1960s. The careers of individuals such as Rory Gallagher and Van Morrison, and bands such as Thin Lizzy and the Boomtown Rats, offered seemingly conclusive proof that a significant impact in the world of international rock could not be made in or from Ireland. The alternative was slow suffocation in the extremely limited market around the larger cities on the island. Many highly talented bands, such as the Blades – contemporaries of U2 – disappeared in this way (Prendergast 1987: 165).

Even after the enormous success of *The Joshua Tree*, U2 remained in many ways a local band. In the late 1980s Dublin did not yet possess the media culture which, most notoriously in Britain, is organised around the constant harassment of celebrities and the invention of news copy if none exists. That situation changed, however, with the onset of the Celtic Tiger and the advent of Dublin Chic. Adam Clayton and Larry Mullen, formerly the least recognisable members of the band, evinced resentment during the early 1990s with regard to their representation in the Irish press and the changing perceptions which prevented a 'normal' relationship with their home town (Flanagan 1994: 393, 442).

Nevertheless, it was important for U2 to remain in Ireland because it enabled them to exploit the island's location between the two main centres of western cultural history: the United States and Europe. It is a cliché in rock music circles to say that U2 were American during the 1980s and European during the 1990s (despite the obvious European influences on *October* and *The Unforgettable Fire*, and the continued engagement with American culture on the recordings of the 1990s); another cliché is that the band underwent one of the most successful 'reinventions' in the history of the genre, from the overblown 'authenticity' of *Rattle and Hum* (1988) to the musical and conceptual sophistication of 1991's *Achtung Baby*. Like all clichés, these have their bases in fact, and the facts themselves emerge from deeper cultural tendencies. As we shall explore at length in the next section, America occupied a highly ambivalent place in Irish popular culture since large-scale emigration began after the Famine of the late 1840s. This place – both 'promised land' and 'land of exile' – provided U2 with a rich store of imagery and cultural memory which they would tap throughout their first decade. This ambiguity is in many ways the informing spirit of their most 'American' record, *The Joshua Tree*. When that vein seemed to have been exhausted, U2 turned to focus on 'Europe', or at least to the idea of Europe reproduced in the influential visions of artists such as Wim Wenders and Brian Eno.

At this stage it is important to grasp that U2 were enabled to engage so fully with these traditions, and to switch so successfully between them, precisely because of Ireland's liminal position in relation to these two postmodern cultural megaliths. In other words, the band exploited Ireland's traditional imaginative location – marginal from Europe, residual to America – to produce deeply compelling engagements with both those large cultural entities. Ireland was nominally and aspirationally European, yet problematically so given the peculiarities of its history and geography. At the same time, given the history of emigration, there were strong cultural and political links with America, yet these also were uncertain, productive of an intense trans-Atlantic cultural traffic in which images of 'home' were exchanged and distorted.

Space, then, figured in U2's career in terms of touring, domicile and imaginative affiliation. Shortly, we shall be focusing on the way in which space is used and evoked specifically in relation to the music. Before that, however, it is interesting to note the regularity with which space, and particularly the issue of Irish space, is invoked in critical responses to U2's music. This is true of a range of discourses, from 'teeny' reviews through 'serious' rock journalism and on to academic commentary. Most analyses respond positively to what is seen as U2's ability to interconnect national and international culture, and to extend the boundaries of 'Irishness' beyond those inherited from a relatively recent model of cultural production based on the primacy of the nation-state.

In the context of an essay collection organised around the issue of emigration and the experience of the Irish overseas, for example, Kieran Keohane examines what he refers to as 'traditionalism and home-lessness in contemporary Irish music'. The premise is that '[aesthetic] political representations of the Irish spirit fluctuate between discourses of communitarian essentialism and the transcendental homelessness of a race of angels' (1997: 302). Keohane suggests that, as a sensitive yet high-profile form of 'aesthetic representation', the great majority of contemporary Irish music (including that emerging from the art and folk traditions) represents a refusal of the 'homelessness' which is at the heart of postmodern experience, and functions instead to support an implicit 'traditionalism'. Bands such as the Saw Doctors are indicted for producing music that remains in thrall to an outmoded notion of 'home'. The role of U2 (and in a somewhat different manner, London-Irish punk-folk outfit the Pogues), on the other hand, is 'to give witness to the zeitgeist and still be in touch with Irish roots' (ibid.: 292). The band members are exemplary 'Zuropeans' in so far as they have managed to overcome the narrow cultural tradition into which they were born, but more importantly in so far as they retain a stake – metaphorically and materially – in that tradition even as they continue to develop a highly sophisticated yet incredibly popular engagement with the postmodern condition. The positive result of this, for Keohane, is that the more U2 emphasises their Irishness, the more that category is rendered problematical.

John Waters' 1994 book *Race of Angels: Ireland and the Genesis of U2* is another representative example in so far as it is a serious though non-systematic attempt to account for the emergence of U2, but (in this context) more significantly in so far as it is imbued with images of space. Attempting to describe his impression upon first hearing 'A Day Without Me' (from *Boy*), Waters writes:

> The sound opens up a picture which, for me, is of a street backing on both sides on to mountains. Or sometimes the dark shaft of a railway tunnel suddenly lit by the frenzy of a locomotive.... I don't know what it's 'about'. All I see is the landscape or the tunnel, which of course are not in the song at all but in my head.... I only know that this song represents a place, described in the reverberating guitar and the climbing bass and the tripping, tumbling drums, a place I need to go to once in a while to breathe and cry. (1994: 25–6)

Similar readings are produced in relation to 'One Tree Hill' (from *The Joshua Tree*) and 'The Wanderer' (from *Zooropa*) (ibid.: 106, 175). Waters' book is in fact innundated with spatial references and metaphors; the fundamental story told by rock'n'roll and its offshoots, he claims, is one 'of a generation of fallen angels caught on the doomed journey from the farmlands to the city, but with neither the motivation nor the inclination to turn back' (ibid.: 177). Like Keohane, Waters is concerned with 'home' and 'homelessness'. The former 'exists not as a place or a set of ideas, but as a metaphysical preoccupation' (ibid.: 140), while the latter is seen less as a positive postmodern response to authoritarian notions of home and more as a cultural reflex of neocolonialism and the free market.

The main point is that U2 were the pre-eminent Irish cultural producers of the late twentieth century, precisely to the degree that their music reflected a matrix of confusing and contradictory spatial affiliations. Waters discusses the band's relation to its 'home' place, and the manner in which individual members were obliged to recreate a sense of home by virtue of the lack of any attractive options in Dublin or Ireland. Rock music creates 'a landscape in which we can place ourselves', he claims, but while '[other] bands make records that reflect them and where they come from . . . U2 make records that reflect their lack of a place to call home' (ibid.: 146). Ironically, this lack of a secure relationship with home is what renders the band quintessentially 'Irish'. 'U2 are an Irish band,' he continues, by which he means 'that they emerged from a place and a time – Ireland in the 1970s – which was the product of a historical and evolutionary process, and that they are as faithful a representation of that place and time as it is possible to conceive of' (ibid.: 121). At the same time, Waters is also keen to locate the band in relation to the United States, Great Britain and Europe, and more specifically in terms of the range of inherited identities of, and relationships between, these categories.

Individual band members have also regularly invoked spatial metaphors when attempting to theorise both the emergence of U2 and the continuing appeal of the band. In conversation with Richard Kearney, Bono drew a parallel between Irish and African-American experience: 'The Irish, like blacks, feel like outsiders. There's a feeling of being homeless, migrant, but I suppose that's what art is – a search for identity' (1988: 190). Later in the same interview he comments: 'Maybe we Irish are misfits, travellers, never really at home, but always talking about it. I met a fisherman who told me we were like salmon: it's upriver all the time, against the odds, the river doesn't want us . . . yet we want a way home . . . but there is no home' (ibid.: 191). The themes of home, homelessness and identity raised here (and elsewhere) emerge time and again, and are essentially a critical reflection upon themes that emerge organically from the creative process.

When we turn to the music itself, we find that U2 were associated with 'big', outdoors music throughout the 1980s. Commentators constantly remarked (usually pejoratively) upon U2's 'big, resounding sound' (cited in Gardner 1994: 23). This was only partly to do with their reputation as a live attraction. Having examined U2's performance and recording techniques between *Boy* (1980) and *Rattle and Hum* (1989) in detail, Allan F. Moore suggested that a sense of space was actually created *in* the music in a number of interrelated ways. These included the songs' characteristically open-ended chord structures; a harmonically and sonically minimal rhythm section (derived at least initially from punk) organised around a pumping bass and solid snare drum; Edge's energetic guitar technique and his highly original use of effects; and Bono's vocal style which, in terms of phrasing, range and volume, was suggestive of large, outdoor contexts (1993: 143–4).

Of these, perhaps the most commonly remarked aspect of the 'U2 sound' is the Edge's guitar style. As remarked in relation to their reputation as a live act, U2 were associated with heavy use of echo, reverb and digital delay throughout the 1980s, and this added to the impression of the band as producers of big, outdoors music. 'Echo', as Bill Flanagan writes, 'fattened the band's sound, covering up the fact that neither the guitarist nor bassist in this band were playing very much. It also gave the early U2 songs a feeling of reverberating size and – not least – laid a coat of common personality over the material. U2 had a *sound*' (1995: 45, original emphasis).

According to Bono, U2 decided to employ echo to get the music 'to another place', because the landscape of sounds offered by the currently dominant types of pop music, especially punk, had 'started to look incredibly limited' (Waters 1994: 26). As the band's success grew, so also did the range of equipment employed by the Edge to enhance his guitar sound. In the early days, the impression of large space was created by ubiquitous and inventive use of a Memory Man Deluxe echo unit.[7] By the time of 'Pop Mart', the band's record-breaking 1996/97 tour, the Edge (and indeed Bono, a notoriously self-deprecating guitarist) commanded a vast array of analogue and digital technology – gadgets rejoicing under names such as the Fuzz Mongoose, the Lovetone Meatball and the Custom Audio Electronics Super Tremolo (Cunningham 1999: 188). Experienced manipulation of this technology, allied with subtle use of pre-recorded loops and creative mixing, enabled the band to reproduce on stage, to an impressive degree, the individual sound required by each song.

Rock music's association with echo is ubiquitous, yet it remains a curious development. As the first popular music to be developed in a technologically sophisticated society, rock has evolved a wide range of conventions regarding its characteristic sounds. One of these is echo which has over the years come to possess definite 'spatial' connotations. In nature, echo relies on the existence of a structure of some kind to bounce back initial sounds and create resonance (Moore 1993: 195). In wide open spaces such as the desert, sounds actually die quite quickly as there is nothing to create resonance. Echo most readily occurs in human-made structures of large size – an amphitheatre or hall, for example. U2's use of echo in relation to their 'outdoors' identity is conventional, but inconsistent and anomalous. It is well documented that when Europeans first encountered the deserts and prairies of the North American continent they were disturbed by its silence. Yi-Fu Tuan quotes the American botanist Thomas Nuttall, who wrote in 1819: 'It is truly remarkable how greatly the sound of objects becomes absorbed in these extensive woodless plains. No echo answers the voice, and its tones die away in boundless and enfeebled undulations' (1993: 74–5).

Of course, an individual sound – especially in the constricted world of rock music – is the result not so much of technology but of the manner in which technology is wielded. The Edge's distinctive guitar style resulted not only from his use of echo, but more fundamentally from an amalgam of idiosyncratic left-hand (fretboard fingering) and right-hand (strumming and picking) techniques. In interview, the guitarist describes how he 'started working with what I later found out to be very Irish musical ideas, like using open strings, alternating those with fretted strings to produce drone type of things' (Gardner 1988: 126). Guitar chords fingered in this way produce complex yet airy sounds far removed from standard rock 'power' chords (based around only the first and fifth notes of the scale). Standard guitar chord shapes tend to be formed from groups of closely clustered notes structured around the progressive repetition of three notes – first, third and fifth in the case of a major scale, first, minor third and fifth in the case of a minor scale. Playing chords high on the fretboard and alternating fretted with open strings allows the guitarist to move away from the rather prosaic sounds of these chords to produce a much more colourful and dynamic range of sounds – emphasising certain notes, letting open strings ring (suggestive of that 'Irish drone'), creating drama by sustaining the same notes and figures over a changing bass line, and so on.

In the studio, U2 songs tended to be layered through a number (although usually two) of overdubbed guitar parts, one rapidly strummed high, 'choppy' figure which could be controlled through use of 'damping' with the heel of the right (strumming) hand, and/or through plectrum technique; the other, some variation on an arpeggio figure (the notes of a chord played in sequence) played on a lower octave with heavy use of echo and digital delay.[8] Besides these aspects, the Edge's guitar style always owed at least as much to what was *not* played as to what was, and the tension and release created by the dialogue of sound and silence. He described his technique as 'minimal': 'Play as few notes as you can, but find those notes that do the most work.... If I could play one note for a whole song, I would' (Gardner 1988: 125).

'I Will Follow', the opening track on U2's first album *Boy*, offers a typical example of a track constructed from these techniques and this philosophy. The song begins with what would become U2's trademark sound for a number of years: a high, repetitive guitar riff played through the Memory Man Deluxe echo unit, underpinned by a pumping bass and a solid snare drum. Bono calls 'I will follow' somewhere in the background, but when the vocal commences the voice immediately moves to the front of the textural register. The riff ceases, the guitar alternates instead between muted chords and dramatic harmonics which subtly fill in the gaps left by the vocal. The signature riff returns between verses and again after the refrain ('I will follow'). The track also includes what might be called the 'early U2 break': the kit and bass revert to a minimal structure (mostly hi-hat and single notes), the Edge plays some resounding guitar harmonics, with Bono expands in seemingly random fashion on the themes already introduced in the earlier part of the song. The full band re-enters for the bridge to the concluding chorus, and the track concludes with the guitar riff repeated a number of times.

Besides these properly 'musical' aspects, 'I Will Follow' initiates a classic spatial trope which perhaps finds its ultimate expression in the songs included on 1984's *The Unforgettable Fire*, but which recurs throughout the U2 canon. The lyric opens with the words 'I was on the outside'. What kind of relationship or structure is the singing persona – 'I' – outside of? Where will he follow 'you', and what is the purpose of the journey both undertake? The 'four walls' of what structure did 'they' pull down? What kind of 'circle' is it that the persona enters? What was he looking at through the 'window', and how does this impact upon his condition of being 'lost' and 'found'? Why is this song of adolescent *angst* cast in such spatial terms, and why have those terms remained such a crucial aspect of Bono's lyrical imagination down to the present? One answer, emerging from the Heideggerean perspective invoked throughout this study, might be that the range of emotions which the teenage persona is experiencing – security and danger, isolation and love, belonging and loneliness – find their 'natural' expression in terms of a spatial discourse organised around the notion of the dwelling.

In any event, these musical and lyrical aspects combined to produce a highly original musical 'texture' in which aural space was created by the dynamism and distance between the different aspects of the music – that is, kit, bass, voice, guitar. For Moore, the typical polarisation of speeds in a U2 song – the steady kit, the pumping bass, the fast guitar – combined with the music's registral layout, 'connotes a sense of open space and grandeur' (1993: 145). Moore also makes a link between the spatial connotations of U2's music during the 1980s and the aura of 'authenticity' which developed around the band as the decade progressed, suggesting that 'the creation of a sense of open space in a style only loosely related may carry connotations of removal from built-up industrial areas, and hence a nostalgic return to the romanticized notion of pre-industrial existence' (ibid.: 146). I now wish to explore the manner in which this particular 'notion of pre-industrial existence' connoted a range of spatial imagery – and one image in particular: the desert – which U2 were to exploit on their most enduringly popular album, 1987's *The Joshua Tree*.

Into the arms of America

In 1994 John Waters suggested that '[the] eight studio albums which U2 has recorded to date may be seen as a journey through both their own experience and through the Irish experience of which they are part. Each album represents a stab at creating a place, a world, a landscape, in which freedom might be attained' (1994: 195). Even if we accept such an interpretation, there could be no way of telling how far this attempt to marry music and space was part of any intentional programme. But certainly, by the time the writing and recording of *The Joshua Tree* began in early 1986, U2 were becoming self-consciously engaged with issues of space. Even the usually anti-intellectual Larry Mullen got in on the act, admitting that 'we wanted to try and capture a place as well as a mood, we wanted to give each song a sense of location' (U2 1987a), while bassist Adam Clayton said: 'I just think the album takes you somewhere' (Gardner 1994: 156). The Edge has since described the band's desire to produce what they and their producers referred to as 'cinematic music . . . a landscape of words and images and themes that made up *The Joshua Tree*' (Flanagan 1995: 51). Elsewhere he described U2's production of a music which 'can actually really evoke a landscape and a place and can really bring you there . . . music that actually brought you somewhere physical as opposed to an emotional place – a real location'.[9]

One of the 'real locations' to which U2 wished to bring their audience was America, and more specifically, the desert. The Edge describes how, quite early in the process, 'Bono started talking about America and particularly the desert south-west of America as a kind of location and metaphor' (King and O'Connor 1999). Bono himself has suggested that the idea arose initially from the time he and his partner spent in Ethiopia after Live Aid: 'I started thinking, "They may have a physical desert, but we've got other kinds of deserts." And that's what attracted me to the desert as a symbol of some sort' (Gardner 1994: 65). However, *The Joshua Tree* took its actual title from the unusual plant found in the Joshua Tree National Forest, located in the Mojave Desert to the east of Los Angeles. This region is only part of a great desert system covering much of the western half of the United States (Hollon 1966: 2). The plant in question was allegedly named by Mormon settlers who saw in its peculiar shape an image of the prophet Joshua pointing the way towards the promised land. The sleeve photographs by Anton Corbijn became an integral part of the package – black and white shots of a very serious looking U2 set against the bleak desert landscape with only some distant hills and a lone Joshua tree to break the monotony.

There was a number of reasons why America loomed large in the band's consciousness at that time. In June 1986, some months into *The Joshua Tree* sessions, U2 headlined the 'Conspiracy of Hope' tour in which a number of high-profile artists played selected dates in the United States in support of Amnesty International. The role and image of America worldwide was therefore of some concern to the band at the time. But U2's fascination with America had grown initially from their early touring days, the enthusiasm with which their music had always been accepted there, and their increasing exposure to various aspects of its culture. Although the previous album, *The Unforgettable Fire* (1984), was in many ways more European in conception and outlook than earlier works, some of its tracks (such as 'Pride [In the Name of Love]', and 'Elvis Presley and America') indicated the direction in which the band were moving.

As remarked earlier, there would appear to be something fundamentally contradictory about the notion of a 'desert music', or at least the kind of broad, resonant, cinematic desert music desired by U2. As Yi-Fu Tuan writes: 'The great hot deserts of the world often fall silent. Under the relentless sun and a sky bleached white by heat, when nothing stirs except an occasional dust devil, one may hear – in a condition of exhaustion mixed with panic – only the thump of one's heart and a hum in the ear' (1993: 74). This evocative imagery, which suggests the overwhelming *silence* of the desert, is paradoxically reminiscent of U2's discourse which employs *sound* (instruments and voice) to evoke many of the same impressions – for example, heat, silence, sun, sky, dust, confusion. The postmodern rock band is much more than its sound, of course, and when it came to creating the appropriate image for *The Joshua Tree*, everything from title, sleeve photography, down to authentic cowboy hats, supported the music's evocation of a spacious, outdoors, natural environment. But still, a number of questions remain to be addressed: How do you go about creating sonic representations of a place primarily characterised by its silence? What are the practical aesthetics of 'desert' imagery? And what kind of spatial genres and traditions were U2 tapping, consciously or unconsciously?

Turning to the latter question first, we find that the associated images of the desert, 'the West' and the wilderness play crucial if ambivalent roles in American cultural history (Short 1991: 19–27; Schama 1995: 573). There are two interesting aspects to this cultural history in the present context. First, the image of the desert in American culture derives in large part from emigrant European sources, and more especially from the response of Irish emigrants to American geography. Second, much of the desert's cultural import derives from religious discourse, the same discourse which infused much of U2's early music and which has continued to resonate (albeit in different forms) throughout their work.[10]

In his essay 'Images of Ireland and America', Fintan O'Toole has suggested that 'the notion of America itself is an Irish invention, the notion of Ireland an American invention' (1990: 133). This situation arose in the first instance from a colonial condition in which the Irish *in* Ireland were widely considered to be savage aboriginals, but on coming to America they aspired towards the superior, civilising, white race which had cast itself against another race of savage aboriginals – the Native Americans.[11] Irish-Americans such as Jesse James and Billy the Kid carried traces of both these narratives, and this in turn coloured the American legends with which they became associated. The result was a paradoxical discourse in which Jesse and Billy were both 'Indian killers and the clearers of the wilderness', 'bad guys' who were also 'good guys' (ibid.: 134). O'Toole's main point is that

> [an] important part of the American psyche, the ambivalence of the desperado as dangerous outlaw and rugged individualist, arises out

of the ambivalence of the Irish in America. . . . This tension between acceptance and exile, between being insiders and outsiders, liberates a set of images that is enormously influential on the development of American culture and therefore on the development of Irish culture. (ibid.: 135)

The contradiction at the heart of cowboy culture in all its high and popular manifestations, he continues, 'has its origins in an Irish-American dynamic' (ibid.: 138). This dynamic, moreover, carries an implicit spatial dimension, to the effect that 'the Wild West' – the cowboy's natural domain – becomes a terrain caught between contradictory desires, those of the 'rugged individualist' in search of a landscape of freedom, and those of the 'dangerous outlaw' using the arid desert terrain to stay one step ahead of the forces of civilisation as represented by the community. O'Toole argues that these contradictions account for the paradoxical representations of each country in the work of another prominent Irish-American, the film director John Ford. In his representation of Monument Valley, the stunning desert landscape that plays such an integral part in many of his films, Ford found an enduring symbol of the paradox at the heart of the America dream, 'both wild, and therefore frightening, and at the same time an alternative wilderness to the wilderness of the American city' (ibid.: 141).

The result is that the desert was and remains a paradoxical image in American culture, a symbol of the freedom that lies at the heart of the American dream, but also of the primitiveness – savage or noble, depending on the context – which must eventually give way to the forces of an inevitably corrupt community. As O'Toole points out (ibid.: 141), it was the mythology of the desert that U2 tapped in the mid-1980s, using it as a symbol of the continuing contradictions at the heart of late twentieth-century American culture, and more specifically as a symbol of their own contradictory role as both (Irish) inventors and (Irish) inheritors of that mythology.

The second issue attending the representation of the West in American culture arises in an essay which is in implicit dialogue with O'Toole's. In religious terms, we recall from Chapter 3 that in first millennium and medieval Ireland, the 'desert' was a place removed from worldly corruption where the anchorite went in imitation of the Desert Fathers to live alone and contemplate God's will as manifested in nature. Already under pressure during the medieval era, this ethos did not survive in Ireland into the modern period. In his essay 'The Myth of the West in Irish and American Culture', Luke Gibbons points out that 'the West' became emblematic of the 'real' Ireland in nineteenth-century cultural nationalist discourse, but the culture of that 'real' Ireland was profoundly recalcitrant to that of the Catholic bourgeoisie which was preparing to assume control of the postcolonial state.

Gibbons argues that the ethos of J.M. Synge's most famous drama, *The Playboy of the Western World*, is anti-Puritan and anti-devotional. The play rehearses and celebrates a form of 'collective passion' (1996a: 30) encapsulated in the organic community.[12] The hero, Christy, emerges from a condition of loneliness and isolation to one of acceptance and intercourse. Synge is suggesting that the individual can come to a full and frank expression of his identity only in the context of a knowable community. Finding the community in which the drama is set too fragmented, already too infected by 'eastern' values, Christy heads off into the sunset, not to return to the lonesome life he knew before, but to find a community worthy of his peculiarly Irish talents – 'drunkeness, sexuality, lying, violence and mob rule' (ibid.: 33). The individual must return from the 'desert', in other words, to confront the task facing all individuals: the concomitant loss and recovery of self in the community.

Gibbons goes on to argue, however, that if in the west of Ireland it is the individual who needs the community, in classic American depictions of the 'the West' it is the community that needs the individual (ibid.: 31). The wilderness (and the desert as one particular form of wilderness) was a favoured place for many Christian sects because it provided them with both a metaphorical and actual distance from what they considered to be the corrupting hand of the centralising state (Hollon 1966: 88–107). The values on which the pioneer spirit was based came in time to inform representations of the cowboy and the places associated with him. 'In its American form, the western is a hymn to individualism,' Gibbons writes, 'a celebration of self-interest and personal liberty evoked in visual terms by the limitless expanse of the great plains and the vast open prairies' (ibid.: 24). The West thus became the mythic location 'of the restless individualism which lies at the heart of the great American dream' (ibid.: 26). One significant aspect of that restless individualism was a form of moral Puritanism. And here, once again, may be found contradictory impulses, for even as the pioneers and settlers cast themselves against the corrupt centralising state, they 'themselves represent the thrust of civilization against the "primitivism" of the Indians' (ibid.: 27); even as the cowboy became the bearer of values encoded in the American dream, that dream was systematically betrayed by the same pioneering spirit – converted into corporate capitalism – which had provided the context for the emergence of the cowboy in the first place.

Although Gibbons does not make the connection, the 'desert' asceticism of medieval Ireland is related in certain fundamental aspects to the puritan asceticism which informs the image of the western cowboy. Whereas the hermits and anchorites of eighth-century Ireland embraced solitude as a precondition for proper contemplation of God's ways, 'the cowboy' as Gibbons puts it, 'embraces solitude as the precondition of freedom and independence' (ibid.: 31). Both take to the desert to realise temperamental and ideological issues that cannot be realised in the community; both were simultaneously acclaimed and mistrusted by communities (religious and politico-economic respectively) for which the ascetic ideal was tactically attractive yet at the same time deeply subversive. And just as the anchorite's ethos found institutional expression within the walls of the community – for example, in the Culdee brotherhood led by Máel Ruain at Tallaght – so the cowboy's rugged individualism came to be paradoxically extolled within the very American institutions – legal, cultural and economic – which were dedicated to its extirpation. The Culdee and the cowboy are blood-brothers, in other words, united in their predilection for the desert and in their vulnerability in the face of powerful institutions wishing to manipulate desert discourse for their own ends.

The religious convictions of U2 (excepting Adam Clayton) are well documented; such indeed was the strength of those convictions that the band came close to splitting after only their second album, *October*, released in 1981 (Dunphy 1987: 207ff). The charismatic Christian emphasis of their beliefs earned U2 a reputation within Ireland as a 'Protestant' band.[13] At the same time, the distance between the Catholic Church and their own notion of spirituality added to U2's perception of themselves as outsiders in their own place. The band's preoccupation with the nature and function of spirituality has metamorphosed over the years but has never been lost. While most of their popular music contemporaries were concerned only to appear 'cool' during the 1980s, U2 were temperamentally and musically equipped to engage with a variety of fundamental human issues which fuelled their reputation as an 'important', or simply 'big', band. This they achieved in *The Joshua Tree* by delving deeper into the religious issues with which they had been concerned from the outset – the nature of belief and doubt, love and justice, life and death. More specifically, they recruited the epic religious imagery associated with the desert for their peculiar artistic vision.

These, then, are some of the musical and wider cultural contexts from which *The Joshua Tree* emerged and with which the album engaged, albeit at a number of disparate, conscious and unconscious, levels: U2's desire to produce 'cinematic' music evocative of 'real places'; the paradox of representing a silent place in sonic terms; the desert as an ambivalent image from Irish and American cultural history; the band's troubled religious concerns. Together, these made for a complex and compelling musical statement. There is also the more obvious point that, as Bono himself put it, he 'didn't know [he] was Irish until [he] went to America', and the band's instinctive impression that '[our] journey to American eventually turned us back to where we came from' (Kearney 1988: 188, 190). At this stage, I wish to expand a little on these issues as they relate to one particular track from *The Joshua Tree*, 'Where The Streets Have No Name' (hereafter 'Streets').

Explicit desert imagery occurs on three tracks ('Streets', 'In God's Country' and 'Trip Through Your Wires'). (It also occurs on a track recorded during *The Joshua Tree* sessions but released on the following year's *Rattle and Hum*, the hauntingly beautiful 'Heartland'.) Yet, the centrality of desert imagery to the entire project is signalled by the fact that 'Streets' is sequenced to open the album. Discussing the track, Larry Mullen said: 'On the original idea there was this feeling of openness, of going down a road through a desert. There was that sort of feel to it. There was no deviation in the guitar, it's just straight ahead. And even with the drums, it's very rhythmic and straight ahead' (*U2 Talkie* 1987). Many of the Edge's recollections of the genesis, composition and recording of 'Streets' are also cast in spatial terms. He refers constantly to 'the landscape' evoked by the song, the 'journey' of the writing and recording process, and 'the place' where the finished text takes the listener (Waters 1994: 254; King and O'Connor 1999). 'Streets', he opined, is one of their most 'cinematic' songs.

The apparent straightforwardness of the track belies its difficult birth. It began as a few bars played on guitar, keyboards and drum-machine recorded by the Edge on a four-track machine. Having introduced it to the rest of the team, the band then spent a great deal of time on the song – 'hours and days and weeks', according to Eno, 'probably half the time that whole album took was spent on that song' (King and O'Connor 1999). At one point, Eno reckoned it would be easier to start the entire song again, and was only just averted from staging an 'accident' which would have wiped the version so laboriously compiled. Band and crew persevered until the musical execution approximated the vision initially glimpsed by the Edge. It is significant, however, that the final album mix was completed not by Eno or Lanois but by Steve Lillywhite (producer of U2's first three albums) who was brought to the project at a late stage to offer a fresh pair of ears.

At a basic level, 'Streets' is 'home-centred' in that it begins in a recognisable key (D major) and modulates through various changes (G, B minor, A) before returning to that key for both minor and major resolutions. The only unusual thing is the introduction of a flattened seventh (C) on the words 'streets' each time, which functions to emphasise that word and to introduce drama into what is otherwise a trouble-free journey along the scale.

Although on their previous four albums U2 had certainly managed to develop a unique and recognisable style, the kind of guitar-based rock music they played simply did not allow much scope in terms of musical structure or composition.[14] That they managed to convey the impression of movement through the vast open spaces of the desert in a song which, in musical terms, does not stray very far from 'home' is a testament to the fact that music is only one of the semiotic codes contributing to the 'meaning' of the postmodern rock song, and that formalist analysis is severely limited if it fails to engage with the ways in which certain cultural effects and practices may develop connotations different, if not entirely opposite, to the established ones. 'Streets' may start and finish in D major, but the emphasis (as Mullen's comments suggest) is not (or not only) on home, but on movement, on journeying, and on what happens to the subject who journeys. The intertextual reference points derive not from classical music theory, but from the cultural sources to which the band had been recently exposed, such as Jack Kerouac's *On the Road* and Norman Mailer's *The Executioner's Song*. The spatial qualities suggested by the music in turn connote some of the wider cultural values (such as safety, danger, freedom and imprisonment) which have been invoked throughout this study, and with which U2 self-consciously undertook to engage on this album.

The introduction, played by Eno on a DX7 synthesizer, is constructed of deep, sustained orchestral chords overlain with what sound like birds calling or a wailing wind. This is immediately suggestive of a wide, majestic landscape, perhaps the Monument Valley so beloved of John Ford, or the Mojave Valley represented on *The Joshua Tree*'s gatefold sleeve. After about 40 seconds, double-tracked guitars enter, one playing a heavily reverbed, four-note arpeggio figure high on the fretboard, the other 'chucking' a dramatic, though minimal chord. After another 25 seconds the tempo changes as the guitars coalesce into a single rapidly strummed chord. At this point the bass enters playing quavers (eighth notes) on the root note of the home key, and this pumping tempo remains more or less constant throughout the song. Finally, the kit enters after a mini-roll, providing a driving rhythm on snare and hi-hat. The only deviation throughout the song is the use of crash cymbal at various moments to emphasise certain musical and lyrical points. The atmosphere is epic, the dominant texture one of felicitous space, with the synthesiser and the guitar providing the high register, the bass and kit grounding the piece, and the vocal occupying the middle ground. Moore has described 'Streets' as possessed of

> a texture of great energy. ... The guitar is present throughout, covering a small range in a single register, with fast, intricate movement. The static bass (keeping to the root of harmonies rather than constructing an independent line) gives great firmness to the texture, while of the kit, only the ride cymbal is allowed to threaten this equilibrium. The guitar remaining above the voice sets up a perfect platform for the voice to dominate as the only sound source that really moves. (1993: 108)

In this sense, 'Streets' is in fact the emblematic song of U2's first decade, musically grounded yet texturally dynamic. The space between the Edge's minimalist guitar and the rhythm section's solid base is filled by the voice which, with Bono singing close to the top of his range, manages to connote conviction and movement without ever deviating too far in terms of melody, or deviating at all in terms of musical structure.

These aspects of 'Streets' are directly linked to the imagery conveyed in the lyrics. At the outset, the persona wishes to 'run' and 'hide' some place far away from 'the walls / That hold me inside'.[15] The city – metonymically suggested here by 'walls' connoting the built environment (as in 'these city walls' from the album's next track, 'I Still Haven't Found What I'm Looking For') – is negatively portrayed, a symbol of what Bono referred to at the time of the album's release as the West's spiritual impoverishment (*U2 Talkie*, 1987). Confusion exists, however, in so far as the city *becomes* a desert where 'love turns to rust' and 'we' are trampled in dust'. The city – whether it be Dublin or New York – is a 'deserted' landscape in so far as it is a place where people come together to 'build' structures and relations based on love, only to burn them down again. But is this something encoded into the very essence of the city – and the image of community which it supports – as a fundamentally flawed and decadent concept, or are there 'good' cities which because of political and cultural factors, become 'bad' and decay into dust?

The ambivalence of the city would become a preoccupation for U2 from *Achtung Baby*. Here it is invoked in contradistinction to the desert which is itself infused with contradictory meanings. Initially, it carries positive resonances as a place offering freedom from the community's spiritual impoverishment. Yet, this 'desert' has 'streets' – that is, traces of human usage and modification. But of course, these 'streets have no name', in keeping with their 'deserted' status.[16] In other words, they constitute a trace of the impact of humanity – which is to say, they would not be 'streets' except for repeated human passage. Yet these streets lack the fundamental property of the name which, as we saw in Chapter 2, is precisely the way in which humans come to know a landscape and locate themselves in relation to it – as property, desired, dangerous, vacant, and so on. The confusion attending the image of the desert here is a reflection of the ambivalence with which the desert (and its close relation, 'the West') has traditionally functioned in both American and Irish cultural history. It is a place of individual freedom, akin to the classical American terrain in which the hero, having settled matters in town, heads off to his 'home on the range'. But when the persona goes to the desert, he will 'go there with you', thus suggesting the possibility of empathy and community.

The lyric functions with reference to a seemingly straightforward dialectic of built (indoors) and natural (outdoors) environments. This is deceptive, however. The city (bad) can become a desert (good), in which case it (the city) would then supposedly become 'good'. In the same way, the desert (good) carries traces (streets) of the city (bad), in which case it (the desert) would then supposedly become 'bad'. 'Streets' trades on these evaluative connotations, both musically and lyrically, creating a rich, yet ultimately incoherent, image of modern western life. 'Coherence' is not necessarily the rock band's remit, however, nor the remit of any artist. As a form of 'desert music' imbued with various key modern spatial images, 'Streets' functions on a number of conventional levels. And as a discrete piece of art, the less 'coherent' it is, the greater number of levels upon which it can exercise its affective function.

Conclusion

Towards the end of U2's second Sydney 'Zoo TV' show on 27 November 1993, Mr McPhisto (one of the alter-egos developed by Bono during the long tour) wearily sang a few lines of the old drinking song 'Show Me the Way to Go Home'. If, on the one hand, this was an indication of the distance U2 had travelled in such a short time from the earnestness of

The Joshua Tree, at another level it also revealed that the issues which had animated the band during the 1980s were maintained, albeit in highly different guise, in their work of the following decade.

The journey from *The Joshua Tree* to *Pop* (1997) was one from desert to city street, and subsequently from street to dance floor and bedroom.[17] The later recordings evince a recognition on the band's part that survival in the modern world requires what Smadar Lavie and Ted Swedenburg describe as 'an on-going negotiation and renegotiation of positionalities, rather than a one-time journey into a faraway wilderness' (1996: 20). This move towards contingent, unchartable urban space may be traced in U2's music, especially with reference to the experimental dance rhythms – industrial, hip hop, techno, ambient, drum'n'bass – embraced by the band during the 1990s.[18] Likewise, the songs on the later albums have been much less 'home'-oriented, more explorative and uncertain in terms of structures, rhythm and direction. From the opening bars of 'Zoo Station' (the first track on *Achtung Baby*) the band increasingly engaged with a range of musical associations which seemed almost directly antithetical to that with which they had been associated in their first decade: where there had been space, there was constriction; where there had been solitude, there was society; where there had been freedom, there was claustrophobia; and where there had been clean sound and deep resonance there was distortion and a self-conscious electrification. Old songs such as 'Streets' were re-encountered in the light of these new ambitions; Adam Clayton claimed that the band had a lot of fun with that particular track on their later tours by rediscovering its latent dance rhythms (King and O'Connor 1999).

Having indicated as late as 1989 that the band were incapable of assuming any identity other than their own, U2 grasped the possibilities of rock mimicry with alacrity (Stein 1999: 285). Dressed in horns, spangly platform shoes and gold lamé suit, plastered in make-up, Mr McPhisto presented an image half a world away from Bono's various 'authentic' looks during the 1980s. He became the representative citizen of 'Zooropa', an imaginary landscape somehow coexisting alongside the 'real' ones that westerners know and travel through; a landscape in which the image could be 'even better than the real thing', in which knowledge and morality were marketable products like any other, and in which, as the song title from *Zooropa* puts it, Daddy will always be there 'to pay for your crashed car'.

Yet, as the musical and lyrical content of *Achtung Baby*, *Zooropa* and *Pop* reveal, beneath the postmodern concern with the surface of things, lies a more fundamental concern with U2's animating spirit: the nature and location of 'home', and the journey one must undertake to get there. Over the years, this has been both a universal human journey and a specifically Irish journey. U2's music is not rooted in a native soil, as Heidegger demanded all genuine art should be; it retains the influence of that soil, yet it is an eclectic and nomad art, drawing on many different sources and impacting in many different contexts. It is an art in which 'uncertainty', rather than denying the subject an authentic sense of where and who he is, can in fact 'be a guiding light'. This same postmodern subject, the hero of so many of the later U2 songs, may, like Mr McPhisto, be slightly drunk and over-dressed; he may be dazzled by the speed with which imagery and reality coalesce and separate; he may be disoriented by the lack of a map or a compass; he may even be self-consciously trying to negotiate what Robyn Brothers in his analysis of late U2 called the 'increasingly problematic intersection of the spiritual, the political, and the technological.'[19] But he is still looking for someone to show him the way home.

Notes

Chapter 1

1. The effect may have been accentuated during the modern period, but Max Oelschlaeger insists that '[local] knowledge versus universal knowledge embedded in philosophy from the beginning.... Through the embrace of alphabetic literacy, Greek intellectuals turned away from the concrete immediacy of place toward the abstract domain of universal and timeless objective truth. The quest for theoretical accounts that explained nature, moving natural phenomena from the domain of myth into the domain of reason, became intellectually dominant' (1997: 375).

2. It is perhaps ironic that one of the progenitors of ecocriticism is also one of the most influential of Marxist cultural critics. Besides *The Country and the City* (for which see the section on 'Marxism' below), Raymond Williams wrote a number of pieces exploring the function of nature and various related issues from a cultural materialist perspective. See the essays 'Ideas of Nature' and 'Social Darwinism' (1980: 67–102), and also 'Socialism and Ecology', 'Between Country and City' and 'Decentralism and the Politics of Place' published in the posthumous collection entitled *Resources of Hope* (1989: 210–44).

3. Although I use the terms more or less interchangeably here, Andrew Dobson maintains a sharp distinction between ecologism and environmentalism. The former 'argues that care for the environment presupposes radical changes in our relationship with it, and thus in our mode of social and political life', whereas the latter 'would argue for a "managerial" approach to environmental problems, secure in the belief that they can be solved without fundamental changes in present values or patterns of production and consumption' (1990: 13).

4. Because of its opposition to a certain form of reason based upon 'Man's' assumed mastery of nature, ecofeminism (and indeed environmentalism in general) is frequently characterised as irrationalism. This is a typical gesture to dismiss criticism within the terms that are themselves in dispute.

5. The literature is vast, but for representative examples see Barnes and Duncan 1992; Benko and Strohmayer 1997; Cresswell 1995; Duncan and Ley 1993; Groth and Bressi 1997; Keith and Pile 1993; King 1996; Lavie and Swedenburg 1996; Mitchell 1994; Philo 1991; Pile and Thrist 1995; Rose 1992; Shields 1991; Shurmer-Smith and Hannam 1994; Sibley 1995.

Chapter 2

1. In an interview entitled 'Questions on Geography', Foucault acquiesced with his interlocutors from the journal *Hérodote* when they pointed out that 'seventeenth-century travellers and nineteenth-century geographers were

actually intelligence gatherers, collecting and mapping information which was directly exploitable by colonial powers, strategists, traders and industrialists' (1980: 75). On the complex historical relations between travel, language and translation, see Cronin (2000).

2. On the history of the human race's quest for ever higher places from which to view and map the world, see King (1996: 177).

3. The difference between Pococke's style – scientific, concise and unemotional according to McVeagh (1995: 20) – and that of Anon. or say James Hall's 1813 account, might be considered with reference to Pratt's distinction between the kind of 'asocial' travel account characteristic of the eighteenth century 'in which the human presence . . . is absolutely marginal' (1992: 51), and the typical nineteenth-century text which her research found to be much more dramatic and subjective. For the Irish context, see Hooper (1998).

4. Foster notes that in the poem 'Killarney' (1772), John Leslie was impressed by 'Majestick Nature's artless symmetry' which united the 'Wonderful, Sublime, and Fair', but found that 'Nature and Art their diff'rent claims maintain, / Divide their empire, and alternate reign' (1991: 20). His point is that the sublime had to compete with residual spatial discourses which were more concerned with balance and decorum.

5. See for example Taylor and Skinner (1778), Tyner (1794) and Wilson (1784). Foster opines that '[it] can be said that the cult of the picturesque created modern tourism, which still depends heavily on "selling" picturesque scenery . . . descriptions of tours in Ireland by doughty and industrious individuals . . . mushroomed during the picturesque period' (1991: 21).

6. With reference to the representation of 'the West' in modern Irish tourist discourse, Byrne, Edmondson and Fahy discuss the 'soft' tourist who 'is quintessentially in search of "liminal" experiences which take him completely out of everyday existence into another, somehow revelatory, world . . . the traveller is invited to escape the mundane or even corrupt quality of city life and exchange it for the purity of the countryside . . . the visitor to a different cultural world comes to experience the functioning of human life as exotic in a way which is not disconnected from his or her daily life but in some way casts light on it. Instead of feeling trapped in everyday sameness, the tourist can experience the fact that it is possible for the world to be different' (1993: 252).

7. In his essay 'Contemporary Travel Writing and Ireland' (in O'Connor and Cronin 1993: 51–67), Michael Cronin concurs when he notes '[a] strong belief that time is ordered differently in Ireland'. He goes on to point out, however, that '[there] is a sense in which the presentness of the past is less to do with the imperialist progress of the colonist's culture than with the very nature of travel writing itself as illustrated by the case of Ireland' (ibid.: 61).

8. The literature on the role and function of 'the West' in the Irish cultural imagination is vast, but in this context see especially Byrne, Edmondson and Fahy (1993); Kneafsey (1995); and Nash (1993, 1996).

9. Sheerin (1998: 48). Regarding the conversion of social experience into heritage products, de Certeau makes a similar point when he writes: '[The] story plays a decisive role . . . it founds spaces. Reciprocally, where stories are disappearing (or else are being reduced to museographical objects), there is a loss of space:

deprived of narrations (as one sees it happen in both the city and the countryside), the group or the individual regresses toward the disquieting, fatalistic experience of a formless, indistinct, and nocturnal totality' (1988: 123).

10. Byrne, Edmondson and Fahy (1993: 253). The cartographer and environmentalist Tim Robinson noted that '[a] current [1990] proposal to site an airport in unspoiled country near Clifden focuses a contradiction between the facilitating of tourism and the conservation of what the tourists come for' (1996: 73).

11. Nicholas Thomas understands nineteenth-century imperialism as part of the larger project of western modernity, 'in the special sense that both the societies internal to western nations, and those they possessed, administered and reformed elsewhere, were understood as objects to be surveyed, regulated and sanitized' (1994: 4). The global significance of mapping/ naming, as a crucial contribution to the surveillance of both western and non-western societies, emerges in this context.

12. Visitors to the Grand Canyon National Park in Arizona, for example, no longer have to brave the demanding terrain, but can experience the full splendour of the landscape for as little as $3 by watching films shown on giant screens near the entrance. Developed by a company called World Odyssey of California, these films are shot in such a way as to reproduce views of the canyon from helicopter, horse and canoe. The implication in their literature is that experiencing the landscape in this way is even better than the real thing.

13. King (1996: 10–11) makes this point with regard to Los Angeles, the supposed capital of postmodernism which yet contains a highly stratified class structure realised in the topography of the megalopolis.

14. Alfred Smyth writes: 'It becomes immediately clear from reading any major work in Early Irish, whether it be a saga or a saint's *Life*, that the cornerstone of ancient Irish antiquarian learning rested on the importance of the association with place.' He continues: 'it is no coincidence that all of these peoples [Celts, Icelanders, Hebrews] built up civilizations in a geographical wilderness and their isolation, each in their separate and distinct environments, promoted a literature characterized by a great sensitivity and feeling for landscape' (1982: 1).

15. It is interesting to compare the attempt to narrativise landscape in *dinnshenchas* with Michel de Certeau's claim that '[the] narration is established on the basis of "primary" stories, stories that already have the function of spatial legislation since they determine rights and divide up lands by acts or discourses about actions. These operations of marking the boundaries, consisting in narrative contracts and compilations of stories, are composed of fragments drawn from earlier stories and fitted together in makeshift fashion. In this sense, they shed light on the formation of myths, since they also have the function of founding and articulating spaces . . . Fragmented and disseminated, the story is continually concerned with marking out boundaries. Stories "go in a procession" ahead of social practices in order to open a field for them' (1988: 122–3, 125).

16. Regarding the dating of *Dinnshenchas Erenn*, Gwynn writes: 'We may tentatively assign as approximate dates – for the First Recension of the prose text, the first quarter of the 12th century; for the Bd.-Ed. text, the second

quarter; for the first draft of the Revised text, the last quarter' (1935: 114). Strongbow, Richard de Clare, landed in Ireland in 1170.

17. The term 'hippie' is used here to denote a certain attitude towards the landscape and environmental issues in general. See Smyth (1999).

18. Robinson (1996: 76). It is interesting that Andrews uses the same phrase to describe his meta-cartographical history of the Ordnance Survey, writing: 'the present work can be no more than an interim report' (1975: ii).

19. Jackson (1988: 72–3); Kiely (1982); Roy (1996: 228); O Tuoma (1985). Jackson's gloss to what he calls Celtic 'Nature' is cast in terms of an age conceit that is particularly revealing: 'Comparing these poems with the medieval European lyric is like comparing the emotions of an imaginative adolescent who has just grown up to realize the beauty of nature, with those of an old man who has been familiar with it for a lifetime and is no longer able to think of it except in literary terms' (1988: 61). Celticism's ageist bias might be usefully read against Bachelard's claims that 'it is not until late in life that we really revere an image, when we discover that its roots plunge well beyond the history that is fixed in our memories. In the realm of absolute imagination, we remain young late in life' (1969: 33).

20. In the introduction to his translation of *Buile Suibne*, O'Keefe wrote: 'Perhaps the outstanding feature of the composition is the extraordinary love of place which it reveals. I venture to say that this is one of the most distinctive features of early Irish literature.... Nor was this love of place a mere convention; I believe it sprang from a very intimate knowledge of the actual place or of the spirit of the place; and I suggest that it will be found on investigation that the descriptions of places given in early Irish literature are in the main accurate' (1913: xxxvii).

21. Heaney uses early Irish nature poetry to support his belief that '[the] love of place and lamentation against exile from a cherished territory is another typical strain in the Celtic sensibility' (1980: 184). He does not include the St Paul fragment in his version of the tale.

22. See Buel (1995); Oelschlaeger (1997). See also Ó Riain (1971–72), who discusses the possible British origins of the legend. Suibne was not the first nor the last 'Wild Man' to take to the wilderness in an attempt to escape society, of course. His flight may be regarded as the archetype of the subject's retreat from society towards a more simple, supposedly more authentic way of life. This movement pervades modern western literature, but is encapsulated in Henry David Thoreau's *Walden*, first published in 1854.

23. *INP* (307, 413). 'Tuaim', Joyce explains, is a cognate of the Latin *tumulus*. In an earlier section on 'Ecclesiastical Edifices', he pointed out that '[the] early missionaries, finding no suitable words in the native language, introduced the necessary Latin terms, which, in the course of time, were more or less considerably modified according to the laws of Irish pronunciation' (ibid.: 287). Not only were words modified, moreover, but the sense in which they were employed was also adapted for use with reference to local landscape and practices. Thus, Dinneen renders *tuaim* as 'a hillock, a funeral mound, a fortified hill' and notes that it is 'common in place-names [such as] Tuam in Galway' (1996: 1262). In his smaller school dictionary, however, *tuaim* loses any association with a burial mound, being given as 'dyke, fence, village,

townland' (1910: 231). In O'Reilly, *tuaim* is given as 'a village, homestead, fortified town; a dyke, fence, fort, hedge; a grave, a tomb, a side' (1877: 537). Greene and Quin suggest that the exact meaning of *túaim* is 'uncertain' (*CDIL* 1948: 335), although they note that it is frequently used in place-names, 'in some cases meaning "burial mound, tumulus"' (ibid.: 336). *Inbear* is less contentious; it is given as 'a harbour, a haven, the mouth of a river, an estuary' by Dineen (1996: 594); 'the mouth of a river, an ostiary' by O'Reilly (1877: 304); and 'a rivermouth, the sea at the point where a river enters it' by O'Daly and O'Sullivan (*CDIL* 1952: 204).

24. The poem is rather enigmatically entitled 'The Pity of Nature – I' in Greene and O'Connor (1967: 100–1). 'The Pity of Nature – II' (ibid.: 179–80) is an extract from *Buile Suibne*.

25. Tree-perching is one of the typical 'states of madness' identified by Ó Riain in his study of Suibne as an exemplary instance of the wild man legend (1971–72: 195–6). It should also be noted that 'cell-building' remained a popular religious practice in Ireland until relatively recent times. Among the first changes commissioned by the Carmelite community after it moved into a new building in Firhouse in 1827 was the conversion of large rooms into individual 'cells'. So they are still called.

26. Bachelard writes: '[Poets] prove to us that the homes that were lost forever continue to live on in us; that they insist in us: that they insist in us in order to live again, as though they expected us to give them a supplement of living.... If there exists a border-line surface between such an inside and outside, this surface is painful on both sides.... In this ambiguous space, the mind has lost its geometrical homeland and the spirit is drifting' (1994: 56, 218). Pain, ambiguity and drifting are fair descriptions of Suibne's plight.

27. More recently, Heaney's poetry has been engaged by the relatively new discourse of ecocriticism which, while retaining the apparent focus on locality, voice and memory, transposes these into an idiom that is less politically specific and more concerned with general environmental issues. See Bate (1991); Fitter (1995); Garrard (1998); Gifford (1995).

28. It is interesting that many of the Heaney's titles contain overt spatial connotations: door, out, station, north, field, island.

29. One such passing is recorded in *The Annals of Ireland*: 'The Age of Christ, 1099 . . . [an] army was led by Domnall Ua Lochlainn and the Clanna-Neill of the North across Tuaim, into Ulidia' (*AFM*, II: 961). We shall have more to say of Domnall Ua Lochlainn and the Northern Uí Neill in Chapter 4.

30. Both the *Oxford English Dictionary* (XVIII: 210) and *Chambers Twentieth-Century Dictionary* (1962: 1159) trace 'tomb' through Old French, Latin and Greek sources; in each case the word connotes a chamber or sepulchre for the reception of the dead. While noting these sources, however, both *Websters New International Dictionary* (1957: 2663) and Klein (1967: 1625–6) also acknowledge its kinship with the Middle Irish word *tomm* (as in *tuaim*, note 5 above), which the former gives as 'hillock' and the latter as 'a small hill'. This kinship inheres in the cognate 'mound', which all sources derive from the Greek *tymbos*, meaning 'sepulchral mound'.

31. The cemetery was an important heterotopic location for Foucault (1986: 25). In so far as tombs, graves and burials seem to be recurring topics in this

book, see also the section entitled 'Burial' in Garrard (1998: 172–3), an essay which examines Heaney's poetry in relation to Heidegger's notion of 'dwelling'. See also Derrida's essay on 'cryptonymy' (1986a) in which the crypt is understood as a place where something or someone both dead and alive is buried. This in turn may be linked to a recurring feature of Derrida's work: the existence, most evident in the literary text, of 'a secret place, a crypt whose coordinates cannot be plotted' (Hillis Miller 1995: 297).

32. In so far as the dead constitute a form of radical 'otherness' for the living, the different practices regarding the relative location of each in various cultures is an important index for a number of disciplines, including anthropology and archaeology. Mitchell and Ryan note a number of composite sites in the Irish neolithic, and suggest that '[this] association between dwellings for the living and burial places may reflect the very complex thinking which evidently lay behind the construction of megalithic tombs' (1997: 180).

33. Coughlan (1991); Picot (1997: 208–9). Nash writes that 'Heaney's poetry celebrates the feminine homeplace and mourns separation from it. It is against the construction of this landscape of the rural home as passive, organic and female that the poet, in distancing himself from it, can assert identity, activity and independence' (1993: 52). As Geoff King points out (and as Lloyd would no doubt concur), the valorisation of the feminine in these terms supports a traditional gendered geography (1996: 170–1).

34. Williams (1975). The classic study is by Glacken (1967), but on the complex history of nature as a concept in western thought see also Adorno (1984); Dobson and Lucardie (1993); Schama (1995).

35. In an essay on the development of the Céide Fields tourist site in Co. Mayo, Moya Kneafsey adopts a Foucauldian perspective to suggest that 'a place has different meanings for different groups in society, and that the identity of a place is not fixed, but is composed of layers of different interpretations and relations between people, their actions, the environment and social structures' (1995: 135–6).

36. 'Mullagh More' (also 'Mullaghmore') translates as 'great summit'. 'Gortlecka' combines *gort* meaning 'tilled field', and *lecka* – Gaelic *leacach* – meaning 'stony'. On the politics of 'interpretation' as it relates to Mullaghmore and other sensitive Irish sites, see the essay 'Tourists in Our Own Land' in O'Toole (1994: 33–50).

37. This interview was conducted before a High Court order directing that the site should be fully restored by 30 May 2001.

38. The Temple Bar Area Renewal and Development Act of 1991 built on the earlier Urban Renewal and Finance Act of 1986 which offered a series of generous tax incentives in an attempt to kick-start inner-city regeneration. Even before the controversies surrounding Temple Bar, there was debate as to whether such area-based renewal packages could be successful in the long term (MacLaran and Murphy 1997).

39. (1998: 9, original emphasis). Corcoran suggests that Temple Bar's iconic building in terms of style and patronage is the Clarence Hotel, owned by U2.

40. (1993: 223). Temple Bar's status as a primarily tourist space was implicit in Taoiseach Charles Haughey's imprimatur: 'The preservation and sensitive

renewal of Temple Bar and its development as Dublin's Cultural Quarter will make it a prominent feature of our capital city in the years ahead, *and give it a special place on the itinerary of visitors'* (quoted in Graeve 1991: 7, emphasis added).

Chapter 3

1. One partial exception is the introduction to John Wilson Foster's (1991) collection of essays entitled *Colonial Consequences*.
2. Hermeneutics, for example, established in European intellectual practice at around the same time as the 'discipline', is implicitly opposed to academic discipline. In their introduction to *Place/Culture/Representation*, James Duncan and David Ley argue that 'hermeneutics ... allows dialogue between the researcher and his or her subject and yet does not misrepresent the power relations that are structured into the Western academy. ... The text disrupts the extra-textual field of reference, by highlighting some elements within the field and deleting others. Elements are reshuffled within the text, thereby splitting up the fields of reference through an act of selection ... the world within the text is a partial truth, a transformation of the extra-textual world, rather than something wholly different from it' (1993: 9).
3. Nietzsche (1956, 1973); Benjamin (1979, 1992); White (1973, 1987). On the contradictory nature of the 'discipline' of literary criticism see Barthes (1972); Smyth (1998: 39–46); and 'The Critic as Artist' (1891) in Wilde (1969: 99–224).
4. There are in fact numerous ways in which an autobiographical discourse could be utilised in critical discourse, some of which I discuss in an essay entitled 'Hippies, Liberals and the Ecocritical Sublime' (1999). The latter term represents a critical engagement with the notion of 'the sublime' invoked in Lyotard (1984), and White (1987: 55–83).
5. Following Thurneysen, Eleanor Knott points out that although based on essentially Leinster traditions, an Ulster dimension was introduced when the tale was first committed to writing some time during the ninth century (1936: xi).
6. The actual location of the Bruidhean Da Derga has been hotly disputed. James Hegarty (1939–40: 72) listed a number of interventions, including Sir Samuel Ferguson (who opted for Donnybrook), and a Mr Henry Morris who argued in an article of 1935 that it was located not in Bohernabreena but further up the valley on Mareen's Brook, one of the Dodder's tributaries. As Christopher Moriarty points out, such speculations bespeak a concern for accuracy unwarranted by either the tale or the genre, although Moriarty himself then opts for the site of Bohernabreena Church, 'built in 1870 on an ancient religious site ... It has a commanding position at the entrance to the enchanted gorge of Glenasmole and a lovely view of Dublin Bay' (1998: 74).
7. Much of the material used in this chapter is taken from a 178-page file entitled 'Firhouse' kindly sent me by Ms Georgina Byrne, senior librarian of the County Library in Tallaght. Although I have tried to trace original

references for these materials as far as possible, when unsuccessful they are listed in a special section of the bibliography entitled 'Firhouse', by letter, file page reference, and with as full a citation as possible. References in the text are given as 'Firhouse', followed by the letter denoting the individual entry, followed by a page reference from the file, if relevant. The reference for O'Curry's Ordnance Survey letters is 'Firhouse B'.

8. One of the motives behind the formalisation of the Fionn cycle in literary form beginning in the ninth century appears to have been a desire to forge a body of southern myth which would function as a counterbalance to the Ulster cycle – including *Táin Bó Cuailnge* – and the Northern Uí Néill who appropriated its great antiquity as part of their lineage claims. At the same time as Fionn has been presented as a pseudo-historical figure within a specific literary genre, however, there is an ancient and enduring popular tradition regarding the exploits of the Fianna. The relationship between these two traditions has proved to be extremely complex (Murphy 1953: xiii–cxvii; Ó hÓgáin 1988: 275–310).

9. 'Plains' – whether the result of human activity or natural conditions – would have been notable topographical features in a landscape dominated by post-glacial forest (Mitchell and Ryan 1997: 163–4). Although I can find no reference in the most modern edition (1991), F.R. Montgomery notes that Ptolemy referred to this particular plain as 'Edrou Heremos', the desert of Eder (1908: 8). The significance of this 'desert' reference will emerge later.

10. Gwynn (1927: 25). In more recent times, Tallaght and Finglas were reunited in very different circumstances in Dermot Bolger's 'journey through unofficial Dublin' (1990).

11. (*MM*: 370). O'Curry goes on to explain that '[it] was during the progress of the late Ordnance Survey of Ireland that this tract came first into notice; and it is no ordinary satisfaction to me to have to say, that I was the first person in modern times that discovered the value of its contents, when under the able superintendence of Colonel Larcom and Dr. Petrie, I brought them to bear, with important results, on the topographical section of that great national undertaking' (ibid.).

12. Ó Riaín's redating of both martyrologies to 828 or later seriously modifies traditional impressions of Oengus's career. If he was in Tallaght seven years before being discovered by Máel Ruain (d. 792), it means that he would have had to have been there for at least 43 years (785–828) altogether, and if we accept the 767 date, probably much longer. Whether this left him time to found a monastery before he went to Tallaght, and return to Clonenagh to die as 'Abbot' is unlikely, but not impossible.

13. The relationship between Máel Ruain and Oengus echoes that between a famous desert anchorite named Macarius who visited the abbot Pachomius in disguise, only to alienate the members of his community by outdoing them all in terms of prayer, deprivation and mortification. On discovering his identity Pachomius reputedly thanked Macarius for the lesson, but continued: 'Now, therefore, return to the place from whence thou camest: we have all been sufficiently edified by thee: and pray for us' (Waddell 1936: 16).

14. (*OED*, IV: 515). An example would be the reference throughout Shakespeare's *As You Like It* to the forest as a 'desert' (1991: 31, 47, 54).

15. *Disert Diarmata* was named for an anchorite named Diarmiad who founded a 'monastery' there in 812 (Mac Airt 1951: 123; Gwynn and Hadcock 1988: 31). Its conversion into 'Castledermot' indicates a Norman interest (Nolan 1982: 23). It also reveals how place-name traditions come to function as highly sensitive indicators of different political cultures and spatial imaginations.

16. Hughes (1966: 185). Both the decision to forsake society and the hermits' feeling for nature recall the story of Suibne the Wild Man. Ó Riain has indeed pointed out that '[in] point of asceticism and diet, [the *gelta* or wild men] are not unlike the *céili dé*' (1971–2: 180).

17. With its conjoining of elements from both the natural (tree) and built (house) environments, 'Firhouse' strikes me as a particularly serendipitous place-name in the light of earlier comments on 'Suibne the Wild Man', and some of the general themes of this book.

18. The present church was built in the early nineteenth century, 'on the site, and partly constructed with the materials of the ancient abbey, of which the lofty square belfry still remains, curiously embattled' (D'Alton 1838: 380–1). My father was buried in the same cemetery after his death in a car accident in 1973.

19. Such has been the growth that in summer 1999 plans were drawn up to split Firhouse into two electoral areas. Firhouse has also applied for official 'Village Status', a designation which would entitle the area to substantial development grants.

20. The Firhouse monastery was owned and run by a small group of Discalced Carmelites, a branch founded in 1594 and inspired by the teachings of St Teresa of Ávila. The original Order of Our Lady of Mount Carmel adhered to the Rule of St Albert of Jerusalem, a monk who made an unsuccessful attempt to revive desert asceticism in Palestine after the Second Crusade.

21. Séamus Ó Néill, long-time resident of Firhouse, reports how, on the last day of September every year, herds of cows would be driven through the village towards sheds in Clanbrassil Street where they would spend the winter months: 'It was like the wild west on that day as all the roads and laneways were crammed with cattle' (n.d.: 15).

22. Higgins (1971). Before instituting the Ionian *familia*, Colum Cille allegedly spent some time with St Mobhi (d. 545) in his monastery at Glasnevin on the north bank of the Liffey. The legend tells how Colum Cille blessed the present well as he rested there during a journey to a friend who lived in a cell near the top of Mount Pelier (Firhouse D). On the holy wells associated with this part of Co. Dublin see Daly (1961–67).

23. The large drinking barns of the 1980s have given way in turn to what Urry calls the 'museumification' (1990: 132) of pubs, a process which in Britain during the 1990s frequently vied, but just as often combined, with what may be termed the 'Irishification' of pubs. Pub architecture is in fact one of the most sensitive ways of tracking Irish economic and cultural fortunes in the last decades of the twentieth century.

24. My last 'big' gig was as bassist to a Tallaght band named Squadron, supporting the well-known local outfit Stepaside at the Baggot Inn on 14 September 1980. This famous Dublin venue was played for the first and only time by U2 on 21 August 1979 (de la Parra 1994: 8).

Chapter 4

1. Frank argued that modernity precipitated a transformation in the aesthetics of the novel, away from its 'naturally temporal' (1963: 57) function towards a vision in which relations are represented and understood 'in a moment of time, rather than as a sequence' (ibid.: 9). He uses the example of *Ulysses* to suggest that '[past] and present are apprehended spatially, locked in a time-less unity that, while it may accentuate surface differences, eliminates any feeling of sequence by the very act of juxtaposition' (ibid.: 59). As an episodic Irish 'novel' with autobiographical overtones and an acute awareness of the power of language, *Reading in the Dark* would obviously bear instructive comparison with *Ulysses*.

2. In 'Region and Class in the Novel' (1991: 229–38), Raymond Williams traced the emergence of British regional fiction, seeing it as a function of the developing bourgeois nation-state with its implicit geography of centre and margin, metropolitan and provincial, universal and local. For Williams, the regionalism which animates the 'regional novel' is quite clearly 'an expression of centralized cultural dominance' (ibid.: 230). On some levels, *Reading in the Dark* represents an obvious deconstruction of that geography. This is true also of the text's representation of an urban milieu, even such a relatively limited one as Derry City. On the development of urban fiction see Wirth-Nesher (1996).

3. The literature is extensive, but for representative examples and surveys, see Carpenter (1977); Duffy (1997); Genet (1991); Harmon (1984); O'Toole (1985); Ward (1988). Although somewhat dated, John Wilson Foster's essay on 'The Geography of Irish Fiction' (1976: 30–43) remains an excellent introduction to the subject. One of Foster's key texts in this essay is Frank O'Connor's *Dutch Interior*, which he sees not as 'an exploration of the constrictions of urban life, but an exploration of the Irish self and the hostile spaces it both creates and is forced to inhabit' (1940: 40). Interestingly, at one point the narrator of *Reading in the Dark* describes an essay by a Heaneyesque character as a 'Dutch interior' (1997: 21).

4. It is not surprising that an American critic so well read in French poststructuralist theory should find in the novel a crisis of representation akin to the one which animated Derrida's early work. But neither should we be surprised that in an essay which functions tacitly to assess the extent of poststructuralism's debt to Heidegger, and given the latter's preoccupation with matters of dwelling and building, Hillis Miller should cast the deconstructive crisis in terms of a spatial discourse.

5. This is not to say that time and space exhaust the possibilities for critical engagement with *Reading in the Dark*. There is, for example, a complex system of colour references running through the text which might be profitably tracked.

6. For an analysis of the intellectual and institutional relations between 'the discipline of fact' and 'the freedom of fiction', see King (1991). See the introduction to Chapter 3 of this volume for a more wide-ranging consideration of confessionalism and genre in modern Ireland.

7. Kirkland (1996: 131–46) has explored the importance of Derry City as a site for Field Day in general and Deane in particular. He quotes the latter's assertion

that Derry is not only 'a symbolic city in the minds of the unionist and nationalist people', but also 'possibly the most sensitive city in Ireland and the site where both cultures meet and collide' (ibid.: 132).

8. Deane's invocation of Aileach here might be read with reference to Heaney's suggestion that '[we] have to retrieve the underlay of Gaelic legend in order to read the full meaning of the name and to flesh out the topographical record with its human accretions' (1980: 132). More interestingly, perhaps, the way in which the gallery in particular is depicted could be usefully compared with the representation of a similar space in 'Toome' as an instance of an ongoing debate between Field Day members, a debate, as Declan Kiberd acknowledged, that 'often proved far more challenging and even abrasive than the critiques of the movement mounted from without' (1995: 618). See note 15 below.

9. Although kin, there was intense political rivalry between the Cenél nEógain and the Cenél Conaill. In so far as '[the] location of political headquarters on boundary lines was a well-established feature of Irish society' (Ó Riain 1972: 23), Aileach would appear to have been deliberately chosen (like Tara and Cashel) for its location on a territorial demarcation point between potentially hostile groups.

10. For genealogical tables and succession lists relating to the Kings of Aileach and subsequently the Mac Lochlainns and O'Neills, see Moody, Martin and Byrne (1982: 128–9, 194–5).

11. O'Donovan (1837: 231). 'Oileach Neid' was also reputedly the site of the act – the murder of a Spanish king named Ith by three Danaan kings – which precipitated the Milesian invasion (Montgomery 1908: 12). See Hogan (1910: 17–18) for a list of references to Aileach in Early and Middle-Irish literature.

12. Although connoting the sun, *grianán* also carries hints of human modification. It is given as 'a summer house; a walk arched or covered over on a hill for a commodius prospect; a royal seat; a green' in O'Reilly (1877: 293). In his supplement, O'Donovan renders it: '1. A beautiful sunny spot. 2. a bower or summer-house ... 4. A royal palace', and notes that in this last sense 'this word is very frequently used in the old Irish historical tales and romances' (1877: 659). Dinneen gives it as 'sunny bower, chamber or palace' (1910: 131), while in Byrne it is 'a sunny chamber, a bower, a soller, an open balcony exposed to the sun, an upper room' (1955: 159). These last two meanings are of special interest in the light of what follows here and in the later section on the house.

13. *Ail* or *aill* is given as 'cliff, rock' in Dinneen (1910: 4); and as 'a stone; rock' amongst many other things in O'Reilly (1877: 14).

14. Mitchell and Ryan describe souterrains as 'underground passages, usually stone-built, leading to one or more chambers. Equipped with creepways which caused the person entering to bend or even crawl and often with changes of level, they were intended as a form of defence' (1997: 264). This description accords with that of O'Donovan (1837: 218). Interestingly, besides the usual stone-related translations of *ail* – for example, 'boulder' – O'Sullivan and Quin also quote uses of it as 'grave-stone, a stone of remembrance ... monument, memorial' (1964: 113). Like *toome*, then, the word *aileach* may derive from ancient Irish burial practices.

15. On the association between death and silence see Tuan (1993: 73). In so far as it 'is capable of juxtaposing in a single real place several spaces, several sites that are themselves incompatible' (Foucault 1986: 25), there are grounds for considering the Grianan, and more particularly its enclosed galleries, as a Northern Irish 'heterotopia' – as Foucault says, a real place which is something like a counter-site: 'a kind of effectively enacted utopia in which . . . all the other real sites that can be found within the culture, are simultaneously represented, contested, and inverted' (ibid.: 24).

16. Tony Pinkney has pointed to the importance of personal and social space for the Gothic novel, arguing that '[when] space had no place in historicist social theory, it fled into a Gothic modernism which was always a utopianism' (1990: 25), and suggesting that the supposed postmodernist rejection of Marxist historicism overlooks the tradition of a 'utopian socialism' to which radical space was central.

17. Having mentioned Heidegger, it should be noted that the three principal spatial figures in his philosophy of authentic dwelling crop up in some or other form in *Reading in the Dark*: the rift marking a point of division; the bridge signifying an ambivalent space of healing and danger; and the ring which 'develops from the interplay of earth, sky, mortals and divinities' (Hillis Miller 1995: 18). These figures have their sources in three essays included in *Poetry, Language, Thought* (1971): 'The Origin of the Work of Art' (15–87) – rift; 'Building Dwelling Thinking' (143–61) – bridge; and 'The Thing' (163–86) – ring.

18. On the question of the inherence of the Other within the Self and the double responsibility that ensues see 'Deconstruction and the Other', Richard Kearney's interview with Jacques Derrida (Kearney 1984: 105–26).

19. Tristram argues that '[throughout] the Georgian period, novels tend to divide between those who travel in order to broaden the mind and those who choose to do so by staying at home' (1989: 3). Recalling the section of 'Travel and Tourism' in Chapter 2 above, Ireland was a popular destination for those choosing the former option. Travel was thus one of the means by which Ireland became an 'unhomely' space for the English traveller, one that could be mapped as Other in relation to the (literally) 'homely' place (the house) in England.

20. In an essay on '. . . an Irish Sense of Place', Angela Martin argues that the kind of nationalism which prevailed in Ireland during the twentieth century was based on a complex of nineteenth-century social and religious attitudes in which '[men] were associated with the fields and the barn, and made frequent trips into town to the market fairs that occurred periodically. Women were associated with the farmhouse, especially the kitchen, which was the central living room of the house, and with the haggard (or farmyard) where they tended chickens, collected water, etc. . . . the proto-typical Mother was a metonym of the House and the authority of the proto-typical Father was enshrined within a heteropatriarchal Law that guaranteed him control over the economic and political realm of the "outside"' (1997: 99, 106). While still relevant, this model is complicated in *Reading in the Dark* by the peculiar political situation of the Northern Irish nationalist community.

21. Literary criticism is only slowly coming to engage with Bachelard's study, but see, for example, Tony Pinkney's study of the novels of Raymond Williams – especially Chapter 2, 'Taking the Feel of the Room' (1991: 18–69).

22. Alan Gailey traces the hearth through eight typological stages in Northern Irish domestic architecture: 'stages in the series were often missed out,' he notes, 'some families even moving from the earliest, free-standing hearth lying on the floor somewhere between the ends of the house, to the latest, a properly built stone or brick chimney with a fire in a grate below, when in the nineteenth century they moved from the rural slums of the landless poor to terraced factory houses in urban areas' (1984: 112). Not surprisingly, some of the earliest traces of human activity in Ireland are 'fragments of worked wood . . . associated with a hearth at Toome Bay' (Waddell 1998: 21).

Chapter 5

1. The 'fifth' Beatle, producer George Martin, described mixing *Sgt. Pepper's Lonely Hearts Club Band* – in many ways a breakthrough album in terms of popular musical texture – and how he 'used to sit forward of the control panel, so that I was right inside the stereo triangle. In this position I could hear the sounds as I panned them, moving right across the imaginary landscape that was called up in me by the song' (1995: 75).

2. Of *The Joshua Tree* (the principal text under discussion here) U2's lead singer Paul Hewson (Bono) said: 'I think [it] is not Irish in any of the obvious senses, but in a much more mysterious way it's very Irish, the ache and the melancholy in it is uniquely Irish' (King and O'Connor 1999).

3. Chambers (1996: 247). For Bono's own extraordinary theories on musical migration and what he has called U2's 'musical wanderlust' (Gardner 1994: 144), see Flanagan (1995: 27ff).

4. An early song 'Rejoice' (from *October*) contains a lyric inspired in part by the cavalier fashion with which modern planners and architects addressed Dublin's problems. Introducing the song at the Hollywood Palladium, Los Angeles on 28 November 1981, Bono said: 'In Dublin they're pulling the houses down in the city centre and they're putting the people out of the city centre and throwing them away in districts outside of the city like if they were something not human. But I say: rejoice!' (de la Parra 1994: 29). He returned to this theme in conversation with Richard Kearney in 1988, saying: 'Dublin, I mean, everybody gives out about Dublin and there lots of things to give out about – unemployment, what the planners have done to the people of Tallaght and Ballymun, the architects who have defaced what was a beautiful city, these are the real vandals . . . but we still love the city' (1988: 191).

5. Andrew Blake writes that '[travelling] rock musicians are part of an international circus, professional nomads plying their trade round the world with comparatively little sense of nationalised selfhood' (1997: 184). Interestingly, U2's Irish concerts have been plagued by criticism and controversy since the early 1980s.

6. In spring 1985 *Rolling Stone* magazine ran a cover feature on U2 with the caption: 'Our Choice: Band of the Eighties'. In April 1987 they were only

the third rock act (after the Beatles and the Who) to appear on the cover of *Time* magazine, with the caption: 'Rock's Hottest Ticket'. U2 were voted 'Best Act in the World Today' in the Q *Awards* (a British rock magazine) in 1990, 1992 and 1993.

7. Mark J. Prendergast writes: '[The Edge's] Fender Stratocaster or Gibson explorer would be fed via a switchbox into two amplification systems, each one set at a different level. The amplification systems were made up of two Memory Man echo-units linked to two separate old fashioned Vox AC30 amplifiers. The powerful sound pulses which this arrangement produced were in some ways better than having platforms of Marshall stacks fed by tens of wah-wah and fuzz pedals. It was an economical innovation with simple technology and very in tune with the better side of the minimalist new wave' (1987: 181).

8. For Moore, the most significant contribution made by the new technology to the creation of rock music texture was 'the use of multi-tracking, with its concomitant control over spatial location' (1993: 105).

9. King and O'Connor (1999). After the release of *Achtung Baby*, Brian Eno published a piece in *Rolling Stone* describing some of U2's working methods and his own understanding of the processes involved. He summed up: 'And this is exactly what I've always liked about pop music: its ability to create crazy emotional landscapes and then invite you to come and dance in them' (Gardner 1994: 170). It is futile to speculate on the precise extent of Eno's influence on U2's interests throughout their association, although his status as the 'godfather of ambient' and his reputation as the creator of complex musical images is surely a significant factor in the development of the spatial dimension to the band's music.

10. David E. Sopher writes that America itself, 'the idea of an ever recreated new home', is a late version of a core religious myth concerned with travel and the journey, thus 'urging a transcendence of both society and geography.... Though transformed into a secular myth, it has not been shorn of its religious roots (1979: 135).

11. John Wilson Foster makes the point that '[the] colonizers at different times paint both an Edenic landscape and a fallen landscape (a "desert" or "waste"). This twofold depiction is both a cause and an effect of the deeply embedded European ambivalence about nature: nature is pristine and prelapsarian, innocent and good, but it is also sullied and savage, wild and unregenerate.' He goes on to suggest that '[the] ambivalence towards nature found a special venue in colonial Ireland' (1997: 28).

12. Interestingly, Synge used a musical analogy to describe the attraction of the organic community. Gibbons writes: 'The kind of communal identity [Synge] sought could be compared, he suggested, to that achieved by a musician in an orchestra: as he expressed it himself, "the collective passion produced by a band working together with one will and one ideal is unlike any other exaltation"' (1996a: 29).

13. In one of the earliest scholarly essays on U2, Barbara Bradby and Brian Torode interpreted 'Sunday, Bloody Sunday' as 'an invitation to us all to march behind a Protestant band, to do battle with infidels... the song's conclusion repeats the military imagery of evangelical Protestantism, familiar in the names of organisations such as the "Salvation Army" and in hymns such as "Onwards Christian Soldiers"' (1984: 76).

14. This was even more the case on *The Joshua Tree* when the band were concerned to be at their most 'authentic' in rock terms. Subsequently, it was the badge of 'authenticity' with which U2 felt they had been lumbered that was so radically reworked on the material released during the 1990s. In the meantime, the true inheritors of the experimental, progressive, 'unhomely' music of the 1960s would eventually emerge in the plethora of club styles characteristic of the 1990s.

15. The persona's recourse to the wilderness as an escape from society's ills recalls Suibne's flight in the face of the madness of battle.

16. Streets with numbers instead of names may be found in many American cities, most famously New York. The image also recalls the ghost towns of the American west, and the cities and towns of Ethiopia, visited by Bono after Live Aid, where, as Bill Graham writes, 'streets are also numbered, not named' (1995: 52).

17. Bill Flanagan wrote that the track 'Zoo Station' 'conjures up an environment like Times Square or Piccadilly Circus at 11 p.m. on a July Saturday' (1995: 19). He goes on to offer an elaborate reading of *Achtung Baby* based on withdrawal from, and return to, the house (ibid.: 43). The Edge has described how '*Zooropa* . . . conjures up for me a certain kind of cityscape – as an album, and particularly the title track' (Waters 1994: 260).

18. In a 1987 interview with *Rolling Stone* Bono expressed the belief that the music of the 1990s would be about 'roots' and 'humanness' (Gardner 1994: 100). In an interview with Richard Kearney published the following year, he expressed doubt as to whether people in the 1990s would be listening to 'machine music' or the 'sophisticated noise of a New York dance club' (ibid.: 191). His prediction of 'simplicity' and 'humanness' as the new regulating aesthetic has not been borne out by U2's engagement with a range of complex dance musics and their exploration of the causes and effects of postmodern dehumanisation.

19. Brothers (1999: 238). Rather more technically, but with reference to some interesting spatial metaphors, Brothers writes: 'If rock culture is plagued by lack of commitment, fragmentation, and cynicism, it must be reinvigorated by its potential to "deterritorialize" and produce desire from within the space of affect and to reconfigure those affects into a map charting political agency' (ibid.: 241).

Bibliography

All titles published in London unless indicated.

Aalen, F.H.A., 'Imprint of the Past' in Gillmor (1993: 72–107)

Aalen, F.H.A. & Kevin Whelan (eds), *Dublin City and County: From Prehistory to Present* (Dublin: Geography Publications, 1992)

Abraham, Nicolas & Maria Torok, *The Wolf Man's Magic Word: A Cryptonymy*, trans. Nicholas Rand (Minneapolis: University of Minnesota Press, 1986)

Adorno, Gretel & Rolf Tiedemann (eds), *Aesthetic Theory* (1970; trans C. Lenhardt; Routledge & Kegan Paul, 1984)

Adorno, Theodor, 'The Beauty of Nature' in Adorno & Tiedemann (1984: 91–115)

Ahmad, Aijaz, *In Theory: Classes, Nations, Literatures* (Verso, 1992)

Andrews, John, *Ireland in Maps* (Dublin: The Dolmen Press, 1961)

—— *A Paper Landscape: The Ordnance Survey in Nineteenth-Century Ireland* (Oxford: Clarendon Press, 1975)

—— 'Paper Landscapes: Mapping Ireland's Physical Geography' in Foster (1997: 199–218)

Appleton, Jay, *The Experience of Landscape* (New York: John Wiley & Sons, 1975)

—— *The Symbolism of Habitat: An Interpretation of Landscape in the Arts* (University of Washington Press, 1990)

Armstrong, Nancy, *Desire and Domestic Fiction: A Political History of the Novel* (Oxford: Oxford University Press, 1987)

Ashcroft, Bill, Gareth Griffiths & Helen Tiffin (eds), *The Post-Colonial Studies Reader* (Routledge, 1995)

Ashworth, John Hervey, *The Saxon in Ireland: or, The Rambles of an Englishman in Search of a Settlement* (Murray, 1852)

Attridge, Derek, Geoff Bennington & Robert Young (eds), *Post-structuralism and the Question of History* (Cambridge: Cambridge University Press, 1987)

Avery, Bruce, 'Mapping the Irish Other: Spenser's *A View of the Present State of Ireland*', *English Literary History* 57.2 (Summer 1990), 263–79

Bachelard, Gaston, *The Poetics of Space* (1958), trans Maria Jolas (Boston, Mass.: Beacon Press, 1994)

Baker, Steve, *Picturing the Beast: Animals, Identity and Representation* (Manchester: Manchester University Press, 1993)

Barnes Trevor J., & James S. Duncan (eds), *Writing Worlds: Discourse, Text and Metaphor in the Representation of Landscape* (Routledge, 1992)

Barrell, John, *The Dark Side of the Landscape: The Rural Poor in English Painting, 1730–1840* (Cambridge: Cambridge University Press, 1980)

Barthes, Roland, 'Criticism as Language' (1963), republished in Lodge (1972: 647–51)

Bate, Jonathan, *Romantic Ecology: Wordsworth and the Environmental Tradition* (Routledge, 1991)

Baudrillard, Jean, *Simulations* (1981), trans. Paul Foss, Paul Patton & Philip Beitchman (New York: Semiotext(e), 1983)

Benjamin, Walter, *One-Way Street and Other Writings*, trans. Edmund Jephcott and Kingsley Shorter (New Left Books, 1979)

—— *Illuminations*, trans. Harry Zohn (Fontana Press, 1992)

Benko Georges, & Ulf Strohmayer (eds), *Space and Social Theory: Interpreting Modernity and Postmodernity* (Oxford: Blackwell, 1997)

Birdsall, Stephen S., 'Regard, Respect, and Responsibility: Sketches for a Moral Geography of the Everyday', *Annals of the Association of American Geographers* 86.4 (1996), 619–29

Blake, Andrew, *The Land without Music: Music, Culture and Society in Twentieth-century Britain* (Manchester: Manchester University Press, 1997)

Boland, Eavan, *Collected Poems* (Manchester: Carcanet Press, 1995)

Bolger, Dermot (ed.), *Invisible Cities: The New Dubliners: A Journey through Unofficial Dublin* (Dublin: Raven Arts Press, 1990)

—— *The Woman's Daughter* (1987; Penguin, 1992)

Bradby, Barbara & Brian Torode, 'To Whom do U2 Appeal?' *The Crane Bag* 8.2 (1984), 73–8

Brady, Ciarán (ed.), *Interpreting Irish History: The Debate on Historical Revisionism* (Dublin: Irish Academic Press, 1994)

—— (1994a) '"Constructive and Instrumental": The Dilemma of Ireland's First "New Historians"', in Brady (1994: 3–31)

Brewster, Scott *et al.* (eds), *Ireland in Proximity: History, Gender, Space* (Routledge, 1999)

Brothers, Robyn, 'Time to Heal, "Desire" Time: The Cyberprophesy of U2's "Zoo World Order"' in Dettman & Richey (1999: 237–67)

Buell, Lawrence, *The Environmental Imagination: Thoreau, Nature Writing, and the Formation of American Culture* (Cambridge, Mass.: Harvard University Press, 1995)

Burke, Edmund, *A Philosophical Enquiry into the Origin of our Ideas of the Sublime and Beautiful* (1757; ed. Adam Phillips, Oxford: Oxford University Press, 1990)

Butlin, R.A. (ed.), *The Development of the Irish Town* (Croom Helm 1977)

Byrne, Anne, Ricca Edmondson & Kathleen Fahy, 'Rural Tourism and Cultural Identity in the West of Ireland' in O'Connor & Cronin (1993: 233–57)

Byrne, Patrick F., 'Ghosts of Old Dublin', *Dublin Historical Record* XXX (1976–77), 26–36

Carpenter, Andrew (ed.), *Place, Personality and the Irish Writer* (Gerrards Cross, Bucks: Colin Smythe, 1977)

Chambers, Iain, 'Review of *Dangerous Crossroads: Popular Music, Postmodernism and the Poetics of Place* by George Lipsitz', *Popular Music* 15.2 (May 1996), 247–8

—— 'Migrancy, Culture, Identity' in Jenkins (1997: 77–81)

Cloonan, Martin, 'Pop and the Nation-state: Towards a Theorisation', *Popular Music* 18.2 (1999), 193–207

Colby, Thomas (ed.), *Ordnance Survey of the County of Londonderry. Volume the First* (Dublin: Hodges and Smith, 1837)

Connell, Paul, Denis A. Cronin & Brian Ó Dálaigh (eds), *Irish Townlands: Studies in Local History* (Dublin: Four Courts Press, 1998)

Connolly, Sean, 'Dreaming History: Brian Friel's *Translations*', *Theatre Ireland* 8 (1987), 41–3

Connolly, S.J., 'Culture, Identity and Tradition: Changing Definitions of Irishness', in Graham (1997: 43–63)

Copley, Stephen & Peter Garside (eds), *The Politics of the Picturesque: Literature, Landscape and Aesthetics since 1770* (Cambridge: Cambridge University Press, 1994)

Corcoran, Lorraine M., Desmond A. Gillmor & James E. Killen, 'An Analysis of Summer Sun Tourists – Outbound Package Holidays from Dublin Airport', *Irish Geography* 29.2 (1996), 106–15

Corcoran, Mary, 'The Re-enchantment of Temple Bar', in Peillon & Slater (1998: 27–38)

Corcoran, Neil, *The Poetry of Seamus Heaney: A Critical Study* (Faber & Faber, 1998)

Cosgrove, Denis & Stephen Daniels (eds), *The Iconography of Landscape* (Cambridge: Cambridge University Press, 1988)

Cosgrove, Denis & Mona Domosh, 'Author and Authority: Writing the New Cultural Geography' in Duncan & Ley (1993: 25–38)

Coughlan, Patricia, '"Bog Queens": The Representation of Women in the Poetry of John Montague and Seamus Heaney' in O'Brien Johnson & Cairns (1991: 88–11)

Cresswell, Tim, *In Place/Out of Place* (Minneapolis: University of Minnesota Press, 1995)

Cronin, Michael, 'Contemporary Travel Writing and Ireland' in O'Connor & Cronin (1993: 51–67)

—— *Across the Lines: Travel, Language, Translation* (Cork: Cork University Press, 2000)

Cunningham, Mark, *Live and Kicking: The Rock Concert Industry in the Nineties* (Sanctuary, 1999)

D'Alton, John, *The History of the County of Dublin* (Dublin: Hodges and Smith, 1838)

Daly (Mrs.) James F., 'Curative Wells in Old Dublin', *Dublin Historical Record* XXII (1961–67), 13–24

Dawe, Gerald, '"What's the Story?": Irish Writing and British Studies', *Irish University Review: A Journal of Irish Studies* 28.2 (Autumn/Winter 1998), 217–26

Dawe, Gerald & John Wilson Foster (eds), *The Poet's Place: Ulster Literature and Society* (Belfast: Institute of Irish Studies, 1991)

Day, Angélique & Patrick McWilliams (eds), *Ordnance Survey Memoirs of Ireland: Volume Thirty-One. Parishes of Londonderry XI, 1821, 1833, 1836–7 South Londonderry* (Belfast: The Institute of Irish Studies in association with the Royal Irish Academy, 1995)

Deane, Seamus, *A Short History of Irish Literature* (Hutchinson, 1986)

—— (gen. ed.), *The Field Day Anthology of Irish Writing*, 3 vols. (Derry: Field Day and Faber, 1991)

—— 'The Production of Cultural Space in Irish Writing', *Boundary 2* 21.3 (1994), 117–44

—— *Reading in the Dark* (Vintage, 1997)

—— *Strange Country: Modernity and Nationhood in Irish Writing since 1790* (Oxford: Clarendon Press, 1997a)

de Breffney, Brian, *Irish Family Names: Arms, Origins, and Locations* (Dublin: Gill & Macmillan, 1982)

de Certeau, Michel, *The Practice of Everyday Life* (1974), trans. Steven Randall (Berkeley: University of California Press, 1988)

de la Parra, Pimm Jal, *U2 Live: A Concert Documentary* (Omnibus Press, 1994)

de Paor, Liam, *The Peoples of Ireland: From Pre-history to Modern Times* (Hutchinson, 1986)

Deegan, Gordon, 'A Community Divided: The Mullaghmore Oral Hearing', *Clare Champion* (Friday 16 July 1999), 6

Delany II Michael, & Michael Delany III, *The Knocklyon Times* (Dublin: n.d.)

Denman, Peter, *Samuel Ferguson: The Literary Achievement* (Gerrards Cross, Bucks.: Colin Smythe, 1990)

Derrida, Jacques, *Of Grammatology* (1967), trans. Gayatri Chakravorty Spivak (Baltimore: Johns Hopkins University Press, 1976)

—— 'Signature Event Context', *Glyph* I (Baltimore: Johns Hopkins University Press, 1977), 172–97

—— *Dissemination* (1972), trans. Barbara Johnson (Athlone Press, 1981)

—— *The Ear of the Other: Octobiography, Transference, Translation: Texts and Discussions with Jacques Derrida*, trans. Peggy Kamuf (New York: Schocken Books, 1986)

—— (1986a) 'Fors: The Anglish Words of Nicolas Abraham and Maria Torok', trans. Barbara Johnson, in Abraham & Torok (1986: xi–xlviii)

—— *Glas* (1974) trans. John P. Leavy Jr. & Richard Rand (Lincoln and London: University of Nebraska Press, 1986b)

—— *On the Name* (1993) trans. David Wood, John P. Leavy, Jr. & Ian McLeod (Stanford: Stanford University Press 1995)

Dettmar, Kevin J.H. & William Richey (eds), *Reading Rock and Roll: Authenticity, Appropriation, Aesthetics* (New York: Columbia University Press, 1999).

Dobson, Andrew, *Green Political Thought: An Introduction* (Unwin Hyman, 1990)

Dobson, Andrew & Paul Lucardie (eds), *The Politics of Nature: Explorations in Green Political Theory* (Routledge, 1993)

Doyle, Roddy, *Paddy Clarke Ha Ha Ha* (Secker & Warburg, 1993)

Dudley Edwards, Ruth, *An Atlas of Irish History* (Methuen & Co., 1973)

Duffy, Patrick J., 'Literature and Art in the Representation of Irish Place' in Graham (1997: 43–63)

Duncan James S., & David Ley (eds), *Place/Culture/Representation* (Routledge, 1993)

Dunphy, Eamon, *Unforgettable Fire: The Story of U2* (Penguin, 1988)

Durand, Jack, *Bohernabreena Reservoirs* (Dublin: Dublin Corporation, 1992)

Eco, Umberto, *Travels in Hyperreality* (1973), trans William Weaver (New York: Harcourt Brace Jovanovich, 1983)

Evans, E.E., *Prehistoric and Early Christian Ireland: A Guide* (B.T. Batsford, 1966)

Feher Ferenc, & Agnes Heller, 'From Red to Green', *Telos* 59 (1984), 35–44

Ferguson, Samuel, *Poems* (Dublin: William McGee, 1880)

Fitter, Chris, *Poetry, Space, Landscape: Towards a New Theory* (Cambridge: Cambridge University Press, 1995)

Fladmark, J.M. (ed.), *Heritage: Conservation, Interpretation and Enterprise* (Aberdeen: Donhead, 1993)

Flanagan, Bill, *U2 at the End of the World* (Bantam Press, 1995)

Flanagan, Deirdre & Laurence Flanagan, *Irish Place Names* (Dublin: Gill & Macmillan, 1994)

Flower, Robin, *The Irish Tradition* (Oxford: Clarendon Press, 1947)

Fogarty, L. (ed.), *James Fintan Lalor: Patriot and Political Essayist* (Dublin: The Talbot Press, 1921)

Foster, John Wilson, *Colonial Consequences: Essays in Irish Literature and Culture* (Dublin: Lilliput, 1991)

—— (1991a) 'The Geography of Irish Fiction' (1976) in Foster (1991: 30–43)

—— *Nature in Ireland: A Scientific and Cultural History* (Dublin: Lilliput, 1997)

—— (1997a) 'Encountering traditions' in Foster (1997: 23–70)

Foucault, Michel, 'Questions of Geography' in Colin Gordon (ed.), *Power/Knowledge: Selected Interviews and Other Writings* (Hemel Hempstead: Harvester Wheatsheaf, 1980), 63–77

—— (a) 'Nietzsche, Genealogy, History' (1971), in Rabinow (1984: 76–100)

—— (b) 'Space, Knowledge, and Power' in Rabinow (1984: 239–56)

—— 'Of Other Spaces', *Diacritics* 16 (Spring 1986), 22–7

—— 'What is an Author?' (1969), trans. Joseph V. Harari, reprinted in Lodge (1988: 197–210)

Frank, Joseph, *The Widening Gyre: Crisis and Mastery in Modern Literature* (Bloomington: Indiana University Press, 1963)

Friel, Brian, *Translations* (Faber & Faber, 1981)

Friel, Brian, John Andrews & Kevin Barry, '*Translations* and *A Paper Landscape*: Between Fiction and History', *The Crane Bag* 17.2 (1983), 118–24

Gailey, Alan, *Rural Houses of the North of Ireland* (Edinburgh: John Donald, 1984)

Gardner Elysa (ed.), *U2: The Ultimate Compendium of Interviews, Articles, Facts and Opinions by the Editors of Rolling Stone* (New York: Hyperion, 1994)

Garrard, Greg, 'Heidegger, Heaney and the Problem of Dwelling' in Kerridge & Sammells (1998: 167–81)

Genet Jacqueline (ed.), *The Big House in Ireland: Reality and Representation* (London: Barnes & Noble, 1991)

Gibbons, Luke, *Transformations in Irish Culture* (Cork: Cork University Press, 1996a)

—— 'Engendering the State: Narrative, Allegory, and *Michael Collins*', *Éire-Ireland: An Interdisciplinary Journal of Irish Studies* XXXI: 3 & 4 (Fall/Winter 1996b), 261–8

Gifford, Terry, *Green Voices: Understanding Contemporary Nature Poetry* (Manchester: Manchester University Press, 1995)

Gilbert John T. (ed.), *Calendar of Ancient Dublin* Vol. I (Dublin: Joseph Dollard, 1889)

Gillmor Desmond (ed.), *Our Way of Life: Heritage, Wildlife, Countryside, People* (Dublin: Wolfhound Press, 1993)

—— 'Tourism Development and Impact in the Republic of Ireland' in Kockel (1994: 17–34)

Glacken, Clarence J., *Traces on the Rhodian Shore: Nature and Culture in Western Thought from Ancient Times to the End of the Eighteenth Century* (Berkeley: University of California Press, 1967)

Glotfelty, Cheryll & Harold Fromm (eds), *The Ecocriticism Reader: Landmarks in Literary Ecology* (Athens, GA: University of Georgia Press, 1996)

Graeve Jobst, (ed.), *Temple Bar Lives! Winning Architectural Framework Plan* (Dublin: Temple Bar Properties, 1991)

Graham, Bill *The Complete Guide to the Music of U2* (Omnibus Press, 1995)

Graham Brian (ed.), *In Search of Ireland: A Cultural Geography* (Routledge, 1997)

—— 'Ireland and Irishness: Place, Culture and Identity' in Graham (1997a: 1–15)

—— 'The Imagining of Place: Representation and Identity in Contemporary Ireland' in Graham (1997b: 182–202)

Graham, Colin, *Ideologies of Epic: Nation, Empire, and Victorian Poetry* (Manchester: Manchester University Press, 1998)

—— '"...Maybe That's Just Blarney": Irish Culture and the Persistence of Authenticity' in Graham & Kirkland (1999: 7–28)

Graham, Colin & Richard Kirkland (eds), *Ireland and Cultural Theory: The Mechanics of Authenticity* (Basingstoke: Macmillan – now Palgrave, 1999)

Greenblatt, Stephen J., *Renaissance Self-Fashioning from More to Shakespeare* (Chicago: University of Chicago Press, 1980)

—— *Learning to Curse: Essays in Early Modern Culture* (Routledge, 1990)

Greene David, & Frank O'Connor (eds and trans.), *A Golden Treasury of Irish Poetry A.D. 600 to 1200* (Macmillan – now Palgrave, 1967)

Gregory, Derek, *Geographical Imaginations* (Oxford: Blackwell, 1994)

Grimes Seamus (ed.), *Ireland in 1804: A Contemporary Account* (Dublin: Four Courts Press, 1980)

Groth, Paul, & Todd W. Bressi (eds), *Understanding Ordinary Landscapes* (New Haven and London: Yale University Press, 1997)

Gwynn, Aubrey & R. Neville Hadcock, *Medieval Religious Houses: Ireland* (Dublin: Irish Academic Press, 1988)

Gwynn, Edward (ed. and trans.), *The Metrical Dindsenchas: Part I–V* (Dublin: Hodges, Figgis & Co., 1903, 1906, 1913, 1924, 1935)

—— (ed.) *The Rule of Tallaght* (Dublin: Hodges, Figgis & Co., 1927)

Haberstroh, Patricia Boyle, *Women Creating Women: Contemporary Irish Women Poets* (Dublin: Attic Press, 1996)

Hall, James, *Tour through Ireland: Particularly the Interior and Least Known Parts* 2 vols. (Moore, 1813)

Hamer, Mary, 'Putting Ireland on the Map', *Textual Practice* 3.3 (Summer 1989), 184–201

Hampson, Norman, *The Life and Opinions of Maximilien Ropespierre* (Duckworth & Co., 1974)

Handcock, William Domville, *History and Antiquities of Tallaght in the County of Dublin* (1876; Dublin: Anna Livia Press, 1991)

Harley, J.B., 'Maps, Knowledge and Power' in Cosgrove & Daniels (1988: 277–312)

—— 'Deconstructing the Map' in Barnes & Duncan (1992: 229–45)

Harmon, Maurice (ed.), *The Irish Writer and the City* (Gerrards Cross, Bucks: Colin Smythe, 1984)

Harrington, John P., *The English Traveller in Ireland: Accounts of Ireland and the Irish through Five Centuries* (Dublin: Wolfhound Press, 1991)

Harte, Liam, 'History Lessons: Postcolonialism and Seamus Deane's *Reading in the Dark*', *Irish University Review: A Journal of Irish Studies* 30.1 (Spring/Summer 2000), 149–62

Hayward, Richard, *This is Ireland: Leinster and the City of Dublin* (Arthur Barker Ltd., 1949)

Healy, Dermot, *The Bend for Home* (Harvill Press, 1996)

Healy, Patrick, 'The Valley of Glenasmole', *Dublin Historical Record* XVl.4 (August 1961), 109–30

Heaney, Seamus, *Door into the Dark* (Faber & Faber, 1969)

—— *Wintering Out* (Faber & Faber, 1972)

—— *Preoccupations: Selected Prose 1968–1978* (Faber & Faber, 1980)

—— *Sweeney Astray* (1983; Faber & Faber, 1984)

—— *Station Island* (Faber & Faber, 1984a)

—— 'Place, Pastness, Poems: a Triptych', *Salamagundi* (Fall/Winter 1985–86), 30–47

—— *The Place of Writing* (Atlanta: Scholars Press, 1989)

Hegarty, James, 'The Dodder Valley', *Dublin Historical Review* vol. II (1939–40), 59–72

Heidegger, Martin, *The Question of Being*, trans. William Kluback and Jean T. Wilde (Vision, 1956)

—— *Discourse on Thinking* (New York: Harper & Row, 1966)

—— *Poetry, Language, Thought*, trans. Albert Hofstrader (New York: Perennial Library, 1971)

Herbert, Máire, *Iona, Kells, and Derry: The History and Hagiography of the Monastic Familia of Columba* (Oxford: Clarendon Press, 1988)

Herder, J.G., *Outlines of a Philosophy of the History of Man* (1784–91), trans. T. Churchill (Johnson, 1800)

Higgins, Columba, *St. Columcille's Well* (Dublin: Good Counsel Press, 1971)

Hillis Miller, J., *Topographies* (Stanford: Stanford University Press, 1995)

Hoagland Kathleen (ed.), *1000 Years of Irish Poetry: The Gaelic and Anglo-Irish Poets from Pagan Times to the Present* (New York: Devin-Adair, 1947)

Hollon, W. Eugene, *The Great American Desert Then and Now* (New York: Oxford University Press, 1966)

Hood, A.B.E. (ed. and trans.), *St. Patrick: His Writings and Muirchu's Life* (Phillimore, 1978)

Hooper, Glenn, 'Writing the Union: James Hall's *Tour Through Ireland* (1813)', in Norquay & Smyth (1998: 181–204)

Horner, Arnold, 'From City to City-region: Dublin from the 1930s to the 1990s', in Aalen & Whelan (1992: 327–59)

Huggan, Graham, 'Decolonising the Map: Post-colonialism, Post-structuralism and the Cartographic Connection', in Ashcroft, Griffiths & Tiffin (1995: 407–11)

Hughes, Eamonn, 'Belfastards and Derriers', *The Irish Review* 20 (Winter/Spring 1997), 151–7

Hughes, Kathleen, *The Church in Early Irish Society* (Methuen & Co., 1966)

Jackson, Kenneth, Hurlstone *Studies in Early Celtic Nature Poetry* (Cambridge: Cambridge University Press, 1935)

—— *A Celtic Miscellany: Translations from the Celtic Literatures* (rev. edn 1971; Penguin, 1988)

Jackson, Val, 'The Inception of the Dodder Water Supply', *Dublin Historical Record* XV.2 (1958–59), 33–41

Jameson, Fredric, 'Postmodernism, or the Cultural Logic of Late Capitalism', *New Left Review* 146 (July/August 1984), 53–92

—— 'Cognitive Mapping', in Nelson & Grossberg (1988: 347–57)

Jenkins Keith (ed.), *The Postmodern History Reader* (Routledge, 1997)

Joyce, James, *Ulysses* (1922), ed. Declan Kiberd (Penguin, 1990)

Joyce, P.W., *The Origin and History of Irish Names of Places* (Dublin: McGlashan & Gill, 1869)

Kearney, Richard, 'Language Play: Brian Friel and Ireland's Verbal Theatre', *Studies: An Irish Quarterly Review of Letters, Philosophy and Science* 72 (Spring 1983), 20–56

—— (ed.), *Across the Frontiers: Ireland in the 1990s – Cultural, Political, Economic* (Dublin: Wolfhound Press, 1988)

Keating, Geoffrey, *Foras Feasa ar Éirinn: Keating's History of Ireland*, ed. and trans. P.W. Joyce (Dublin: M.H. Gills & Son, 1880)

Keith, Michael & Steve Pile (eds), *Place and the Politics of Identity* (Routledge, 1993)

Keohane, Kieran, 'Traditionalism and Homelessness in Contemporary Irish Music' in Mac Laughlin (1997: 274–303)

Kerridge, Richard & Neil Sammells (eds), *Writing the Environment: Ecocriticism and Literature* (Zed Books, 1998)

Kerrigan, John, 'Earth Writing: Seamus Heaney and Ciaran Carson', *Essays in Criticism: A Quarterly Journal of Literary Criticism*, XLVIII.2 (April 1998), 144–68

Kiberd, Declan, *Inventing Ireland* (Jonathan Cape, 1995)

Kiely, Benedict, 'A Sense of Place' in Mac Réamoinn (1982: 93–109)

Killen, James, 'Transport in Dublin' in Aalen and Whelan (1992: 305–23)

King, Geoff, *Mapping Reality: An Exploration of Cultural Cartographies* (Macmillan – now Palgrave, 1996)

King, Richard, 'The Discipline of Fact/the Freedom of Fiction?', *Journal of American Studies* 25.2 (August 1991), 171–88

Kinsella Thomas (ed.), *The New Oxford Book of Irish Verse* (Oxford: Oxford University Press, 1986)

Kirkland, Richard, *Culture in Northern Ireland Since 1965: Moments of Danger* (Harlow: Longman, 1996)

Kneafsey, Moya, 'The Cultural Tourist: Patron Saint of Ireland?' in Kockel (1994: 103–16)

—— 'A Landscape of Memories: Heritage and Tourism in Mayo' in Kockel (1995: 135–53)

—— 'Tourism and Place Identity: A Case-study in Rural Ireland', *Irish Geography* 31.2 (1998), 111–23

Knott Eleanor (ed.), *Togail Bruidne Da Derga* (Dublin: Stationery Office, 1936)

Kockel Ullrick (ed.), *Culture, Tourism and Development: The Case of Ireland* (Liverpool: Liverpool University Press, 1994)

—— *Landscape, Heritage and Identity: Case Studies in Irish Ethnography* (Liverpool: Liverpool University Press, 1995)

Lavie, Smadar & Ted Swedenburg (eds), *Displacement, Diaspora, and Geographies of Identity* (Durham, NC and London: Duke University Press, 1996)

Lebow, R.N., *White Britain and Black Ireland* (Philadelphia: Institute for the Study of Human Issues, 1976)

Lee, Joseph (ed.), *Ireland: Towards a Sense of Place* (Cork: Cork University Press, 1985)

—— (1985a) 'Centralisation and Community' in Lee (1985: 84–98)

Leerssen, Joep, *Remembrance and Imagination: Patterns in the Historical and Literary Representation of Ireland in the Nineteenth Century* (Cork: Cork University Press, 1996)

Lefebvre, Henri, *The Production of Space* (1974), trans. Donald Nicholson-Smith (Oxford: Basil Blackwell, 1991)

Lincoln, Colm, 'Dublin and the Discovery of Urban Heritage' in O'Connor & Cronin (1993: 203–26)

Lipsitz, George, *Dangerous Crossroads: Popular Music, Postmodernism and the Poetics of Place* (Verso, 1994)

Lloyd, David, *Anomalous States: Irish Writing and the Postcolonial Moment* (Dublin: Lilliput Press, 1993)

Lodge, David (ed.), *Twentieth-Century Literary Criticism* (Harlow: Longman, 1972)

—— (ed.), *Modern Criticism and Theory: A Reader* (Longman, 1988)

Lyotard, Jean-François, *The Postmodern Condition: A Report on Knowledge* (1979), trans. Geoff Bennington & Brian Massumi (Manchester: Manchester University Press, 1984)

Mac Airt, Seán (ed.), *The Annals of Inisfallen* (Dublin: Institute for Advanced Studies, 1951)

MacAlister, R.A. Stewart (ed.), *Lebor Gabála Érenn: The Book of the Taking of Ireland*, Parts I–IV (Dublin: Irish Texts Society, 1938, 1939, 1940, 1956)

Macan, Edward, *Rocking the Classics: English Progressive Rock and the Counterculture* (Oxford: Oxford University Press, 1997)

Mac Giolla Léith, Caoimhín, 'Dinnseanchas and Modern Gaelic Poetry' in Dawe & Foster (1991: 157–68)

MacLaran, Andrew & Laurence Murphy, 'The Problems of Taxation-induced Inner-city Housing Development – Dublin's Recipe for Success?', *Irish Geography* 30.1 (1997), 31–6

Mac Laughlin, Jim (ed.), *Location and Dislocation in Contemporary Irish Society: Emigration and Irish Identities* (Cork: Cork University Press, 1997)

MacNeill, Máire, *The Festival of Lughnasa: A Study of the Survival of the Celtic Festival of the Beginning of Harvest* (Oxford: Oxford University Press, 1962)

Mac Réamoinn, Seán (ed.), *The Pleasures of Gaelic Poetry* (Allen Lane, 1982)

Mahoney, Elizabeth, 'Citizens of its Hiding Place: Gender and Urban Space in Irish Women's Poetry' in Brewster *et al.* (1999: 145–56)

Martin, Angela K., 'The Practice of Identity and an Irish Sense of Place', *Gender, Place and Culture* 4.1 (1997), 89–119

Martin, George, *Summer of Love: The Making of Sgt Pepper* (Pan, 1995)

Massey, Doreen, 'Politics and Space/Time' in Keith & Pile (1993: 141–61)

McCourt, Frank, *Angela's Ashes: A Memoir of Childhood* (HarperCollins, 1996)

McCullough, Niall, 'Urban Design' in Quinn (1996: 26–9)

McDonald, Frank, *Saving the City: How to Halt the Destruction of Dublin* (Dublin: Tomar Publishing, 1989)

McErlean, Thomas, 'The Irish Town Land System of Landscape Organisation' in Reeves-Smith & Hamond (1983: 315–40)

McManus, Ruth, 'Heritage and Tourism in Ireland – An Unholy Alliance?', *Irish Geography* 30.2 (1997), 90–8

McVeagh, John (ed.), *Richard Pococke's Irish Tours* (1752) (Dublin: Irish Academic Press, 1995)

Meinig, D.W. (ed.), *The Interpretation of Ordinary Landscapes: Geographical Essays* (Oxford: Oxford University Press, 1979)

Meyer, Kuno, *Selections from Ancient Irish Poetry* (Constable, 1911)

Mitchell, Frank & Michael Ryan, *Reading the Irish Landscape* (rev. edn, Dublin: Town House, 1997)

Mitchell, W.J.T. (ed.), *Landscape and Power* (Chicago: University of Chicago Press, 1994)

Montague, John, *The Figure in the Cave and Other Essays* (Dublin: Lilliput Press, 1989)

—— *The Rough Field* (1972; Newcastle upon Tyne: Bloodaxe Books, 1990)

Montgomery, F.R., *The Midland Septs and the Pale: An Account of the Early Septs and Later Settlers of the King's County and of Life in the English Pale* (Dublin: Sealy, Bryers and Walker, 1908)

Moody, T.W., F.X. Martin & F.J. Byrne (eds), *A New History of Ireland: Volume IX – Maps, Genealogies, Lists* (Oxford: Clarendon Press, 1984)

Moore, Allan F., *Rock: The Primary Text* (Buckingham: Open University Press, 1993)

Moriarty, Christopher, *Down the Dodder: Wildlife, History, Legend, Walks* (1991; Dublin: Wolfhound Press, 1998)

Murphy, Andrew, 'Reviewing the Paradigm: A New Look at Early Modern Ireland', *Éire-Ireland: An Interdisciplinary Journal of Irish Studies* XXXI: 3 & 4 (Fall/Winter 1996), 13–40

Murphy, Denis (ed.), *The Annals of Clonmacnoise, Being Annals of Ireland from the Earliest Period to AD 1408*, trans. Connell McGeoghagan (1627) (Dublin: Dublin University Press, 1896)

Murphy, Gerard (ed. and trans.) *Early Irish Lyrics: Eighth to Twelfth Century* (Oxford: Clarendon Press, 1956)

—— (ed.), *Duanaire Finn: The Book of the Lays of Fionn* (Irish Texts Society), Parts II (London, 1933) and III (Dublin, 1953)

Murray, Christopher, *Twentieth-Century Irish Drama: Mirror up to Nation* (Manchester: Manchester University Press, 1997)

Nash, Catherine, 'Remapping and Renaming: New Cartographies of Identity, Gender and Landscape in Ireland', *Feminist Review* 44 (Summer 1993), 39–57

—— 'Reclaiming Vision: Looking at Landscape and the Body', *Gender, Place and Culture* 3.2 (1996), 149–69

—— 'Embodied Irishness: Gender, Sexuality and Irish Identities' in Graham (1997: 108–27)

Nelson, Cary & Lawrence Grossberg (eds), *Marxism and the Interpretation of Culture* (Macmillan – now Palgrave, 1988)

Nietzsche, Friedrich, *The Birth of Tragedy* (1872) *and The Genealogy of Morals* (1887), trans. Francis Golffing (New York: Doubleday & Co., 1956)

—— *Beyond Good and Evil* (1886), trans. R.J. Hollingdale (Harmondsworth: Penguin, 1973)

Nolan, William, *Tracing the Past: Sources for Local Studies in the Republic of Ireland* (Dublin: Geography Publications, 1982)

Norquay, Glenda & Gerry Smyth (eds), *Space and Place: The Geographies of Literature* (Liverpool: Liverpool John Moores University Press, 1998)

O'Brennan, Lily, 'Little Rivers of Dublin', *Dublin Historical Record* III (1940–41), 19–25

O'Brien Johnson, Toni & David Cairns (eds), *Gender in Irish Writing* (Milton Keynes: Open University Press, 1991)

O'Connell, Jeff W. & Anne Korff (eds), *The Book of the Burren* (Kinvara, Galway: Tír Eolas, 1991)

O'Connor, Barbara, 'Myths and Mirrors: Tourist Images and National Identity' in O'Connor & Cronin (1993: 68–85)

——, & Michael Cronin (eds), *Tourism in Ireland: A Critical Analysis* (Cork: Cork University Press, 1993)

Ó Cróinín, Dáibhí, *Early Medieval Ireland 400–1200* (Harlow, Essex: Longman, 1995)

O'Curry, Eugene, *Lectures on the Manuscript Materials of Ancient Irish History* (1861; Dublin: Four Courts Press, 1995)

O'Daly, John (ed.), *Transactions of the Ossianic Society for the Year 1858: Vol. VI – Fenian Poems* (Dublin: John O'Daly, 1861)

O'Donovan, John, 'Grianan of Aileach' in Colby (1837: 217–32)

—— (ed. and trans.), *The Banquet of Dun na N-Gedh and the Battle of Mag Rath: An Ancient Historical Tale* (Dublin: Irish Archaeological Society, 1842)

—— (ed. and trans.), *The Topographical Poems of John O'Dubhagain and Giolla Na Naomh O'Huidhrin* (Dublin: Irish Archaeological and Celtic Society, 1862)

Oelschlaeger, Max, 'Geography in a Time of Cultural Crisis: Helping Philosophy Find its Place', *Ecumene: A Journal of Environment, Culture, Meaning* 4.4 (1997), 373–88

O'Faolain, Nuala, *Are You Somebody? The Accidental Memoir of a Dublin Woman* (Dublin: New Island Books, 1996)

Ó hÓgáin, Dáithí, *Fionn mac Cumhaill: Images of the Gaelic Hero* (Dublin: Gill and Macmillan, 1988)

O'Hearn, Denis, *Inside the Celtic Tiger: The Irish Economy and the Asian Model* (Pluto Press, 1998)

O'Kearney, Nicholas (ed.), *Transactions of the Ossianic Society for the Year 1853: Vol. I – The Battle of Gabhra* (Dublin: John O'Daly, 1853)

O'Keefe, J.G. (ed. and trans.), *Buile Suibhne: The Frenzy of Sweeney* (Irish Texts Society, 1913)

O'Kelly, Michael J., *Early Ireland: An Introduction to Irish Prehistory* (Cambridge: Cambridge University Press, 1989)

O'Meara, John J. (ed. and trans.), *The History and Topography of Ireland by Gerald of Wales* (1951; Harmondsworth, Middlesex: Penguin, 1982)

Ó Néill, Séamus, *Firhouse: History, Legends, People, Places* (Dublin: Scoil Treasa, n.d.)

Ó Riain, Pádraig, 'A Study of the Irish Legend of the Wild Man', *Éigse: A Journal of Irish Studies* 14 (1971–72), 179–206

—— 'Boundary Association in Early Irish Society', *Studia Celtica* VII (1972), 12–29

—— 'The Tallaght Martyrologies Redated', *Cambridge Medieval Celtic Studies* 20 (Winter 1990), 21–38

O'Toole, Fintan, 'Going West: The Country versus the City in Irish Writing', *The Crane Bag*, 9:2 (1985), 111–16

—— *A Mass for Jesse James: A Journey through 1980's Ireland* (Dublin: Raven Arts Press, 1990)

—— *Black Hole, Green Card: The Disappearance of Ireland* (Dublin: New Island Books, 1994)

Ó Tuama, Seán, 'Stability and Ambivalence: Aspects of the Sense of Place and Religion in Irish Literature' in Lee (1985: 21–33)

Peillon, Michael & Eamonn Slater (eds), *Encounters with Modern Ireland: A Sociological Chronicle 1995–1996* (Dublin: Institute of Public Administration, 1998)

Philo, Chris (ed.), *New Words, New Worlds: Reconceptualising Social and Cultural Geography* (Aberystwyth: Cambrian Printers, 1991)

Picot, Edward, *Outcasts From Eden: Ideas of Landscape in British Poetry since 1945* (Liverpool: Liverpool University Press, 1997)

Pile, Steve & Nigel Thrist (eds), *Mapping the Subject: Geographies of Cultural Transformation* (Routledge, 1995)

Pinkney, Tony, 'Space: The Final Frontier', *News From Nowhere: Journal of Cultural Materialism* 8 (Autumn 1990), 10–27

—— *Raymond Williams: Postmodern Novelist* (Seren, 1992)

Pratt, Mary Louise, *Imperial Eyes: Travel Writing and Transculturation* (Routledge, 1992)

Pred, Allan, 'Re-presenting the Extended Present Moment of Danger: A Meditation on Hypermodernity, Identity and the Montage Form', in Benko & Strohmayer (1997: 117–39)

Prendergast, Mark J., *Irish Rock: Roots, Personalities, Directions* (Dublin: The O'Brien Press, 1987)

Quane, Michael, 'Speaker Conolly', *Dublin Historical Record* XXV (1971–72), 25–32

Quinn, Patricia (ed.), *Temple Bar: The Power of an Idea* (Dublin: Temple Bar Properties, 1996)

Rabinow, Paul (ed.), *The Foucault Reader: An Introduction to Foucault's Thought* (Penguin, 1984)

Reeves-Smith, Terence & Fred Hamond (eds), *Landscape Archaeology in Ireland* (Oxford: British Archaeological Reports, British Series 116, 1983)

Regan, Stephen, 'Review of *Reading in the Dark*', *Irish Studies Review* 19 (Summer 1997), 35–40

Relph, Edward, *Place and Placelessness* (Pion, 1976)

Reynolds, Horace (ed.), *W.B. Yeats: Letters to the New Island* (Cambridge, Mass.: Harvard University Press, 1934)

Richards, Shaun, 'Way out West: Binary Oppositions in Recent Irish "Texts"', unpublished paper, n.d., 1–10

—— 'Placed Identities for Placeless Times: Brian Friel and Post-colonial Criticism', *Irish University Review: A Journal of Irish Studies* 27.1 (Spring/Summer 1997), 55–68

Robinson, Tim, *Oileáin Árann, The Aran Islands, Co. Galway: A Map and Guide* (Roundstone: Folding Landscapes, 1976)

—— *The Burren: A Map of the Uplands of North-west Clare* (Roundstone: Folding Landscapes, 1977)

—— *Stones of Aran: Pilgrimage* (1986; Penguin, 1990)

—— *Connemara: Part One, Introduction and Gazetteer; Part Two, A One-Inch Map* (Roundstone: Folding Landscapes, 1990)

—— *Stones of Aran: Labyrinth* (Dublin: Lilliput Press, 1995)

—— *Setting Foot on the Shores of Connemara and Other Writings* (Dublin: Lilliput, 1996)

Roche, Anthony & Jody Allen-Randolph (eds), *Eavan Boland: A Special Issue of the Irish University Review* 23.1 (Dublin, 1993)

Rose, Gillian, *Feminism and Geography: The Limits of Geographical Knowledge* (Cambridge: Polity Press, 1992)

Roy, James Charles, *The Road Wet, The Wind Close: Celtic Ireland* (Dublin: Gill and Macmillan, 1986)

—— 'Landscape and the Celtic Soul', *Éire-Ireland: An Interdisciplinary Journal of Irish Studies* 31.3 & 4 (Fall/Winter 1997), 228–54

Salleh, Ariel, *Ecofeminism as Politics: Nature, Marx and the Postmodern* (London: Zed Books, 1997)

Schama, Simon, *Dead Certainties (Unwarranted Speculations)* (Granta Books, 1991)

—— *Landscape and Memory* (New York: Alfred A. Knopf, 1995)

Shakespeare, William, *As You Like It*, edited by Agnes Latham (London: Routledge, 1991)

Sheerin, Emer, 'Heritage Centres' in Peillon & Slater (1998: 39–48)

Shepherd, John, *Music as Social Text* (Cambridge: Polity Press, 1991)

Shields, Rob, *Places on the Margins: Alternative Geographies of Modernity* (Routledge, 1991)

Short, John Rennie, *Imagined Country: Society, Culture and Environment* (Routledge, 1991)

Shurmer-Smith, Pamela & Kevin Hannam, *Worlds of Desire, Realms of Power: A Cultural Geography* (Routledge, 1994)

Sibley, David, *Geographies of Exclusion: Society and Difference in the West* (Routledge, 1995)

Smith, David, *The Tallaght Chronicles* (Tallaght: privately published, 1983)

Smith, Neil & Cindi Katz, 'Grounding Metaphor: Towards a Spatialized Politics' in Keith & Pile (1993: 67–83)

Smith, Robert, *Derrida and Autobiography* (Cambridge: Cambridge University Press, 1995)

Smyth, Alfred P., *Celtic Leinster: Towards an Historical Geography of Early Irish Civilization, A.D. 500–1600* (Dublin: Irish Academic Press, 1982)

Smyth, Gerry, *The Novel and the Nation: Studies in the New Irish Fiction* (Pluto Press, 1997)

—— *Decolonisation and Criticism: The Construction of Irish Literature* (Pluto Press, 1998)

—— 'Hippies, Liberals and the Ecocritical Sublime', *Keywords: A Journal of Cultural Materialism* 2 (1999), 94–110

Smyth, William J., 'Explorations of Place' in Lee (1985: 1–20)

Soja, Edward, *Postmodern Geographies: The Reassertion of Space in Critical Social Theory* (Verso, 1989)

Somerville-Large, Peter, *Dublin* (Hamish Hamilton, 1979)

Sopher, David E., 'The Landscape of Home: Myth, Experience, Social Meaning', in Meinig (1979: 129–49)

Steedman, Carolyn, *Landscape For a Good Woman: A Story of Two Lives* (Virago, 1986)

Stein, Atara, '"Even Better than the Real Thing": U2's (love) songs of the self' in Dettmar & Richey (1999: 269–86)

Stokes, Martin, *Ethnicity, Identity and Music: The Musical Construction of Place* (Oxford: Berg, 1994)

Stokes, Whitley (ed.), *Togail Bruidne Dá Derga: The Destruction of Dá Derga's Hostel* (Paris: Librairie Émile Bouillon, 1902)

—— (ed.), *Félire Óengusso Céli Dé: The Martyrology of Oengus the Culdee* (Henry Bradshaw Society, 1905)

——, & John Strachan (eds), *Thesaurus Palaeohibernicus: A Collection of Old-Irish Glosses, Scholia, Prose and Verse* vol. 2 (Cambridge: Cambridge University Press, 1903)

Stout, Geraldine & Matthew Stout, 'Patterns in the Past: County Dublin 5000 BC–1000 AD', in Aalen & Whelan (1992: 5–41)

Swiss, Thomas, John Sloop & Andrew Herman (eds), *Mapping the Beat: Popular Music and Contemporary Theory* (Oxford: Blackwell, 1998)

Tambling, Jeremy, *Confession: Sexuality, Sin, The Subject* (Manchester: Manchester University Press, 1990)

Taylor, George & Andrew Skinner, *Maps of the Roads of Ireland* (Dublin: William Wilson, 1778)

Thomas, Nicholas, *Colonialism's Culture: Anthropology, Travel and Government* (Cambridge: Polity, 1994)

Thoreau, Henry David, *Walden* (1854; Edinburgh: David Douglas, 1884)

Thurneysen, Rudolf, *Old Irish Reader, With a Supplement to A Grammar of Old Irish* (1909), trans. D.A. Binchy & Osborn Bergin (Dublin: Institute for Advanced Studies, 1949)

Tristram, Phillipa, *Living Space in Fact and Fiction* (Routledge, 1989)

Tuan, Yi-Fu, *Space and Place: The Perspective of Experience* (Edward Arnold, 1977)

Tuan, Yi-Fu, *Passing Strange and Wonderful: Aesthetics, Nature, and Culture* (Washington, D.C.: Shearwater, 1993)

Tyner, George, *The Traveller's Guide Through Ireland* (Dublin: Byrne, 1794)

Urry, John, *The Tourist Gaze: Leisure and Travel in Contemporary Studies* (Sage, 1990)

Virgil, *Georgics*, trans. James Rhoades (Kegan Paul & Co., 1881)

Waddell, Helen, *The Desert Fathers: Translations from the Latin* (Constable, 1936)

Waddell, John, *The Prehistoric Archaeology of Ireland* (Galway: Galway University Press, 1998)

Wainwright, Hilary, 'Raymond Williams and Contemporary Political Ecology', *Keywords: A Journal of Cultural Materialism* 2 (1999), 81–93

Ward, Catherine, 'Land and Landscapes in Novels by McLaverty, Kiely, and Leland', *Éire-Ireland: An Interdisciplinary Journal of Irish Studies* 23.3 (Fall 1988), 68–78

Waters, John, *Race of Angels: Ireland and the Genesis of U2* (Belfast: Blackstaff Press, 1994)

Whelan, Kevin, 'Beyond a Paper Landscape – John Andrews and Irish Historical Geography' in Aalen & Whelan (1992: 379–424)

White, Hayden, *Metahistory: The Historical Imagination in Nineteenth-Century Europe* (Baltimore: Johns Hopkins University Press, 1973)

—— *The Content of the Form: Narrative Discourse and Historical Representation* (Baltimore: Johns Hopkins University Press, 1987)

Whiteley, Sheila, *The Space Between the Notes: Rock Music and the Counter-Culture* (Routledge, 1992)

Wilde, Oscar, *Intentions and The Soul of Man under Socialism* (London: Dawsons of Pall Mall, 1969)

Wilde, William, 'Upon the Unmanufactured Animal Remains belonging to the Academy', *Proceedings of the Royal Irish Academy* 7 (Dublin: M.H. Gill, 1862), 181–212

Williams, J.E. Caerwyn, & Patrick K. Ford, *The Irish Literary Tradition* (Cardiff: University of Wales Press, 1992)

Williams, Raymond, *Culture and Society 1780–1950* (1958; Penguin 1979)

—— *The Country and the City* (1973; St. Albans, Herts: Paladin, 1975)

—— *Problems in Materialism and Culture: Selected Essays* (Verso, 1980)

—— *Resources of Hope: Culture, Democracy, Socialism,* edited by Robin Gable (Verso, 1989)

—— *Writing in Society* (Verso, 1991)

Wilson, William, *The Post-Chaise Companion: or Traveller's Directory through Ireland* (Dublin: Author, 1784).

Wirth-Nesher, H., *City Codes: Reading the Modern Urban Novel* (Cambridge: Cambridge University Press, 1996)

Wood, Denis, *The Power of Maps* (New York: Guildford Press, 1992)

Yeats, W.B., 'Browning' (22 February 1890) in Reynolds (1934: 97–104)

Young, Arthur, *Tour in Ireland 1776–1779* 2 vols., ed. A.W. Hutton (George Bell & Sons, 1892)

Other Sources

Bartholomew Touring Map of Ireland (Bartholomew/HarperCollins 1994)

The Beatles, *Sgt. Pepper's Lonely Hearts Club Band* (1967)

Bord Fáilte, *Developing Sustainable Tourism: Tourism Development Plan 1993–97* (Draft Summary) (Dublin, Bord Fáilte: 1992)

Bunreacht na hÉireann (Constitution of Ireland) (Dublin: Stationery Office, 1937)

Burren Action Group Website, http://homepages.iol.ie/^burrenag

Cairns, R.P.S., *Burren National Park Entry Point at Gortlecka: Environmental Impact Statement* (Cork: R.P.S. Cairns, 1999)

Chambers Twentieth-Century Dictionary, ed. William Geddie (Edinburgh: W. & R. Chambers, 1962)

Claudius Ptolemy, *The Geography*, trans. and ed. by Edward Luther Stevenson (New York: Dover, 1991)

Connolly, S.J. (ed.), *The Oxford Companion to Irish History* (Oxford: Oxford University Press, 1998)

Contributions to a Dictionary of the Irish Language (Dublin: Royal Irish Academy)

—— David Greene & E.G. Quin (arrangers), *T-tnúthaigid* (1943)

—— David Greene & E.G. Quin (arrangers), *to–tu* (1948)

—— Máirín O'Daly & Anne O'Sullivan (arrangers), *I* (1952)

—— Mary E. Byrne (arranger), *G* (1955)

—— Mary E. Byrne & Maud Joynt (arrangers), *degra–dodelbtha* (1959)

—— Anne O'Sullivan & E.G. Quin (arrangers), *A* (1964)

—— Máirín O Daly & P. Ó Fiannachta (arrangers), *L* (1966)

Davidson, Mary Gray, 'Ireland's Ghosts: An Interview with Seamus Deane', *Common Ground* (USA Radio, 6 September 1998)

Department of Tourism and Transport, *1989–1993 Operational Programme for Tourism* (Dublin: Stationery Office, 1988)

Dinneen, Patrick S., *Foclóir Gaedhilge agus Béarla: An Irish-English Dictionary* (1904), enlarged edn. 1927 (Dublin: Elo Press, 1996)

—— *A Smaller Irish-English Dictionary for the Use of Schools* (Dublin: M.H. Gill and Son, 1910)

Dun Laoghaire/Rathdown County Council, *Southern Cross Route Motorway, Map and Newsletter* (December 1998)

Government of Ireland, *Operational Programme for Tourism, 1994–1999* (Dublin: Stationery Office, 1994)

Hennessy, William M. (ed. and trans.), *The Annals of Ulster: A Chronicle of Irish Affairs* vol. I (Dublin: Alexander Thom, 1887)

Hogan, Edmund, *Onomasticon Goedelicum: Locorum et Tribuum Hiberniae et Scotiae: An Index, with Identifications, to the Gaelic Names of Places and Tribes* (Dublin: Hodges, Figgis & Co., 1910)

Illustrated Road Book of Ireland with Gazetteer, Itineraries, Maps, & Town Plans (Dublin: The Automobile Association, 1963)

King, Philip & Nuala O'Connor (dirs.), *Classic Albums: U2's The Joshua Tree* (Britain, Independent Television, 27 November 1999)

Klein, Ernest, *A Comprehensive Entymological Dictionary of the English Language* 2 vols (London: Elsevier Publishing Company, 1967)

Lewis, Samuel, *A Topographical Dictionary of Ireland* 2 vols (S. Lewis & Co., 1849)

McArt, Pat (ed.), *Irish Almanac and Yearbook of Facts 1999* (Donegal: Artcam Ireland, 1998)

MacCarthy, B. (ed. and trans.), *The Annals of Ulster: A Chronicle of Irish Affairs* vol. II (Dublin: Alexander Thom, 1893)

O'Donovan, John (ed.), *Annala Rioghachta Eireann: Annals of the Four Masters of the Kingdom of Ireland from the Earliest Period to the Year 1616* 7 vols (Dublin: Hodges & Smith, 1848–51)

Ordnance Survey, *Rathfarnham 1912* (Dublin: Phoenix Maps, 1989)

O'Reilly, Edward, *An Irish-English Dictionary, New Edition with a Supplement by John O'Donovan* (1817; Dublin: James Duffy & Sons, 1877)

The Oxford English Dictionary 2nd edn., prepared by J.A. Simpson & E.S.C. Weiner, 20 vols, (Oxford: Clarendon Press, 1989)

Simington, Robert C. (ed.), *The Civil Survey A.D. 1654–1656. Vol. VII – County of Dublin* (Dublin: Stationery Office, 1945)

Temple Bar Website, http://www.temple-bar.ie

Temple Bar Properties, *Development Programme for Temple Bar* (Dublin: Temple Bar Properties, 1996)

U2, *Boy* (Island, 842 296–2, 1980)

—— *October* (Island, 842 297–2, 1981)

—— *War* (Island, 811 148–2, 1983)

—— *The Unforgettable Fire* (Island, 822, 898–2, 1984)

—— *The Joshua Tree* (Island, 842, 298–2, 1987)

—— *The U2 Talkie: U2 in Interview with Dave Fanning* (Island, UK U2CC-1, 1987a)

—— *Rattle and Hum* (Island, 842 299–2, 1988)

—— *Achtung Baby!* (Island, 510 347–2, 1991)

—— *Achtung Baby: The Videos, the Cameos, and a Whole Lot of Interference from Zoo TV*, dir. David Mallet (Island Visual Art/Polygram Video, 1991)

—— *Zooropa* (Island, 518047–2, 1993)

—— *Zoo TV Live from Sydney*, dir. David Mallet (Island Video, 1994)

—— *Pop* (Island 524 334–2, 1997)

Various Artists, *Across the Bridge of Hope: In Aid of the Omagh Fund* (White Records, 1998)

Websters New International Dictionary of the English Language 2nd edn, editor-in-chief, William Allan Neilson (Cambridge, Mass.: G. & C. Merriam, 1957)

Welsh, Robert (ed.), *The Oxford Companion to Irish Literature* (Oxford: Clarendon Press, 1996)

Firhouse File

A (58) 'The Faction-fighting near Terenure', *Irish Times* (24 June 1880)

B (92–102) Michael O'Flanagan (ed.), *Letters Containing Information Relative to the Antiquities of the County of Dublin Collected During the Progress of the Ordnance Survey in 1837* (Bray, 1927)

C (106), 'The Fur House' and environs, from John Rocque's Map of Co. Dublin (1760)

D (145–6) 'St. Columcille's Well' by Doirin Doyle

E (161–64) 'Tallaght, Co. Dublin: Its Monastery and its Castle' (*Dublin Historical Record*) by Reverend C. Scantlebury, S.J.

Index